The Gig Academy

Reforming Higher Education: Innovation and the Public Good

William G. Tierney and Laura W. Perna, Series Editors

The Gig Academy

Mapping Labor in the Neoliberal University

Adrianna Kezar, Tom DePaola, and Daniel T. Scott

 Johns Hopkins University Press

Baltimore

Johns Hopkins University Press
2715 North Charles Street
Baltimore, Maryland 21218-4363
www.press.jhu.edu

Library of Congress Cataloging-in-Publication Data

Names: Kezar, Adrianna, author. | DePaola, Tom, 1987– author. | Scott, Daniel T.,
    1988– author.
Title: The rise of the gig academy : mapping labor in the neoliberal university /
    Adrianna Kezar, Tom DePaola, and Daniel T. Scott.
Description: Baltimore : Johns Hopkins University Press, 2019. | Series: Reforming
    higher education : innovation and the public good | Includes bibliographical references
    and index.
Identifiers: LCCN 2019001229 | ISBN 9781421432700 (hardcover : alk. paper) |
    ISBN 9781421432717 (electronic) | ISBN 1421432706 (hardcover : alk. paper) |
    ISBN 1421432714 (electronic)
Subjects: LCSH: College teachers' unions—United States. | College teachers, Part-time—
    United States. | College teachers—Employment—United States. | College teachers—
    Professional relationships—United States. | Universities and colleges—United States—
    Faculty. | Universities and colleges—United States—Administration.
Classification: LCC LB2335.865.U6 K49 2019 | DDC 378.1/2—dc23
LC record available at https://lccn.loc.gov/2019001229

A catalog record for this book is available from the British Library.

*Special discounts are available for bulk purchases of this book. For more information, please
contact Special Sales at 410-516-6936 or specialsales@press.jhu.edu.*

Johns Hopkins University Press uses environmentally friendly book materials, including
recycled text paper that is composed of at least 30 percent post-consumer waste, whenever
possible.

Contents

....

Acknowledgments   vii

Introduction   1

1   Putting the Gig Academy in Context
    Neoliberalism and Academic Capitalism   13

2   Employees in the Gig Academy
    Insecure, Isolated, Exploited, and Devalued   36

3   Disintegrating Relationships and the Demise of Community   76

4   How Employment Practices Negatively Impact Student Learning
    and Outcomes   97

5   The Growth of Unions and New Broad-Based Organizing Strategies   120

6   Whither the Struggle
    Future Trends, Policies, and Actions   144

Notes   171
References   211
Index   245

Acknowledgments

....

We wish to thank all students, workers, educators, and organizers on the front lines building solidarity and fighting, sometimes at great risk, to create better educational conditions, to reform higher education to better realize its democratic and collectivist values, and ultimately to build a better future for all. Their critical dialogue and action around the future of higher education deeply influenced this work.

We would like to thank our generous reviewers—Tim Cain, Peter Magolda, John Curtis, and Sue Doe—for their thoughtful comments that helped us improve the manuscript. We want to dedicate this book to Peter, who passed away recently and who fought for those who have been disenfranchised. We would also like to thank the many partners of the Delphi Project on the Changing Faculty and Student Success (www.thechanging faculty.org) for championing and supporting action to better support educators, realizing they are integral to students' success.

The Gig Academy

Introduction

A temporary agency in Michigan now recruits, hires, pays, and deploys faculty to college campuses.

The University of California system outsources staff technology jobs to India.

Postdoctoral positions are becoming mandatory in many fields and increasing in length, with science fields averaging six to eight years after the doctoral degree prior to another form of employment, usually as contingent research faculty.

Positions in residence halls, bookstores, custodial work, and dining services are all outsourced to private firms that offer no benefits, do not pay overtime, and fire workers who complain.

Non-tenure-track faculty members, now 70 percent of the faculty within US higher education, average pay of $22,400 for teaching eight courses, making less than most fast-food workers and often with less job security and benefits than fast-food workers.

Graduate students unionize, realizing that they often teach or conduct research for close to a decade with poverty-level wages and poor job prospects after these long apprenticeships.

These news items are all excerpted from real headlines that illustrate massive changes in employment practices on college campuses. Recently, the shift to colleges' reliance on largely contingent faculty has finally garnered attention after nearly two decades of indifference. Fed up with their working conditions, contingent faculty workers began to band together—to speak about their plight and to unionize. Given their high levels of education and traditional social or public power, contingent faculty had the agency to voice their concerns to external audiences, even as the decline in tenure eroded that power. Surprisingly, they have found few stakeholders to take up their cause. As a result, contingent faculty are unionizing across the country.

The plight of contingent faculty has received much attention, but staff roles at academic institutions are also undergoing massive, mainly unnoticed, changes. The growth of postdoctoral and graduate student labor also has gone largely undocumented. This book outlines and connects the various changes in labor occurring across American higher education, at all types of institutions and within all job categories, because of neoliberalism. The book provides an overarching framework—through the notion of the Gig Academy—to understand these transformations.

These trends in labor have not yet been documented in one place to demonstrate their breadth and depth, and our hope is to illuminate a meta-pattern that has gone largely unnoticed. These labor trends are tied directly to neoliberal philosophy and resultant policies of academic capitalism that have transformed campuses over the past decades. Slaughter, Leslie, and Rhoades documented the rise of these neoliberal policies and academic capitalism throughout the 1980s and 1990s.[1] At that time, a public-good regime still existed that competed with academic capitalism. But by 2018, academic capitalism and neoliberal policies had become the dominant regime in higher education, leading to this wholesale shift in labor. Fueled by the larger gig economy that has become part of the fabric of business and society, the neoliberal trends are amplified and embedded within academe in recent years.

We hope not just to document these trends for the first time in one place but also to examine the implications of these changes. Given the invisibility of these trends, there are very limited data about their impact. However, where there have been studies of impact, there are documented adverse effects—most prominently on student outcomes and on campus communities and relationships. We use conceptual and theoretical literature to bridge empirical gaps and evaluate the detrimental impact of the Gig Academy on student success and outcomes, building on very solid theoretical evidence from various streams of social learning theory to support our case. Given the decades that it often takes for research programs to demonstrate a significant impact, combined with the lack of interest among funding agencies and those in power to explore these trends, we know it is imperative to document these trends and suggest implications for our institutions, even as empirical evidence is still scant.

We argue that the higher education enterprise, at its core, is a relational and people-driven enterprise and that the exploitation of the people that support and maintain the enterprise is not sustainable or ethical. Exploitation and dehumanization of labor are damaging higher education's primary mission—student success and learning—as well as secondary activities, such as scholarship, community engagement, and social critique. Learning is social—all evidence points to the central role that relationships, community, and support play in learning, particularly for first-generation, low-income, and traditionally underserved students.[2] Positive social bonds and relationships are necessary for higher education to accomplish its mission. Today, relationships, community, and social bonds are becoming extremely strained, dangerously close to collapsing the enterprise as we know it. Current labor models are not sustaining a quality learning environment, and trends suggest the future will be even worse. Chambliss and Takacs' recent ten-year longitudinal study of college students (one of the longest and most comprehensive studies of students' experience and outcomes) concluded that relationships were the most important factor for student development, learning, and future success. Add to this the recent Gallup finding that students who have the most positive outcomes after college report having a mentor in college, usually a faculty member, and the Gig Academy's labor models seem counter to common sense.[3]

Take the findings from one seminal study by Kuh et al. as an example of this issue.[4] The research examined twenty campuses that have strong success in supporting students and developing meaningful learning, finding that institutional agents were critical in fostering high levels of student engagement. Faculty and staff made it a priority to interact with students in myriad ways, ranging from supporting a student organization to sharing a cup of coffee or answering late-night e-mails. On one of the campuses, many students mentioned a staff member, Elaine, in the dining hall who was interested in their achievements, asked about their personal life, and always made sure they got enough food to make it through a hard day at school. On another, students talked about a bus driver, Eddie, who asked about their studies, inquired about exams, comforted them on a rough day, and even provided advising support. Because Eddie was a longtime staff member with a full-time position and was included in staff development, he was able to provide support for the students he interacted with on a day-to-day basis. Many students noted they could not imagine being successful in the first year of college without Eddie. We challenge institutions to make employment decisions that prioritize these everyday people—the bus driver and the cafeteria worker—whose key roles on campus have been so long overlooked.

Most student success initiatives focus on technology, interventions (novel approaches to a process like remediation or advising), and silver bullets (such as adopting a transfer policy). But these technologies and interventions will not work without people to support them. And in the end, as researchers and students themselves know, it is people who make students successful. Policy, technology, and programming do support students, but not in the absence of well-supported people to enact them.

We hold little hope that data and reasoned arguments alone will create change in the absence of political will and power. There have long existed data to support the argument that we are making this book. While we are synthesizing the data in novel ways, we are very aware that these patterns have been brought to the attention of campus leaders over the years with little or no action. As we will report on when we review trends for postdocs, sixty years of repeated reports recommending the same changes have not been heeded. Postdocs are now working collectively to create changes for themselves. And we want to make explicit that we do not see higher education as having had some golden age to which it needs to return. While working conditions are getting worse, there always have been inequalities and discrimination on campus. We wish to provide a vision for a type of workplace democracy in higher education that has yet to exist.

Rather than a report to those in power, our book is more a call to arms to bring together various groups—faculty, staff, postdocs, graduate students, and administrative and tenure-track allies—to fight the Gig Academy and neoliberalism. If there is enough collective action, then changes are possible. And while we describe unionization, we speak to multiple forms of collective action that extend beyond unions as ways to advance workplace democracy. The few advances that have been made today are based on collective action and unionization. Perhaps some administrators will be persuaded by the damage occurring to higher education institutions, and maybe others will see the inevitability of change to create better employment standards and will work to be proactive rather than reactive.

We see the following as our original contributions in this volume:

- An introduction to the Gig Academy, an extension of neoliberalism, and how it has shaped and will continue shaping the future of higher education unless action is taken;
- A review of how faculty, staff, postdocs, and graduate students' positions have been altered based on the logics of neoliberal philosophy and the Gig Academy, which will continue to further alter these positions;
- A description of the growing divide between employees and administrators based on changing employment conditions embedded in a more corporate approach;
- An understanding of the impact of the shift in employment for the overall mission of the institution, including teaching and learning as well as campus community and relationships that shape learning;
- A review of trends in unionization, more generally, that demonstrate the promise of this strategy going forward;
- A set of predictions about the future of higher education without a course correction;
- Recommended future collective actions and policy given the current tensions and chasm between employees and administrators; and
- Ideas to shape and frame employment policies and practices within the Gig Academy to offer protection from its worst iterations until broader and more sweeping changes can be made.

No other book today has addressed these important issues. And while one of the authors of this book has written extensively about the issues of non-tenure-track faculty, this volume offers a whole new set of insights into today's campus employment practices.[5]

This book is organized into six chapters that all build on a core idea: that the gig economy has become embedded into higher education and created the Gig Academy. The book divides into three sections. Chapters 1 and 2 outline the features of the Gig Academy and new labor practices; chapters 3 and 4 designate the impacts of this reorganization of the academy; and chapters 5 and 6 examine possible directions forward to ameliorate the Gig Academy and implications if no collective action or policymaking takes place in the coming years.

In chapter 1, we outline the elements of the Gig Academy—a cheap and deprofessionalized workforce, fissured workers through outsourcing, automation and uses of technology to reduce labor costs, offloading repro-duction costs onto employees, an ethic of micro-entrepreneurship, and managerial control over labor supply and demand. We also establish the Gig Academy within its roots of neoliberalism, connected to the values of corporatization, marketization, and privatization, and lay out the four-decade progression to today's labor conditions. After establishing what the Gig Academy is, in chapter 2, we provide detailed evidence of how it has shaped the labor of most higher-education workers. We demonstrate how it has shifted the working conditions of faculty and staff; expanded traditionally educational apprenticeships into labor and thus created a new set of employees, academic professionals; and altered the composition and work of administrators. What we underscore in chapter 2 is that the labor conditions of most workers in higher education have eroded dramatically.

Chapters 3 and 4 begin to examine the way the Gig Academy is shap-ing and impacting higher education. In chapter 3, we discuss the ways that the Gig Academy has eroded a sense of community on campuses. Community is essential for the public-good goals of higher education and learning, which is the focus of chapter 4. We outline the contours of how both neoliberalism and the Gig Academy have an underlying project to dismantle community, as it can be the underpinnings of collective action. Individualism can serve as an ethic that disrupts the collective conscious-ness necessary for questioning and disrupting unequal power conditions. With the breakdown of community also comes many other problematic outcomes, including disengagement, poor morale, and alienation, that are hindering higher education in meeting its outcomes and being effective. Chapter 4 explores how the Gig Academy's labor practices shape students' educational outcomes. Learning is social and requires relationships and community—thus the breakdown of community outlined in chapter 3 has real consequences for the mission of higher education, student learning. The rise in attrition, lowered graduation rates, and lower transfer rates between two-year and four-year institutions among many other outcomes can all be associated with the changing labor practices. We review social learning theory, which provides an empirical framework for understanding why learning and student outcomes are compromised by the changing working conditions for faculty and staff.

Chapters 5 and 6 consider actions for the future that are grounded in more democratic approaches to organizing higher education. Chapter 5 starts by examining unionization in higher education—looking at its growth, goals, strategies, and impact. From this empirical base, particularly its impact, a strong case can be made for unions successfully stemming some of the Gig Academy practices. However, we outline social, policy and legal challenges to unionization that limit this strategy. Chapter 6 outlines the democratic workplace as a framework for thinking differently about policymaking around working conditions. Using ideas from the democratic workplace, we draw several potential means of ameliorating some aspects of the Gig Academy to better support workers in fulfilling their essential roles in ways that preserve their dignity and provide more sustainable conditions. We also outline what will happen to the academy without collective action, demonstrating that the very soul of higher education is being eroded by practices that dehumanize workers and compromise learning.

In addition to the Gig Academy, which is an undercurrent across all chapters, there are a few themes we want to make explicit in the introduction. Power is a pervasive theme. Faculty and staff have lost power, and administrators are centralizing and gaining power. Postdocs and graduate students are asserting power as they find themselves as laborers. We argue that the consolidation of power among administrators does not serve higher education institutions. Our ultimate recommendations are centered around workplace democracy that is based on notions of power redistribution to ameliorate existing labor problems. We see collective action in multiple forms, including unionization, as the main avenue for moving forward. Collective action is articulated in chapters 5 and 6 in particular but is an undercurrent throughout the book. The world is a dynamic stage where we see workers can take action and curb the centralization and unilateral use of power that has become common today.

Values are also an important theme. Higher education espouses values such as academic primacy, equity, collegiality, shared decision-making, and egalitarianism. Yet higher education practices favor exploitation, competition, top-down authority, and efficiency. In chapter 6, we offer recommendations to create better alignment between these espoused and enacted values. Throughout the book we make note of the disconnect between our values and our practices.

A note about language: We use the term "adjunct" to refer to part-time faculty off the tenure track, as it is familiar, but we note that it is a problematic term and that "contingent part-time" is often favored by unions. "Non-tenure-track" and "contingent" refer to both full-time and part-time non-tenure-track faculty.

Audience

Our main audiences are the very faculty, staff, postdocs, and graduate students who are experiencing these changes to their working conditions. The first two chapters are helpful for assisting groups on campus to understand and see broad trends that are not apparent to individuals and can be very effective for unions and other collective groups. These groups can also use the first two chapters as data to support their case for working across different employee groups to facilitate collective action. Chapter 3 and 4 can be used for collective bargaining, to garner support from reluctant employees, and for consciousness-raising. Chapters 5 and 6 help to demonstrate the promise of union efforts as well as where and how to target union efforts.

While we see the groups affected by these changes as the primary audience, policymakers can greatly benefit from the book. State policymakers who allocate resources should use this book as they examine campus budget conditions that have long privileged facilities and technology over staffing. Policymakers may need to step in and provide more parameters around how campuses allocate funds and around employment policies and practices. While these are areas that have not been traditionally part of policymaking, the trends outlined in this book suggest that policymakers need to rethink their focus. They can align with accreditors and other groups that care about the outcomes of higher education. Furthermore, policymakers can use the book to help argue for more funding for staff and faculty as needed to meet the mission of institutions.

We see administrators as another audience for this book. Many administrators have inherited the employment patterns that exist today, and some would like advice to move higher education in a new direction. For administrators who wish to be more effective and meet their educational goals with integrity, we suggest using this book to ask questions about the current employment patterns on your campus, to ask for data about salary, benefits, and outsourcing trends, and to encourage research on the impact of changes in employment on student outcomes, learning, and campus community. Administrators might also use the suggestions and data offered in this book to guide their work with unions in collective bargaining or offer direction in policymaking.

About the Authors

In writing a book about academic labor with the goal of creating a broader coalition of actors to pursue changes in the employment trends in higher education, it is important to talk about who we are as authors. Adrianna Kezar is a tenured professor at the University of Southern California. Adrianna began her career as an adjunct at the George Washington University (GWU). She also served in a research staff role at GWU and has been in all the roles described in this book except a postdoc. She has dedicated the last fifteen years to the study of changing labor conditions, particularly related to contingent faculty. She also has written about change in higher education such as implementing improved pedagogies and curriculum and making campuses more inclusive for diverse populations over the last three decades. It is in her work on educational improvement that led her to explore the changing labor practices affecting higher education's fundamental mission. Adrianna is also dedicated to issues of equity and has explored this issue in myriad ways including improving access and success for low-income, first-generation, or underserved minority students; exploring the discrimination that women and faculty or staff of color confront; infusing curriculum and pedagogy with an awareness of historical power conditions; and combating the lack of diversity among higher education leaders. She also has a background in studying organizational practices that are more democratic in practice, such as shared governance, grassroots leadership, social movements, and collaborative approaches to working in higher education. All this work informs the ideas and focus of this book—changing labor practices, support for all faculty and staff, democratic organizational processes and approaches, equity and inclusion, and educational reform. Adrianna started The Delphi Project on the Changing Faculty and Student Success that aims to bring resources to better support faculty nationally and to create changes in policy and practice.[6] She has also been an activist her own campus to better support non-tenure-track faculty and for improved shared governance, and she works with institutions across the country on these issues.

Tom DePaola is a PhD candidate in higher education at the University of Southern California. His adviser is Adrianna, and she codirects the Pullias Center for Higher Education, where Tom works as a research assistant. They have collaborated on multiple writing projects centered on the changing nature and politics of academic labor. Tom previously earned a double bachelor's degree in literature and philosophy, graduating from the State University of New York (SUNY) at Purchase in 2010 and entering the workforce precisely at the Great Recession's nadir. Crushed by student loan payments that ate more than half of his paycheck as a part-time, low-wage barista in New York City, he lucked into a job at Bronx Community College (BCC) within the City University of New York (CUNY), working as an academic adviser and activity coordinator in the social science department. There he bonded with many of BCC's students, faculty, and administrators and found a deep appreciation for the many convergent institutional and socioeconomic forces that made the work they did so relentlessly challenging. In time, he developed a social-justice-oriented internship program and took up additional work as an adjunct instructor in the first-year program, honing his interest in critical feminist and antiracist pedagogy and fueling his drive to become an activist scholar.

After being admitted to USC's doctoral program in the Rossier School of Education, Tom underwent a stark transition from work at an under-resourced community college to an elite private research university, which, though jarring, greatly expanded his thinking about postsecondary inequality. His dissertation examines the intersection of land and labor issues within urban academic spaces. He is also a highly invested member of the graduate student organizing committee, working alongside many his peers to form a union of graduate workers at USC. Tom aspires to a career pursuing more equitable distributions of power in the academy and beyond through praxis-based teaching, research, and organizing. He is committed to advancing radical democratic movements and realizing the promise of more just cities—places like Los Angeles and New York that he has called home—and ultimately a better world through shared struggle.

Daniel Scott is also a research assistant and PhD student—that is to say, a graduate worker—at the University of Southern California. Having been a union member in professional roles in higher education, Daniel is aware of the important role that organizing plays in protecting the interests of workers and preserving recourse to collective agency. Carrying forward his emphasis on shared power, Daniel works with Tom on the graduate organizing committee at USC. As a first-generation college graduate, Daniel is dedicated to helping people bring about individual and collective social transformation through higher education. Daniel grew up in a working-class family torn apart by addiction, incarceration, and poverty. He was able to find escape, relief, and a sense of agency by processing and contextualizing these traumas through studies in literature and philosophy, consequently dedicating his life to seeking knowledge to meaningfully engage social problems and help others do the same.

As an undergraduate philosophy major, Daniel sought to become a professor so he could pass on his passion for learning and exploration to others, and through this personal journey he observed the working conditions of many new faculty who were teaching at his alma mater. Daniel's mentors compassionately alerted him to the great challenges he could face in aiming for a faculty career in philosophy—scarcity of opportunity, likelihood of long-term undercompensation, and steep competition for PhD funding—hoping to prepare him for the potentially difficult path ahead. Already weighed down by student debt, Daniel considered how many other aspiring students like himself were seeking to become philosophy professors as well and how faculty working conditions made life that much harder for them. Rather than take on the risk of an academic career trajectory, he resolved to keep his passions alive but work in college administration, where, by contrast, employment was plentiful. He hoped this work would provide a platform for improving the conditions that prevent so many from pursuing their scholarly passions.

Working as a professional staff member in a public university, and subsequently in the nonprofit sector, he took advantage of tuition remission to pursue a graduate degree part-time in preparation for possible employment in administrative leadership down the line. While in these positions, Daniel was exposed to the challenging working conditions faced by staff who, like faculty, were passionate about supporting students yet felt stymied by dismal working conditions. These experiences further cemented his desire to understand and ultimately reform the structures of employment in socially minded sectors like education. Under the mentorship of Adrianna, he is grateful to be sharing some of the first fruits of those efforts.

With our purposes, arguments, organization, audience, and selves described, we now move into our text, beginning with the Gig Academy.

ONE

Putting the Gig Academy in Context
Neoliberalism and Academic Capitalism

....

The crisis of the academy may be approaching its apotheosis. For at least two decades, scholars and commentators have been sounding the alarm around the threat of neoliberal restructuring, exhorting all who will listen to consider what stands to be lost when corporate higher education takes over. We are rapidly closing in on the institutional dystopia long feared by those who see universities as our only bulwark against the many forces that threaten free inquiry and undermine the democratic function of higher learning. This book is an attempt to unpack the deteriorating state of post-secondary labor and situate the academy within a broader constellation of trends that broadly define our new reality of precarious work and its connection to unraveling the public good role of higher education. To understand the changes that have occurred in higher education labor, we provide some conceptual frameworks that help outline why and how these changes have occurred. We begin at the broadest conceptual level by sketching neoliberalism and the shifts in logic that commonly attenuate it before turning to the way scholars theorize the neoliberal changes that have taken place within higher education under a rubric of academic capitalism. We then discuss the concept of the "gig economy"[1] as an outgrowth of neoliberalism, which emphasizes a collection of concerns with labor and approaches to workforce management.

Neoliberalism and Academic Capitalism
....

The conceptual boundaries of neoliberalism are not easily traced at a high level of abstraction because "neoliberal" can take on different shades of meaning depending on the object it describes. It can be used to characterize an ideological tendency, organizational structure, political/economic/social policy, cultural attribute, or mode of power. The features attributed to neoliberalism have manifested differently across history and regional context, with inconsistencies and contradictions. For these reasons it is perhaps best understood not as a kind of fixed order but as a normative rationality that gradually reconfigures relationships between citizens, societies, states, and markets.[2]

General neoliberal tendencies include prioritizing individual freedoms over collective liberty and personal responsibility over shared welfare. They also include a preference for shifting responsibility over the provision of basic needs and public goods from democratic institutions to private enterprises.[3] Neoliberalism animates a wide array of contemporary social arrangements. Ultimately it is only by proving examples of this normative rationality in real-world contexts that we glimpse and comprehend the extent to which neoliberalism has transformed the way we live and work at every scale, from the individual all the way up to the national and supranational.

Analyzing the neoliberalization of the academy is not new. A key point in the history of this work came over two decades ago, when the concept of academic capitalism was introduced into the lexicon of critical scholarship by Leslie and Slaughter. The theory received more robust theorizing in a follow-up volume by Slaughter and Rhoades, *Academic Capitalism and the New Economy*.[4] In it, they analyze structural shifts in higher education since the late 1970s that fundamentally altered the operational logics and institutional character of colleges and universities at every organizational level. They describe the commercialization of research through the rise in patents and copyrights, the commodification of parts through contracts, trademarks and logos, the positioning of students as consumers, and the corporatization of management through accountability schemes. At the time, Slaughter and Rhoades identified neoliberalism in higher education as an ascendant regime, as opposed to a totalizing structure. The authors make it clear that the adoption of neoliberal strategies was not something done to universities by forces external to them. Rather, much of this profound transformation was self-directed, even if structural factors like public disinvestment and federal legislation like the Bayh-Doyle Act did help to cultivate an environment that was more amenable to neoliberal restructuring.[5] *Academic Capitalism* argues that tension exists between free-market logic and a residual public-good regime that is more collectivist and egalitarian in its aims, and that this has helped constrain neoliberal proclivities that could damage the polity.

The rise of academic capitalism brought many systemic changes to universities, perhaps none more consequential than those imposed on the workers and relations of academic production. Slaughter and Rhoades' work did not focus on the shift in labor on campus. One of our major contributions is to extend their argument by focusing on academic labor. The most prominent scholarship in this area focuses on faculty, particularly the dwindling number of tenured or tenure-track faculty and concomitant growth in contingent hires (including both part-time adjunct and full-time faculty off the tenure track). Contingent faculty—a minority in the workforce just a few decades ago—now make up nearly three-quarters of all instructors.[6] Contingent faculty working conditions are detailed in chapter 2, but it is important to note that these positions often lack a living wage, benefits, pension, long-term contract, paths for career advancement, involvement in governance, protection of academic freedom, and autonomy to define one's role and work, all of which are features of professional roles. As we explore in later chapters, this shift had drastic, negative consequences on many aspects of university life, many of which continue to be understudied.

The decreased availability of permanent appointments altered the balance of power in university governance by leaving more decisions and processes to be managed by university administrators, reducing faculty autonomy and contributing to long-term deprofessionalization of the professoriate. Contingent faculty roles are often deprofessionalized through a range of material indignities caused or compounded by imposed economic insecurity. Lack of job security and poor levels of compensation have made housing and food instability surprisingly common among contingent and part-time faculty, with reports of periodic homelessness, reliance on campus food pantries, and wage-supplanting work in the underground economy, including sex work. The Labor Center at UC Berkeley recently reported that a full quarter of part-time instructors receive some kind of public assistance. These faculty shifts have proven detrimental to students; the working conditions of contingent instructors can negatively affect the overall quality of learning and decrease student success in empirically demonstrable ways, which we review in subsequent chapters.[7]

However, faculty changes are just one dimension of the large-scale shifts in academic production, even if they tend to attract the most attention. The fact is, the majority of all nonmanagement university workers, both academic and nonacademic, are employed on a part-time, temporary, or contingent basis, sometimes called "at-will," "on-demand," or "just-in-time" hiring. This book is an attempt to analyze the spectrum of postsecondary contingency more comprehensively than has been done before. We discuss the increasingly fractured professoriate, certainly, but we also strive to be more inclusive of groups that are frequently overlooked: graduate and postdoctoral employees, clinical and research-only faculty, and a wide array of nonacademic workers, from administrative support staff to service workers. All of these workers are indispensable to the functioning of the institution.

The pervasive insecurity foisted on most college employees, regardless of the particular job duties they perform, is a key strategy used to regulate the postsecondary workforce writ large. The structural lack of stability imposed by the so-called gig economy is a key part of a broader regime for regulating a surplus labor supply, which it has intentionally fabricated. It is to this concept of the gig economy—a contemporary variant of neoliberalism which sprang into our cultural consciousness in recent years—that we now shift our attention.

Gig Economy

Industries have a long history of trying to contain production costs by replacing full-time, permanent workers with short-term, contingent ones. Yet even amid union decline in the last quarter of the twentieth century, according to Rosenfeld, labor regulations seemed reasonably effective at maintaining some fundamental worker protections, such as a minimum wage and overtime. Katz and Kreuger's data on contingent labor available show that nationally, the contingent workforce has increased by more than 50 percent in the last twenty years, rising from 10.7 percent of the total workforce in 1995 to 15.8 percent in 2015. Though some critics contend the true figures might be lower, others have suggested that the Federal Labor Statistics tend to underreport contingent labor because the reporting categories fail to capture many individuals in these roles. For example, the firm Intuit, owner of TurboTax software, recently estimated that more than double that percentage work contingently, based on an analysis of the data it has from 2016 tax filings. Perhaps more ominously, researchers found that expansion of this labor segment accounts for around 95 percent of the net growth in employment in the two decades since 1995.[8]

The nature, frequency, and regulation of contingent labor fundamentally shifted with the introduction of a novel segment of businesses capitalizing on widespread mobile internet access by creating peer-to-peer markets in which to exchange goods and services: the gig economy. These new technological spaces of commerce are one factor driving the dramatic increase in contingent laborers across many sectors. One strange development in this iteration of contingent labor markets is the extent to which contingency and withdrawal of protections have been culturally reconfigured as virtuous markers of self-reliance. These widespread changes are significant to higher education, where workers confront a similar transformation in conjunction with the proliferation of digital-age knowledge and information commodities. Standard gig economy firms (e.g., Uber) breed a contingent workforce by incentivizing micro-entrepreneurship, say, by offering a convenient way to rent out resources people already possess but underutilize—whether a means of transportation, guest bedroom, skill set, or perhaps simply time and attention.[9] Companies extract profits by in turn renting access to proprietary digital platforms that facilitate these transactions as independent contracting arrangements. Redefining workers as independent contractors is a way of legally circumventing a formal employee designation—a convenient regulatory loophole through which firms can avoid offering workers benefits and job protections.[10]

Workers in the gig economy are construed by the system's advocates as empowered with the flexibility of choosing when and when not to work. While some may find gig work practical and lucrative, the vast majority earn well below a living wage. A recent survey found nearly half of all workers in the gig economy today depend on such jobs as their primary source of income. The same poll showed that 41 percent of gig economy workers report experiencing economic anxiety, compared to 32 percent of full-time workers. The most recent edition of "Freelancing in America," the largest existing study of the independent labor force, projects that if trends continue at the current rate, freelance workers in the United States could outnumber traditional workers as soon as 2027.[11]

Even if work in the gig economy is plentiful, because wages are so low, many workers find the promised flexibility to be an illusion, since they must work longer and longer hours to make ends meet. A recent in-depth qualitative study of sixty-five gig workers by Petriglieri et al. found that every one of the participants, regardless of how much they claimed to appreciate the additional flexibility of gig-work schedules, reported some degree of personal, social, or economic anxiety linked to the precariousness and isolation of at-will employment.[12] Even the most financially successful participants reported persistent fears about income, reputation, and identity. Those who dealt with these anxieties most effectively did so by actively cultivating connections to places, routines, purposes, and people. For many postsecondary contingent workers, particularly those compelled to take part-time, short-term contracts at multiple institutions, that strategy may not be tenable.

The term "gig economy" is often used as a leitmotif for our high-tech, postindustrial era in general. Informality aside, it can also provide a useful construct for elaborating and updating a key dimension of Slaughter and Rhoades' theory: academic capitalism's effect on working relations and conditions in higher education.[13] Where their landmark book tends to emphasize processes of external market-seeking by universities, our work examines the dynamics of internal labor-restructuring in more depth and looks at how the university as a workplace has grown more complex over time.

In this chapter we explore the usefulness of the gig economy as a metaphor. Does it offer a way of framing the changing nature of college work now that academic capitalism has guided postsecondary policy for nearly three decades? Few attempts have been made to seriously analyze the features and tropes of the gig economy alongside the neoliberal university. Aside from a handful of editorial pieces,[14] to the best of our knowledge, there is only one existing long-form publication from a scholarly press that directly sets out to theorize some of these linkages. Hall, in an extended essay published as part of a series highlighting provocative analyses of "in-process" phenomena, reflects on what he terms the "Uberfication" of higher education. He explores several changes that have plausible parallels in the "sharing economy" (Hall's preferred nomenclature, synonymous with "gig economy"), drawing on Foucault's theories of disciplinary power and entrepreneurialism much as Slaughter and Rhoades did years earlier, as did more recent authors such as Bousquet and Brown. Hall's short book is a meditation on what befalls the university as advanced capitalist nations continue lurching toward a society not of people but of individual enterprises—blurring the distinctions between brand and citizen within an economy defined increasingly by the attempts of "platform capitalists" to reimagine every activity as source of rents. Platforms like Uber and Airbnb encourage individuals to rent their labor and property to one another, and charge everyone rent on the space of transaction itself. Others, such as the music "sharing" platform Spotify, normalize rent-based modes of consuming media and other intellectual property, which concentrates their ability to regulate access and force down wages. Universities, like these firms, leverage their status as platforms to surveil, de-skill, and devalue the labor they need to function, charging rents to students and workers alike for platform access and instilling the notion that contingency is best overcome individually through competitive rent-seeking instead of collectively through solidarity.[15] Hall explores several themes with which our own analysis overlaps. In some ways, this book contributes further support for his arguments by providing empirical data and trends and by offering a more thorough account of the overarching shifts to contingent labor that Hall covers largely in abstract terms. We hope this deeper dive can help usher in a more nuanced conversation as we continue to grapple with the cascade of changes in how we live, work, and learn in our increasingly tech-augmented society.

Universities' need for highly trained workers means that they must produce their own cheap workforce. For years, they have simultaneously expanded the number of doctoral degrees granted while constricting the number of stable academic jobs, creating a system in which low wages and precariousness are standard terms of employment for the least *and* most educated workers alike.

Today this means the working conditions of most nonmanagerial employees on campus are becoming more similar to each other than ever, regardless of the kind of labor performed. Contingency pervades college work in ways that has universalized certain experiences of devaluation and vulnerability. This state of affairs ought not be perceived as normal, natural, or inevitable but as the product of institutional choices. We select the term "Gig Academy" as a way to encompass this cluster of mutations that long-term restructuring toward cheap and disposable labor in higher education has wrought and to signal its relation to changes in the broader knowledge economy. So we now shift from a discussion of the contours of the gig economy to that of the Gig Academy.

Contours of the Gig Academy

There are several philosophical and values shifts that undergird the Gig Academy as well as forms of labor restructuring that characterize it. In this section, we review the values shifts that have become embedded into and support new forms of work, including a fissured and misclassified workforce; unbundled, deprofessionalized, and atomized roles; forced micro-entrepreneurship; managerial influence over labor supply and demand; offloading costs onto workers; technological means of reducing labor costs; and increasing structural discrimination. While several of these exist within academic capitalism—particularly unbundling and contingency—they are further deployed or transformed within the Gig Academy.

Fissured Workers through Outsourcing and Misclassification

Economists from the Roosevelt Institute, among others, are sounding the alarm that union decline is not the sole explanation for evaporating worker power and wage stagnation—there are related issues involving disproportionate market power and uses of technology. Labor outsourcing is an important culprit, whereby workers are disaggregated from full-time employment into franchised, part-time, temporary contracting, or subcontracting arrangements. Neither the Wagner Act nor the current regulatory system or safety net is in a position to mitigate these effects, especially for the United States' 2.9 million temporary workers, 5.7 million involuntary part-time workers, and 25 million independent contractors. The information technology, human resources, and finance sectors in recent years have seen rapid shifts to outsourcing economy-wide, including in higher education. Industry analysts at Deloitte are confident outsourcing will continue to surge in 2018 and beyond. And recent commentary suggest that current reports greatly underestimate the volume of contingent workers due to the way the Bureau of Labor Statistics collects data, which itself may be helping outsourcing practices to continue growing without effective scrutiny or regulation.[16]

Contingency is of course widespread in higher education, but divisions within that label are increasingly multifaceted. The Gig Academy is heavily infused with outsourced employment in many nonacademic staff and service positions. In addition to cutting labor costs, this fragments the workforce into de-linked sets of working relations, increasing legal and administrative barriers to any sort of cooperative action. These discrete blooms of subcontracted employees constitute what Weil calls the "fissured workplace," which is a result of the rising tendency for firms and organizations to separate core functions from auxiliary ones and transfer responsibility for the latter to third-party vendors.[17] College campuses are one among many types of workplaces that are rapidly fissuring in the new economy.

Where workers in housing, dining, security, maintenance, landscaping, tech support, and other areas once had a shared claim to the status and rights of university employees, now each of these areas can be staffed separately at a discount using private companies, each with its own distinct (largely part-time or contingent) supply of labor. Because employees work for many different employers, they are separated and constrained in their ability to organize at a scale that might constitute a threat. Imposed contingency is thus a crucial instrument for managing the workforce mediated through networks of subcontractors. For university administrations, outsourcing not only frees up resources (for administration) but simplifies the process of acquiring a fluid supply of labor available on demand, at any scale, with no additional commitment of time or human resources required of the institution.

Weil, for his part, was proactive during the three years he served as Administrator of Wage and Hour Division with the Obama-era Department of Labor about moving to close legal loopholes that gig economy firms, among others, were known to exploit. Chief among his efforts was the drafting and implementation of new regulations taking aim at widespread worker misclassification. Under these rules, workers who are repeatedly hired as independent contractors, but for whom their "economic reality" reveals a relationship of economic dependency to the employer, would be considered misclassified and mandated to the status of full employees. These misclassifications matter, particularly to workers on the receiving end, who lose basic protections of employment, including minimum wage and overtime protection, as well as social safety net protections, such as workers' compensation and unemployment insurance, because independent contractors do not contribute to those funds. But they also matter to the polity, since misclassified workers can be used to craft exemptions from payroll taxes, which would otherwise cycle back into the public coffers.[18]

Worker misclassification happens throughout the economy and is not unique to employment in app-based gig services. At the same time, virtually none of the research addressing the problem examines its prevalence in higher education. Some university managers undoubtedly perceive misclassification as offering multiple tactical benefits—not only cost-effectiveness but also sidestepping antidiscrimination regulations, obscuring race and gender inequity in hiring, and making unionization efforts intrinsically more difficult.[19] Many contingent instructors hired on short-term contracts and classified as independent would not pass Weil's "economic reality test," since they both depend on this work to survive and tend to be rehired semester after semester under the same erroneous designation.

Unbundling Roles to Deprofessionalize and Atomize Workers

Because of the complexity of occupations such as medicine, law, and scholarship, professional associations and forms of professionalization emerged to protect the integrity and quality of these jobs by ensuring that decisions about working conditions remained in the hands of qualified and committed experts.[20] But autonomous, collective decision-making by faculty inhibits the ability of administrators to optimize resource flows and production processes, so undermining these professional entitlements became a central preoccupation of academic restructuring.

For this reason, unbundling is a crucial arrow in the quiver of Gig Academy managers. This trend developed directly out of the discourse on "scientific management," also known by the moniker "Taylorism," after its creator. The key is to study complex work processes and devise ways to reproduce them by disassembling the tacit expertise of highly skilled workers into the simplest components. Each of these components is standardized in order to distill the process down to a mechanical sequence that can be delivered far more cheaply by substituting or supplementing low- to middle-skilled labor.[21] In this manner, the contemporary university has managed to break down complicated professional roles like those of academic faculty, which paved the way to displace large portions of work onto contingent hires.

By unbundling traditional faculty roles, administrators can assume a greater degree of control over institutional resource flows and reconfigure them to optimize return on investment. Advisement can be accomplished far more efficiently as a separate job than when professors advise students in a decentralized, idiosyncratic fashion. Often with the help of data tools, academic progress is monitored by dedicated workers who do nothing but track indicators for signs of students at risk of failing, which in its repetitive simplicity does not command the premium compensation afforded to permanent faculty. Instruction suffers the same fate—since far more people can communicate course content to undergraduates than can win prestigious grants, these positions are vulnerable to being unbundled and casualized. But students need advice about careers and networking opportunities from faculty that technology cannot supply. When positions are deprofessionalized, key aspects of roles are often lost.

Meanwhile, faculty who are fortunate enough to work free of contingency are increasingly insulated from responsibilities thought to be central to the job of a professor, including teaching, advisement, assessment, grading, and course design, once performed alongside scholarly activities like research and writing for publication. And today's faculty have less involvement and sway in matters concerning institutional governance. There is little evidence to attest that this kind of unbundling actually produces any long-term gains in efficiency, cost-effectiveness, or student learning outcomes.[22] In fact, it seems to be the opposite: faculty whose roles are unbundled are often stymied in their ability to provide high-quality instruction.

Faculty can even avoid much of the rudimentary work of actual research and serve merely in an oversight capacity, with contingent labor conscripted to meet the needs of scholarly production: postdocs, graduate students, research-only appointments, and the like. The combined cost of workers from these segments is far short of what it would cost to have permanent faculty produce the same research. Unbundling not only fragments the university workforce into highly complex chains of production but is undertaken despite its documented negative effects on teaching and learning.[23] It is reasonable to conclude that these trends reflect a desire to concentrate power rather than strengthen educational missions. While deprofessionalization is most prominently documented among faculty, it is also seen commonly among staff, whose roles are also being routinized and professional expertise de-emphasized. For example, many student affairs roles are being automated, and the advice and decisions they once provided to students have been replaced with computer alerts and data analytics.

The Academic Micro-Entrepreneur

Originally the parlance of jazz musicians and other artists, the term "gig" can evoke cultural assumptions about the person undertaking it—that is to say, gigs are usually interpreted as the kind of short-term work people motivated by passion, drive, and creativity do.[24] By implication, under-remuneration and experiential compensation are socially acceptable for this kind of work. Gig work conjures the image of the artist and bohemian, who seeks to remain untethered and therefore free to pursue activities of passion—a freedom which may be culturally signaled at least in part by a rebellious indifference to long-term planning for financial security. Universities no doubt benefit from a detrimental tendency of many aspiring academics to romanticize the life of the mind as a liberating career, as Bousquet illustrates:

> Universities, digital industry, and other employers of "mental labor" have succeeded in interpellating intellectual workers more generally with the "bohemian" ideology that previously was reserved for artistic occupations: large new sectors of intellectual labor have proved willing to accept not merely the exploitation of wage slavery but the super-exploitation of the artist, in part because the characteristics of casual employment (long and irregular hours, debt subsidy, moonlighting, the substitution of reputation for a wage, casual workplace ethos, etc.) can so easily be associated with the popular understanding of normative rewards for 'creative' endeavor.[25]

Universities discovered how to monetize their employees' aspirations in order to produce academics with the discipline to tolerate gig work as long as possible before giving up on professional advancement. Passion is not the only useful pressure point; there is also a common need to recoup the exorbitant costs of doctoral studies, which for some can lead to motivated reasoning in a desperate attempt to stave off the terrifying possibility that so much training and sacrifice could become worthless. "I'll give it one more year" has doubtless become a tragic refrain for many qualified would-be faculty. To be clear, this is not to say that colleges successfully or even actively sell a romanticized version of the academy to prospective contingent hires; rather, persistent misconceptions about contemporary academia and the viability of a career in it are simply an advantageous byproduct of more diffuse neoliberal attitudes that success or failure is determined solely by level of dedication and keeping the large patterns of labor and hiring hidden. And some tenure-track (as well as non-tenure-track) faculty become extremely talented at tapping external revenue sources and begin to hire their own gig workforce with labs with dozens of postdocs or contingent faculty. These academic capitalists replicate the labor practices of administrators.

As Slaughter and Rhoades argue using Foucault, neoliberal market logic is disciplining not only in the way it elicits worker compliance but in the way it seeds the very subjectivity of individuals as more and more domains of social interaction become vulnerable to reconstitution in the style and mode of a competitive enterprise. Entrepreneurialism is a way that competition becomes embedded in workers and working conditions. As Brown among others point out, one distressing side effect of this is that when everyone is fixated on the task of cultivating their own personal brand, the notion of a university's public good mission starts to become unmoored from egalitarian values of collectivism and citizenship and increasingly bound up in neoliberal terms that prize individual advantage.[26]

If professorial fantasies can draw academics into extended periods of contingency, other workers across the organization may be compelled by virtuous notions of education as a sacred calling and a desire to work in service of a social good. This applies to many kinds of staff members, who may tolerate lower wages partly because they believe in the mission of universities and feel that employment on campus is more meaningful. Women who dominate the clerical and staffing positions at universities have long been attracted to college and university employment through this lure, and the Gig Academy leverages this perceived ethos to support worker complacency.[27]

Managerial Influence on Labor Supply and Demand

High-level management plays a critical role in maintaining the Gig Academy. With authority over the size and composition of the contingent workforce, they make hiring decisions that work to constrain the academic labor market as a whole and actively put downward pressure on wages to generate cost savings. These administrators have the collective incentive to reduce demand for primary (secure) workers while increasing the supply of primary job seekers. Once the latter are sufficient in number, they become less resistant to participation in the secondary labor market, recalling Marx's industrial reserve army. By restricting secure and well-paid positions to upper management and a smattering of faculty, while at the same time engineering a surplus of PhDs many times what the job market can absorb, institutions capitalize on the depressed value of labor which they have collectively brought about through systemic overproduction. In other words, human capital waste is built into the production process as a function of neoliberal governance.[28] Prior to the era of academic capitalism, mass contingency could not possibly sustain universities because the number of people with advanced training was scarce relative to the needs of the expanding postsecondary system. It is no accident this is not the case anymore.

Gig economy firms maintain a similarly stratified workforce, on the one hand keeping a modest number of stable, well-compensated managers and employees (executives, lawyers, supervising engineers, various marketing and technical experts, etc.) while on the other generating profits by cultivating reserve populations of interchangeable drivers, shoppers, etc., and channeling them as needed into single-use contracts. Platform owners and their algorithms set the prices and choose the level of rent to extract from the transaction. In both the Gig Academy and the gig economy, the reserve army is the key to providing instant delivery; the only difference is the level of skill required. Whether one needs a car ride to the airport in two minutes or an instructor to teach one semester of English in two weeks, it can be delivered cost-effectively only if the labor required exists in sufficient oversupply that someone can always be mobilized on demand.

Shifting Economic Risk onto Workers

As we have argued, the Gig Academy employs the tools of scientific management to unbundle work and to deprofessionalize and atomize workers in the service of flexible accumulation. Once everything has been unbundled into the simplest units of work, each one can be administered in the manner of a gig—that is, as a self-contained production process. Similar to the managers of gig economy platforms, this allows academic managers to simultaneously maximize institutional returns and flexibility over workers while minimizing risks and waste. One factor that makes this possible is the way this arrangement allows employers to foist all costs of reproduction back onto the worker. Consider a comparison of how this can unfold in each domain.

An Uber driver is responsible for the costs of owning, maintaining, and repairing all equipment necessary to perform the work; in short, with the only relevant measure of value of work being the outcome of an individual task, every delivery cost is forced back upon individual workers. A two-mile ride hail nets the driver four dollars whether the trip takes five minutes or an hour; meanwhile, the platform skims a 30-percent cut regardless of absolute cost to the worker.

It is not so different for the typical adjunct, who must provide their own office space, computer supplies, copies, telephone, internet, and so forth, not to mention healthcare and insurance. If they sign a contract to teach forty people three credits' worth of instruction in English and composition over four months for a fee of three thousand dollars, that rate is fixed regardless of whether the professor commutes five miles or fifty, whether it takes twenty minutes or two hours to grade an exam, and whether or not they must manage a chronic health condition, provide for children, or care for elderly family members. Staff face the same challenge, with campuses increasingly hiring marketing, development, recruitment, and other staff through contingent appointments. These staff also are expected to provide their own office supplies, telephone and internet service, and benefits. The employer's concern can be confined to the wage and nothing else. Since the dawn of the labor movement such arrangements have been considered an unacceptable and dehumanizing violation of labor protections and basic dignity.

Technological Means of Reducing Labor Costs

Technology plays an important role in the story. The "just-in-time" service mantra of the gig economy appears again and again with the waves of hype around every new "innovation." Technology can be used thoughtfully to support student learning, and faculty and staff can be involved in decisions about its use. However, in the Gig Academy, technology is often deployed in problematic ways. One commonly decried example of this is the development of massive open online courses, or MOOCs, initially heralded as a postsecondary "revolution" by Moody's. The rising popularity of platforms like Coursera, Udemy, and Udacity became a lightning rod in the debate over higher learning in the digital age. Yet despite the confidence of venture capital, within a just few years the imminent threat of MOOCs was revealed to be overblown. Recently the vice president of Udacity in an interview bluntly admitted that MOOCs are "dead." Prior to fizzling out, universities that offered free courses on Coursera searched for new ways to monetize the platform, including using it as an interface through which various support services could be purchased on demand, such as academic tutors, translators, and discussion moderators. Had it come to fruition, this would have essentially provided a way for universities to squeeze additional value out of graduate and undergraduate workers and contingent faculty by using Coursera as an instant labor contractor, much like other digitally mediated freelance work, while creating streams of transactions from which the university could extract surplus. In other instances professors can be encouraged to design course content for other on-demand e-learning ventures.[29] Likely, contingent staff would be hired to manage online courses—to advice, assess, and provide student support. These practices are already common in for-profit models of higher education.

Another place the technological side of the gig economy is gaining a foothold in higher education is in the evolution of workforce management software. As more postsecondary work is unbundled and workers become outsourced to many different staff providers, the use of human capital management (HCM) tools such as Oracle and Workday with the capacity to manage large organizational ecosystems of contingent labor has started to proliferate in higher education. Workday, for instance, is an increasingly popular HCM software system which is advertised as "uniquely designed for higher education." Targeting colleges and universities specifically, Workday's website describes "uniting financial and workforce planning" within one "flexible, modern platform that can adapt to your changing needs."[30]

Among the features it offers are tools to "support workforce restructuring [and] optimization," allowing for the easy processing of contingent hires, and algorithms to guide staffing decisions that help determine which configurations are most "conducive to growth." It eliminates many transaction costs of hiring internationally, since the platform can integrate workers across the globe and automatically resolve currency exchange and compliance issues through its payroll systems. Many elite research institutions are counted among its clients, including Yale, Cornell, Brown, Penn, Carnegie-Mellon, and the University of Southern California. Much like the scheduling software notoriously used by fast food restaurants and other low-wage employers, which shaves labor costs through erratic shift assignments and hour totals that have been surgically calculated to avoid triggering benefits eligibility, Workday allows academic managers to hire adjuncts for last-minute course additions while accounting for budget impacts in real time. Academic workers, however seamlessly conscripted and dismissed, are not quite as functionally interchangeable as say, Uber drivers; still, this approach essentially mimics the same labor structure. As digital labor intermediaries, Workday and Uber both serve as interfaces built to manage a flexible workforce that can provide services on demand.

Among the major technology systems controlling faculty are course management systems, particularly for faculty who primarily teach online. These days most faculty are expected to have their courses administered through these systems. Some faculty are asked to design courses that are embedded into such systems so that individual faculty lose intellectual property rights to the courses they create. Managers can use these systems to control and audit faculty work, to replace aspects of faculty work, and potentially to fully supplant faculty.

Another major area where technology platforms have taken off in higher education is intrusive student tracking and advising. Increasingly, technology systems are being developed to replace the traditional work of staff and faculty in advising students. For-profit companies are developing technologies intended to automate various postsecondary functions with the promise that these can "disrupt" many expensive and outdated processes traditionally done by professionals by offering something cheaper and scientifically optimized. However, even assuming they work as advertised, most of these technologies only streamline a portion of the work, perhaps a single task that has been abstracted from the organic learning environment, which leaves support gaps that can undermine student success and fragment the student experience. These technologies are unlikely to replace the integrative social and emotional supports many students need to persist and develop as college students, as studies in social learning and educational neuroscience have demonstrated.[31]

Systems that are designed to make aspects of the university more Uber-like in their delivery undermine both worker protections and privacy rights. This marks a new way of conceptualizing work in the Gig Academy: When using or cooperating with various human-capital or learning-management platforms is a condition of being hired, submitting oneself to data surveillance and therefore shouldering substantial privacy risks actually becomes a de facto job duty. This suggests that discussions of insecurity among contingent workers ought to take a dual meaning: these workers are made vulnerable not only to arbitrary dismissal but also to exposure of their valuable personal data—a risk that can multiply with adjuncts working part-time at multiple institutions that all use different data platforms.

None of these developments were natural or inevitable, which is why it is important to analyze technologies that enable and benefit from contingent labor as a key part of the ecosystem of postsecondary restructuring. Information and communications technology is not automatically a tool for deprofessionalizing and devaluing work; it can be augmentative. Advancements in educational technology sometimes genuinely enhance work that remains the respected purview of dedicated professionals. In this case the Gig Academy's techno-entrepreneurialism contributes to altered relations of production: any digital platforms that stand a chance of getting adopted (purchased) are almost certain to reinforce existing power imbalances in the institutional structure as a basic precondition.

Structural Discrimination

The Gig Academy, like the gig economy, is rife with workplace discrimination, some of which is due to quality control issues that intrinsically manifest when large, fluid populations of contingent workers are involved in production. University managers may try to partly address the problem through outsourcing. By subcontracting with a labor provider that has its own review and quality control procedures, the institution can be absolved of liability for most accusations of discrimination, exploitation, or harassment, so long as workers answer to the external firm. This strategy generally only works with service workers and support staff.

For contingent instructors, quality control processes are similar to those for gig economy workers like Uber drivers—both work through crowdsourcing. App-based services achieve cost efficiencies from independent contracting arrangements because they are made using an algorithm rather than a thinking human resources professional. Those who sign up to be drivers or hosts are not typically vetted by another person before they can begin accepting customers. Instead, the gig economy relies on customer reviews and star ratings that aggregate over time to form a supposedly objective metric of quality which has been distilled by the free market. But as Hannák et al. recently uncovered in their study of bias in app-based freelance work, women and people of color face significant job discrimination, as structural social biases also get aggregated in the form of negative customer feedback and lower ratings, which ultimately reduces their earnings. Worse, these services often enforce minimum rating standards, meaning workers can find themselves permanently banned from the platform at a moment's notice and without recourse if they fail to meet the minimum level of customer satisfaction, undoubtedly a fate more likely to befall those who already experience arbitrary social bias.[32] This same structural discrimination is at work in the Gig Academy.

Contingent faculty and their advocates have long criticized universities for relying on student evaluations to assess the re-employability of adjuncts and the nontenured, which, along with a glance at course passing rates, has all but replaced any other means of assessment. In a 2015 interview with the *Chronicle of Higher Education*, the founder of Udemy (a prominent MOOC platform) argues that student ratings are the ideal form of instructional quality control: "In an open marketplace where there

Figure 1 Amazon's published demographics.
Diversity at Amazon, "Our Workplace Demographics," July 2016, www.amazon
.com/b/ref=tb_surl_diversity/?node=10080092011.

is competition, if you're an instructor and you can't teach well or you don't
know what you're talking about, students will say so with ratings . . . *If
you're not providing value, you won't make money*—only the best teachers go to the top." The most obvious problem with this statement is that
there is a great deal of empirical evidence to show that student evaluations
of teaching are not always measures of instructional quality, and they
show clear bias on the basis of race, gender, and perceived political orientation. Furthermore, because adjuncts know their chances of getting rehired can depend largely on student evaluations of teaching and passing
rates, they have strong incentives to placate students, dilute assignments,
avoid sensitive topics, and inflate grades. Regardless of actual merit, if an
instructor's evaluations are too low, a department chair could simply decide not to renew their contract, which again, is more likely to happen to
nonwhite, nonmale adjuncts.[33]

Universities and gig economy firms alike have learned to mask underlying inequities through strategic counting. In carefully deciding what
employees should be counted and how to count them, contingent workers can be instrumentally included or omitted to serve the institution's image.
Gig employment platforms have been known to count concentrations of
workers of color in low-wage, contingent positions to skew their diversity statistics. For example, by including all workers and disaggregating by
race but not the role they serve in, Amazon is able to deflect some scrutiny
and (partly) obscure the full extent of its widespread race and gender
stratification (figure 1).[34]

Despite such arithmetical sleights of hand, it remains well known that
women and people of color are woefully underrepresented among the
ranks of CEOs, technical officers, and well-paid engineers that build and

maintain these applications, and that any who do make it that far tend to face routine harassment—something which is also true of higher education's upper echelons.[35]

Universities can use other means of obfuscation as well. If they have subcontracted most campus services and support functions, they have no obligation to report the demographics of workers in these sectors, which in all likelihood contain problematic patterns. Decentralized reporting structures often give departmental discretion over how or whether contingent faculty hires are tracked, which makes it challenging to aggregate data across departments. Omitting contingent workers from any official figures gives some universities a way to maintain an institutional ignorance about the size and demographics of the contingent workforce. At the same time and perhaps unsurprisingly, the most secure and prestigious positions—executive administrators, tenured faculty—remain considerably overrepresented by white men.[36]

Even before considering race and gender gaps among faculty, contingent appointments created in the process of unbundling are deprofessionalized in many ways beyond undercompensation and insecurity. Teaching-only faculty, for instance, may be recruited at the last minute and forced to use prefabricated course syllabi with prescribed texts, assignments, and other teaching materials such as slideshows or activities, undercutting whatever agency and respect they would normally be afforded based on professional expertise.[37] When race and gender discrepancies are added on top of this, the disproportionately harmful impact of contingent arrangements comes into sharp relief.

Limits of a Metaphor

Analogizing the contemporary university with a gig economy firm, we argue, can in fact help us understand neoliberalism's evolved role in restructuring postsecondary labor markets. Still, the analogy is not a perfect fit, and it is important to highlight some key differences between contemporary higher education and the gig economy.

If we imagine students as the users of gig service platforms, one major difference emerges in the arena of consumer cost. The meteoric rise of gig services and popularity among consumers is due not to their convenience—after all, on-demand services have always been available to those with enough wealth. The novelty is competitive pricing that allows for instant delivery on an industrial scale. Firms offer these discounts in two ways: first by using a drastically underpaid contingent workforce and second by subsisting on venture capital, initially operating the enterprise at a loss (sometimes for years) in order to undercut the competition into oblivion and corner the market. These two pillars constitute the primary strategy of Uber and their ilk, but higher education is constrained in its ability to fully replicate this model. Even as universities shift to leaner production methods for their educational mission, the costs to consumers have still grown exponentially. Whatever purpose labor restructuring in higher education has served, it is clearly not being used to make college costs more competitive.

So where does the institutional savings obtained from contingent workers go if not to the consumer? Generally, toward noneducational aims that help universities function as sites of accumulation. In chapter 2, we detail how some of college and university costs have gone to hire highly paid administrative staff to manage the contingent staff. Additionally, studies show that revenues are going to noninstructional activities that enhance the universities' reputations and rankings, such as massive research infrastructures and physical plant improvements. Physical campuses with all of the infrastructure and equipment necessary to carry out academic production represent a vital base of assets for most institutions—and thus infrastructure costs are far more substantial for universities than for firms digitally aggregating gig work. This focus on infrastructure development is particularly true today when so many institutions have embraced a growth strategy rooted in amenities-driven development and a luxe student experience.[38]

Additionally, gig economy services generally broker commodities exclusively offering use value, while higher education sells products with a complicated assemblage of both use and exchange values. Because gig economy firms are motivated exclusively by shareholder returns, social power is leveraged only when necessary to support that aim. Universities, however, are driven by more than revenue—there is a broader economy of prestige intersecting the Gig Academy, which currently has no parallel in the consumer gig economy.[39] This alters the business calculus significantly. Universities wield social power through their role in knowledge production, not merely to accrue more wealth but to compete for superior recognition. This helps further account for the tuition problem: in a world where price is a convenient proxy for quality, rising degree costs are a necessary component of prestige-signaling within the academic capitalist regime. The point is for others to recognize the institution's high value. Students today pay tens of thousands of dollars more per year on average for an undergraduate degree than preceding generations, a fact about which few need to be reminded.[40] Yet unlike in the past, most of the workers hired to service nearly every aspect of the intellectual, social, and aesthetic experience of college today are exploited.

Higher education differs from the gig economy in another respect: the general absence of algorithmically mediated "peer-to-peer" commerce. Among app-based gig enterprises like Uber, labor markets are directly regulated by software, as opposed to formal agencies that place people into temporary employment. Such temporary employment agencies have been used for corporate downsizing and outsourcing for years. The app-based platform replaces this form of intermediary and provides a thick digital buffer between workers and anyone with whom they could attempt to lodge a complaint. This also means that universities, unlike gig firms, have human managers that can be more easily made into clear targets of collective action. By contrast, app workers cannot confront management; management is not a person but an algorithm.

Only by grappling much more deeply with ongoing changes in the organization of postsecondary work can we arrive at some plausible ways of contesting neoliberalism within higher education. The pervasive spread of contingent, deprofessionalized, and precarious employment in institutions of higher education suggests we need a new way of thinking about collective solutions, something along the lines of what Platzer and Allison call "ecological solidarity," capable of finding commonality for a heavily segmented and fragmented workforce.[41] We explore collective solutions in the book's conclusion.

The epithet "gig economy" did not exist when Slaughter and Rhoades published *Academic Capitalism*, but as an insurgent construction in the popular consciousness, it is useful for bounding the constellation of trends we focus on in this book.[42] In the chapters that follow we review empirical data about how the Gig Academy has transformed the postsecondary workforce.

TWO

Employees in the Gig Academy

Insecure, Isolated, Exploited, and Devalued

In 1998, Rhoades's landmark study, *Managed Professionals*, described how tenured and tenure-track faculty were gradually ceding more and more power to university administrators over crucial areas of academic decision-making.[1] This work appears in retrospect as an urgent warning that went unheeded. Although it earned wide praise at the time and accrued hundreds of citations, over the twenty years since its publication the neoliberal reorganization of work on college campuses has only accelerated and continued to spread into nearly every job that remains in higher education today. In this way, it has brought about what we are calling the Gig Academy: a university that has become fully dependent on a patchwork of loosely connected contingent workforces to service both its central missions and its day-to-day operations. Today we have moved beyond traditional faculty as managed professionals into an era of comprehensively managed *institutions*, rendered as such to obtain maximum rates of continuous growth.

In this chapter, we survey many ways the state of labor has been transformed on college campuses. The overall trends across each group show many similarities. The characteristics of contingent, temporary, and part-time work in the Gig Academy include a reduced salary (often below a living wage) and benefits, unbundled and outsourced roles, forced entrepreneurship, deprofessionalization, minimal autonomy, and maximum external control. For faculty, important protections like academic freedom and inclusion in governance are withheld. In the Gig Academy, a growing proportion of faculty, postdocs, graduate students, and staff have quite similar poor working conditions: subsistence wages; lack of benefits, retirement funds, and vacation time; no influence over conditions of work or structures of advancement; and constant anxiety over the possibility of arbitrary termination. These trends impact all institutional types, but they are often more drastic at public institutions and poorly resourced institutions such as community colleges. To be sure, these employment trends parallel those of other sectors in the wake of the neoliberal turn and rise of the gig economy. But unlike other professionals who face contingency but earn higher salaries in lieu of loss of insurance and other benefits, such as doctors and lawyers, for faculty it is the opposite. In no other sector has contingency among high-skill professionals come with such dramatic wage decreases.

Staff employment changes more closely parallel other sectors. Some postsecondary staff in higher education once enjoyed special benefits, such as tuition remission for themselves or their children or flexible work schedules to accommodate family obligations. For years this made the sector attractive for many kinds of workers and supported intergenerational mobility, but these benefits have largely disappeared.

It is unsurprising that these trends produce workers with lower satisfaction and morale, who feel more alienated from their work and the campus community and incur greater levels of disrespect and marginalization. Magolda's recent study of the working lives of campus custodians observed that these staff have gone from feeling like part of a community in which they were connected to the faculty, staff, and students to feeling they are no longer respected or even visible and increasingly under the thumb of corporate administrators.[2] As greater proportions of faculty, staff, graduate students, and postdocs come to feel exploited by organizations nominally linked to the common good, any shared notion of campus community suffers, a theme we explore in the next chapter in more detail.

First, we review how the work trends across various labor segments in higher education reveal consistent patterns of exploitation, alienation, and devaluation, which are destroying satisfaction and morale among employees across the postsecondary spectrum. We begin the chapter describing staff, as they tend to be overlooked in discussions of the changing labor, and follow by discussing contingent faculty, postdocs, and graduate student employees. We end the chapter by describing the consistent growth of administrators in number, power, and salary over the years. Examining this contrast is instructive for understanding the widening gulf that separates academic managers from the rest of the campus community, which itself continues to grow more fragmented. Throughout this chapter we will define these groups and clarify what we mean when we refer to staff, faculty, or administrators, as these are large umbrellas which contain many within-group differences.

Staff

University staff are a frequently overlooked category of workers in terms of the structural changes that have transformed their employment relations over time. As noted by Mello: "Despite the noticeable growth in and important organizational functions carried out by support staff, this population has neither been extensively written about nor examined."[3]

According to the National Center for Education Statistics, the postsecondary sector had over 2 million staff members in 2016. Colleges and universities are made up of a wide variety of staff—the website Higher Ed Jobs, for instance, divides these workers into dozens of different subcategories.[4] Nearly half (45 percent, or 770,033) of the higher education support staff workforce is comprised of support/service professionals, 25.8 percent (442,287) is represented by clerical and secretarial, followed by service/maintenance (13.7 percent or 234,541) and technical/paraprofessionals (11.8 percent or 201,867). The smallest group is skilled crafts, representing nearly four percent (62,575) of the higher education support staff population.

Decreasing Number of Employees and More Work

Staff have borne the brunt of cost-cutting measures in higher education over the last two decades, and their numbers on college campuses have decreased significantly.[5] The decrease in staffing is even worse at two- and four-year institutions that face more pressure on finances. Reductions in clerical and maintenance staff have been the most significant. In 2017, Rosser documented changes in just a two-year period.[6] The number of staff decreased by 181,601 (11.2 percent) between 2012 and 2014. Librarians, curators, and archivists experienced the largest cuts: 23,490 employees or

−34.92 percent. Office and administrative support workers showed a substantial decrease as well, 37,409 employees or −7.45 percent, and healthcare practitioners and technical workers report a similar figure, 9,279 staff members or −7.39 percent. Other areas showed less dramatic shifts—sales and related occupations (574 employees or −3.11 percent); production, transportation, and material moving (551 or −2.75 percent); natural resources, construction, and maintenance (1,811 or −2.36 percent); and service occupations (643 employees or −0.26 percent).

As a result of these declines, staff workloads have increased over the last ten to fifteen years, largely in the wake of the 2007 financial crash. As Rosser notes: "drastic reductions in hiring new support professionals accompanied these cutbacks. The inability to fill existing and new vacancies is demoralizing the remaining loyal, hardworking professionals who are asked to do much more with much less." Unsurprisingly, new hires declined during this same period and have generally stayed flat since.[7]

Contingency

Since 2016 there have been some increases in employment availability compared to the previous ten years, with more jobs posted, although many are part-time. Most recently, Rosser reports that 32 percent of office and administrative staff are now part-time. Headlines from employment news over the last decade generally suggest that full-time employment trends have been in continuous decline in higher education, and part-time positions have swelled.[8]

Salary and Benefits

Staff salaries have contracted in the last twenty years, compared to prior decades, with minimal increases related to cost of living. In 2017, Rosser tracked income across staffing groups and identified the annual salary (based on average minimum wage for all states) as $16,655, compared to an annual poverty rate of $18,850.[9] That many staff in higher education earn sub-poverty wages should be a major conversation on college campuses, but is rarely discussed beyond some occasional student protests. Historically, these salaries were already low relative to other comparable occupational domains, particularly for those in clerical support, and with no raises, their salaries are declining.

Benefit packages are likewise being pared back, with employee health-care premiums rising as employers offload more of these costs. Further, the range of medical benefits has narrowed, tuition benefits are being withdrawn, and available vacation and sick days are decreasing as well. Workers' compensation and disability benefits are disappearing as part of a growing trend. Finally, while many staff are not offered pensions, those who are have seen greater reductions in that benefit. As Conley notes: "A long-term view reveals a trend toward defunding retirement and benefits, most notably in the form of shifting responsibilities [to workers] beginning about 1980. The recent economic downturn propelled a pension reform movement with short- and long-term consequences."[10] The substantial declines in worker pay and protections adhere to the Gig Academy's general approach to labor reorganization.

Outsourcing

Staff positions are increasingly being outsourced to external labor providers to save on costs. Longtime university employees are let go and often rehired by a contracting firm, continuing to work for the institution only now without benefits, a living wage, or relative job security. Universities and colleges prefer these arrangements since they allow the institution to grow or shrink the worker population at will, while lowering overall costs. Bushman and Dean provide arguments for colleges about the value of outsourcing what they consider to be nonessential staff, that is, anyone not directly involved in instruction (which is ironic, since instructors themselves face comparatively poor conditions). They argue outsourcing is necessary to reduce costs and provide institutional flexibility. They report bookstore workers are being outsourced 50 percent of the time, food services 75 percent of the time, vending 63 percent of the time, and groundskeeping 20 percent of the time. There are some variations by job type, but it is clear across-the-board outsourcing is on an upswing. They contend that for some positions, like food services, outsourcing has become common and uncontroversial. But core functions are now also being targeted for outsourcing, including admissions, financial aid, housing, budget management, human resources management, and information technology. Unfortunately, staff not outsourced are not much better off, since contingent and part-time appointments are still growing.[11]

Promotion and Advancement

Research on staff shows they feel deprived of opportunity and full membership in the college community. For example, Johnsrud and Rosser report staff generally have limited opportunities for promotion and advancement and are frustrated with the lack of mobility their positions afford. Johnsrud also found restricted opportunity for skill building and professional development to enhance their prospects for advancement. While staff marginalization has always been a problem on campuses, it has grown over the last two decades.[12]

Declining Morale

Staff on college campuses report less satisfaction with their positions and working environment, exhibiting lower morale overall than in previous decades. Like other employees described in this section, staff also consistently claim to receive second-class treatment and disrespect within their institutions. Rosser cites interpersonal relations as an area of growing concern, particularly around second-class citizenship, lack of respect from both administration and faculty, lack of clear communications and organizational inclusion, and hostile supervisory relations. Marginalization and respect issues were the most commonly reported by respondents, problems that in turn affect managerial oversight issues like communication and workplace inclusion. Asked about their working conditions, staff reported high levels of disappointment, citing low salary, unreasonable workload, and forced transition to part-time contracts. Like contingent faculty in the Gig Academy, staff experience heightened insecurity about their jobs and are overwhelmed with official and unofficial responsibilities.[13]

Alienation and Fear

As draconian employment conditions continue to spread, staff feel more and more marginalized, alienated, and deprofessionalized. They report anxiety and fear about their insecure status and the possibility of surprise layoffs due to downsizing. Their worries further extend to involuntary transfers, forced work outside their official assignment, and the immanent possibility of sudden outsourcing. Many also fear for their health and safety, reporting that supervisors often do not take proper protections to ensure worker safety.[14]

Johnsrud explains how, because support staff have so few job protections, they fear retaliation if they were to ever expose illegal or unethical activities at work.[15] Often these workers are not even covered by typical protections for whistleblowers. Collective bargaining agreements can enforce protections around safe incident reporting, grievances, health or safety violation concerns, or workplace discrimination. These tend to be rare, however. For the most part, employees shoulder substantial risk of being fired or transferred if they speak out about concerns in their work environment. Occupational cultures of fear, control, and abuse appear to be growing among a multiplicity of staff worker domains in the Gig Academy.

Loss of Power and Control

Finally, staff report a rising concern over the lack of input they are afforded in the workplace and express disappointment in tighter managerial control over their work. In previous eras, support staff were traditionally included in institutional decisions to a much greater degree and were sought out for advice, but campuses today have centralized decisions that affect their work. Staff generally lack agency and autonomy in their workplace regardless of skill or experience and resent the pervasively marginal treatment they receive, not to mention increased surveillance and accountability. Magolda discusses the growing prevalence of audits imposed on the janitorial workforce and the stress and increased workload it causes.[16] Staff understand the need for quality control but feel that managers assume employee incompetence. This new apparatus of organizational control is a shared attribute of employment across different strata of the postsecondary workforce. We end this section by calling for more studies of campus staff to explore the ways their jobs are being transformed and to better understand their impact on colleges' missions and operations. We now move to the employee category that has received the most attention—contingent faculty.

Contingent Teaching Faculty

The contingent workers who tend to receive the most attention in higher education scholarship (though still a relatively modest amount) are instructors—full-time or part-time non-tenure-track (NTT) professors. In reorganizing the work of faculty, the Gig Academy employs a dual strategy. First, decoupling teaching from the faculty role allows for a large reserve of instructors to be cultivated without the need to provide job security, academic protections, support, or opportunities afforded to those with tenure. Second, the more recent decoupling of the research function allows the work of actual knowledge production to be shifted onto a set of cheaper, research-only faculty. Together these moves permit the continued functioning of core university operations without generating new employment costs or legal obligations to workers.

Rising Contingency

One of the most significant employment shifts has been the dramatic decline of tenure-track faculty, who now only make up 30 percent of faculty nationally. Tenure-track faculty maintain a decent salary (although lower than other professional employees or administrators on campus), benefits, and job security. They also are provided many job supports including in-depth socialization and orientation, professional development, promotion and advancement opportunities, and institutional resources and support. But now more than 70 percent of current instructional faculty are non-tenure-track. With little or no job security they are typically hired semester-to-semester or year-to-year, often within weeks or days of the semester's beginning, so they have very little ability to predict their work schedules, obligations, and even income. In fact, a study by the Center for the Future of Higher Education found last-minute hiring to be rampant, with more than a third of contingent instructors reporting they were hired within just three weeks of the start of classes and more than a sixth within two weeks. Full-time non-tenure-track faculty report concern about the time frame under which the institution provides notification of contract renewal. Some faculty receive only a month's or two weeks' worth of notice before the next academic year, making it extremely difficult to find another full-time appointment if necessary. They also can be scheduled to teach and then learn days before the start of classes that their section has been cancelled, in which case they receive no pay regardless of the time and effort spent preparing the course. Until recently, part-time contingent faculty could not receive unemployment benefits when their appointments were not obtained or renewed, leaving them vulnerable to a total salary loss for extended periods of time. Employment is therefore often highly unpredictable and income-volatile. Most part-time contingent faculty expressly seek a full-time position but accept contingent ones because of a lack of full-time opportunities. Three of four open positions today are contingent, meaning the opportunity for tenure-track roles is quite remote. Yet information about these hiring trends is neither readily available nor typically publicized in graduate school.[17]

Contingent faculty are classified either as part-time or full-time, but all are non-tenure-track. Part-time faculty, often termed "adjuncts," may be employed at several institutions simultaneously. They are a diverse group including retirees, working professionals, and freelancers, but most are aspiring academics who have been unsuccessful thus far in landing secure, full-time employment. These instructors experience the greatest degree of contingency, as their contracts are commonly renewed on a semester-to-semester basis. The status of "part-time" can be deceiving, though, as studies have found that some part-time faculty teach full-time loads. Such individuals teach full-time while typically earning even lower wages than nontenured faculty formally hired as full-time. Part-time faculty account for the most substantial rate of employment growth over the last four decades and now make up roughly 52 percent of all postsecondary instructors. To illustrate this growth another way, one study found the number of part-time faculty increased by a staggering 422 percent between 1970 and 2003, compared to just over 70 percent among all full-time faculty—both on and off the tenure track—during the same period.[18]

Full-time non-tenure-track faculty are still contingent but tend to have annual contracts. These contracts are varied and can include teaching, research, administrative, or service work. We will discuss the exclusive research positions in the next section. Some may also have multiyear (usually two- or three-year) contracts, a trend which seems to be on the rise among full-time NTT faculty. Full-time NTT positions are also increasing, but at a slower and more uneven rate than part-time faculty positions. In 1969, full-time NTT faculty made up about 3 percent of the faculty. The share peaked at 18.8 percent of faculty positions nationwide in 2007 and then contracted slightly to 16.7 percent by 2015.[19]

Salary and Benefits

Salary, benefits, and support services vary significantly between full-time and part-time contracts. National studies found that part-time faculty earn approximately 60 percent less hourly than comparable full-time tenure-track faculty. Adjunct salaries are extremely low, averaging about $2,700 a course nationally, for an annual salary averaging between $18,000 and $24,000, equivalent to fast food workers' salaries. Twenty years ago, median salaries of full-time non-tenure-track faculty were roughly 25–30 percent less than those of full-time tenure-track faculty, but this gap has narrowed slightly, and today they generally have salaries closer to those of tenure-track faculty—anywhere from $49,000 to $122,000 per year depending on appointment and field. They also tend to enjoy similar benefits and are able to take advantage of professional development and other privileges. These faculty are more likely to have regular salary adjustments and are sometimes part of a promotion and evaluation system. Though their study was not national, Hollenshead et al. found 71 percent of full-time non-tenure-track faculty received pay raises for good performance.[20]

Part-time faculty, though, are typically excluded from benefits. While national figures are not available, the largest-scale study of the topic found that less than 23 percent indicated they had access to employer-based health benefits; among those respondents, 4.3 percent indicated that the college or university paid for health care, 14.6 percent that benefit costs were shared by the employee and employer, and 3.6 percent that access to coverage was offered by the employer but all costs were borne by the employee. Gappa and Leslie discovered that institutions will often elect not to rehire part-time faculty precisely because they might become eligible for benefits based on length of continuous employment. They also found that institutions tend not to make information available about benefit options that do exist for part-timers, and that part-time faculty would have used benefits had they been informed. In some cases, full-time non-tenure-track faculty receive benefits that resemble those on the tenure track, though they still lack other means of long-term stability and security.[21]

One unfortunate result of the Affordable Care Act has been that part-time faculty teaching loads have been reduced in order to keep these employees from becoming eligible for health insurance. This was a widespread change occurring from 2012 to 2015 that has now become standard practice. Part-time faculty end up with no benefits and lower salaries by having fewer courses.

Workload and Overload

Various studies identify how contingent faculty roles are rarely properly defined, often leading to de facto unpaid overtime and increased workloads. The workload of non-tenure-track faculty is typically outlined in terms of teaching (as well as research, discussed in the following section), but work requirements such as office hours, class preparation, and communicating with students are frequently ambiguous to most non-tenure-track faculty (unless they happen to have a collective bargaining agreement). Studies have also found that NTT faculty may be asked to conduct administrative tasks, supervise clinical practicums or fieldwork, train or mentor teaching assistants, or participate in service work without clarity about pay. Studies further show that faculty conduct additional work even knowing they will not be paid, as they do not feel they could responsibly satisfy their professional role and ethics if they refused to meet with students, respond to their questions, or adequately prepare for their lessons.[22] They also often do so in hopes of obtaining a full-time position if one should become available.

Advancement and Promotion

Part-time faculty typically lack any promotional opportunities or bridges to secure employment. This means they have little recourse to substantially grow their salary or earn rewards for good performance. Even years of positive student evaluations can do little to help their case. Data suggest that approximately 50 percent of institutions offer some type of promotional opportunity for full-time non-tenure-track faculty, but this has not been studied recently and the figure is likely outdated. Some institutions use rankings similar to those for tenure-track faculty and have non-tenure-track faculty move through the ranks of assistant, associate, and full professor. Other institutions have simpler designations of lecturer and senior lecturer. Even when promotional tracks do exist, they are not guaranteed to increase salary. Some institutions offer title-only promotions as a more of a symbolic token.[23]

Outsourcing

Adjuncts are also experiencing outsourcing, a disconcerting trend that may be on the rise. Right now there are just a handful of examples, but it is conceivable that more adjuncts will be outsourced to temporary agencies. Around 2013, a set of community colleges in Michigan decided to have a temporary agency recruit, hire, and manage payroll for adjuncts. The community college administrator in the news story notes: "that they are overwhelmed with hiring so many adjuncts constantly and managing the process, so looking to outside solutions as the sheer number of adjuncts grows." When adjuncts are hired and managed by a temporary agency, the institution can abdicate responsibility for benefits or pay increases in perpetuity, knowing they can never be conceived of as formal employees of the institution. One can see how this logic would be attractive to other campuses overwhelmed with the staggering logistics of semester-to-semester hires. More recently, in 2017, faculty at the University of Tennessee Knoxville and members of a statewide union fought the university's efforts to outsource facilities staff to a private firm, Jones Lang LaSalle. While worker advocacy prevented this outsourcing, the example points out that institutions are beginning to discuss and test this approach. Twenty years ago no one could have imagined that faculty might be outsourced and hired by a temporary agency, but that is exactly what has occurred in two state systems.[24]

While the direct outsourcing of adjuncts is still rare, a different form of outsourcing is quite common: working with a for-profit (and sometimes not-for-profit) organization to deliver programs and courses. For example, both Missouri State and Florida Atlantic Universities have agreed to let the Poynter Institute—a Florida-based nonprofit organization that focuses on noncredit journalism training for students and professionals—teach an introductory journalism course online for traditional credit. In 2008, three universities formed partnerships with Higher Ed Holdings, a Texas-based company: Arkansas State University (to develop a master's degree in education), the University of Texas at Arlington (to develop education and nursing programs), and Ohio University (to develop a nursing degree). The arrangement at Arkansas State has received decidedly mixed reviews, engendering intense faculty objections due largely to lack of faculty involvement in the early stages of the negotiation process. A second course-outsourcing model is illustrated by the contract signed in 2009 by the California Community College Chancellor's Office and Kaplan University. Under this agreement, community college students can take online courses from Kaplan to fulfill some of their associate degree requirements. Recently, Purdue University purchased Kaplan University from Kaplan, Inc., and transformed the entity into Purdue University Global, which formally launched in April 2018. Kaplan, Inc., will remain a for-profit subsidiary of the Graham Holdings Company and will basically run Purdue University Global, collecting 12.5 percent of profits generated by the partnership. This allows for the entity to avoid the liabilities, regulation, scrutiny, and suspicion leveraged against for-profit colleges and universities without having to change any of the for-profit practices that brought about such scrutiny in the first place. Dozens, perhaps hundreds, of such arrangements now serve as a precedent for instruction to be administered by outside providers rather than university faculty and employees.[25]

Deprofessionalization

Another neoliberal trend within the Gig Academy is widespread deprofessionalization of employees and greater consolidation of control among academic managers and administrators. One key area that has traditionally defined academic professionals is involvement in shared governance. Part-time faculty are typically excluded from governance processes and often not even permitted to attend departmental or institutional meetings. If they are invited to attend, they are usually not compensated for such participation. Adjuncts have consistently expressed concern over lack of involvement in decision-making and governance, particularly regarding the courses they teach and the professional development programs aimed at them. Baldwin and Chronister report that full-time NTT faculty are more actively involved in governance, with about 50 percent of their sample institutions inviting them to participate in the faculty senate and other forms of governance, and 75 percent extending an invitation to participate in departmental affairs. Consistently, though, non-tenure-track faculty (both part-time and full-time) register concern about not having input on decisions that directly affect them.[26]

Another crucial dimension of academic professionalization is having the autonomy to define one's work. However, the unbundling of the faculty role into discrete categories of teaching-only and research-only has largely eroded this degree of freedom. Faculty contracts now routinely stipulate with a high level of specificity the type and structure of activities expected, which provides little room for faculty to direct their own work.

Finally, academic freedom has long been a core component of the faculty role. Academic freedom involves the right for faculty to teach what they conclude is important in their classrooms and to conduct research on topics they feel are significant to advancing knowledge, without fear of institutional interference or professional retaliation. Because faculty off the tenure track have no job security, many argue that they have no academic freedom and can be let go for espousing controversial ideas. Reports in the media describing non-tenure-track (and sometimes tenured) faculty fired for criticizing their institutions are common. Baldwin and Chronister note that some full-time NTT faculty expressed concern about academic freedom—not in teaching and scholarship as much as in shared governance or threat of termination due to critical remarks about the administration.[27]

This book focuses primarily on the patterns that appear across different employment categories. However, many other employment conditions that limit, deprofessionalize, and marginalize non-tenure-track faculty have been written about in other sources, including lack of opportunity to participate in professional conferences, absence of involvement in curriculum planning and learning goals, last-minute hiring, insufficient socialization, lack of feedback and evaluation, exclusion from resources and support structures, and restrictions on teaching, such as being primarily focused on remedial and introductory courses and excluded from teaching upper-division courses.[28] We review some of these areas in chapter 4 in examining how today's working conditions inhibit faculty from providing a quality teaching and learning environment.

In addition to a dramatic rise in teaching faculty, studies also show a steady rise of research faculty in the few pockets of higher education where rates have been documented. For example, research by the Association of American Medical Colleges showed a rise from 12 percent of total faculty in 1980 to 20 percent in 2000 to 28 percent in 2014 among medical schools (the most-studied institution type overall). Similarly, dental schools have doubled the number of research faculty employed off the tenure track. The magnitude of growth is hard to establish. In one of the few large-scale studies, Bergom et al. interviewed a total of 123 research faculty at five institutions and found that none of the institutions had reported employing contingent research faculty in their Integrated Postsecondary Educational Data System (IPEDS) data, though the authors conducted interviews and focus groups with these very faculty. They concluded that research faculty are even less likely to be known on their own campuses or reported as part of institutional and federal data, suggesting that their numbers are underestimated. Still, studies of individual institutions with strong data capacity show the research faculty typically doubling and tripling in size over a decade. So while we have no national statistical data, case studies of individual campuses consistently demonstrate broad growth.[29]

Rising Contingency

The reason behind such immense growth is that these faculty can conduct the research typically conducted by tenure-track faculty, but with no job security, lower pay, limited professional career track or pay raises, short-term commitment to benefits, and essentially zero risk for the employer. Research faculty typically raise their own salaries through grants and projects. Faculty on research appointments face job insecurity and typically are funded through soft money; when a grant ends, they no longer have employment. Such faculty members are constantly searching for new grant opportunities to fund their own employment. Bergom et al. reported that research faculty find this precarious employment extremely stressful. They often have full-time appointments, but their appointments vary depending on the grant funding they receive.[30]

Salary and Benefits

Research-only faculty are underpaid for their professional expertise but much more highly compensated then other workers described in this chapter, with an average annual salary of around $71,000.[31] This is likely because grants or contract agencies, not the institutions, pay their salaries.

Advancement and Promotion

Some institutions have a promotional track for research faculty, as for other full-time non-tenure-track faculty. But is also quite common for them to have no promotional track, with no path for an increase in pay, rank, or title over time. Those institutions that do have a professional career advancement opportunity often have unclear criteria or processes.[32] Research faculty, like other full-time non-tenure-track faculty, may have access to benefits similar to tenure-track faculty. However, once the grants run out, the benefits do too.

Workload and Role

Similar to other contingent employees, research faculty report that they are often asked to conduct work outside the scope of their contract. For example, Bergom et al. found they are frequently expected to do work unrelated to their research focus, assist other faculty in obtaining grants, and even mentor graduate students.[33] This creates a sense of conflict for research faculty: they are paid through a grant, but the institution is asking them to conduct work that they are not strictly contracted to do by the grant funding agent. This can lead to ethical and practical dilemmas because if they disappoint their employing institution they can still be fired, even when the reasons relate to work outside their contract.

Isolation and Alienation

In addition to the problems noted earlier, including job insecurity from having to secure funding for their own salaries and an absence of clear and consistent policies governing appointment and advancement, Bergom et al. reported widespread feelings of alienation and second-class status among research-only faculty.[34] Having few peers with whom to network, these faculty may try to reach out to permanent faculty colleagues, only to be ignored. Contingent teaching faculty have very different roles and so are not necessarily colleagues they can identify with. Isolation is pervasive among research faculty.

Bergom et al. argue that the concerns of contingent research faculty essentially boil down to three persistently toxic working conditions: insecurity, invisibility, and isolation. The authors draw links between two observed employment trends. First, many research faculty are hired only after a series of postdoctoral appointments ultimately failed to yield a permanent faculty offer. With no better alternative, they opt to press on as research faculty and hope it will enhance their professional image, despite little or no change in working conditions. Second, many others tend to arrive after working in government, nonprofit, or industrial research sectors. A common motivation is the belief that university employment offers a way to engage in more varied types of research than other sectors permit, plus that it ostensibly comes with the benefits of autonomy and academic freedom. In some cases, these faculty report high degrees of satisfaction, particularly when they have the agency to creatively collaborate with others and retain some control over the shape of their work with students and postdocs. At the same time, according to Baldwin and Chronister, research faculty tend to report the lowest satisfaction among all full-time NTT workers and are least interested in ever returning to work in academe again after leaving, due to experiences of alienation, isolation, and disrespect in the workplace.[35]

Forced Entrepreneurship

Under the neoliberal regime within the Gig Academy, two type of workers are prevalent: deprofessionalized workers and entrepreneurs. Adjunct faculty and staff fit the trend of deprofessionalized workers. Research faculty conditions, on the other hand, conjure the neoliberal model of the entrepreneur: they are individuals who must hustle to raise the money to support their salary. Because they generate their own funding, they are not subject to the dramatic decrease in wages and benefits experienced by other employees. Postdoctoral scholars are aligned with research faculty in their categorization as entrepreneurs. But as seen from studies of research faculty, being an entrepreneur leads them to be among the most unsatisfied workers in higher education. They are constantly plagued by an awareness of their job insecurity, and because they are hustling for funds, they have no time to forge networks and garner the relationships that make work meaningful. They feel their role is constructed in an impossible way—they have to be constantly raising funds, managing those grants, and meeting the implicit obligations of the institution—all without any institutional support. This is not to say there are not individual research faculty who enjoy the autonomy of their roles and the ability to focus on research. But the majority of research faculty report problems in the role's current configuration.

Postdoctoral Employees

Postdoctoral researchers represent another rapidly growing, yet sparingly studied segment of the postsecondary work force—one that is highly useful to the Gig Academy. The National Postdoctoral Association (NPA), National Science Foundation (NSF), National Institutes of Health (NIH), National Academy of Sciences (NAS) and National Research Council (NRC) all define a postdoc as "an individual who has received a doctoral degree (or equivalent) and is engaged in a temporary and defined period of mentored advanced training to enhance the professional skills and research independence needed to pursue his or her chosen career path."[36] This definition implies that what sets postdocs apart is that their role is meant to be both structurally educational and temporary, designed to enhance professional experience and expertise. As we show, despite the original vision of postdoc employment, these workers too are vulnerable to the caprices of neoliberal logics and the Gig Academy.

Rising Contingency

The most recent surveys by the National Science Board suggest the number of postdocs working at US universities currently exceeds 90,000, the majority of which are in STEM fields that tend to be favored by federal grant programs. Since 1980 the domestic postdoc population rose from under 20,000 to around 79,000 today, according to the NAS. In reality the number is likely to be even higher given the upward trend and the amount of time that has elapsed since the last time data were gathered. Available research suggests the number of STEM postdocs employed between 2000 and 2012 grew by anywhere from 50 to 150 percent, depending on the discipline. Meanwhile, the typical length of time spent by early-career scholars at the postdoc level has surpassed the three- to four-year window that used to be typical. Today researchers are likely to spend six years or more of their fledgling career at this rung of the academic ladder. Many simply take on a series of postdoc appointments, largely due to a lack of better alternatives, until eventually they get dismissed as so-called permadocs. Postdocs once served as a distinct complement to the work of permanent faculty, which created measurable returns to creativity and productivity. Today these workers are more often seen as yet another cost-effective substitute for traditional faculty, as are contingent faculty. With postdocs the labor savings are found in research rather than teaching, cutting those costs by as much as half. Principal investigators of research projects have come to rely on postdocs as the main labor source for their research projects and yield immense amounts of power in providing opportunities for postdocs—or destroying their careers.[37]

Many casual commentators are quick to identify oversupply as the problem, suggesting the postdoc population is simply expanding at a rate that exceeds what the tenure-track market can absorb. This is a problematic framing for reasons we explore more deeply in the following section on graduate workers. Nevertheless, according to one estimate, 65 percent of all PhDs go on to a postdoctoral appointment, while only 15–20 percent of them are ever able to find academic positions on the tenure track.[38]

One institutional response has been to try capping the number of years a postdoc can be employed. Postdocs may even be pushed out of academe altogether if they fail to obtain a faculty position by the time the limit is reached. Another response seen at some institutions involves the creative use of ambiguous job titles to manipulate the employment status of research faculty (addressed in previous section) as a way to seamlessly shift the postdoc into a new contract researcher position that generally preserves all of the same structural elements (contingency, overwork, cut-rate salaries, etc.) while managing to circumvent rules around employment duration. Yet even without being subject to a time limit, many grow frustrated with the ever-tighter job market and reach a point where low wages, insecurity, and contingency are no longer sustainable. As these scholars are forced into jobs in nonresearch fields, their extensive training suddenly becomes worthless, something that should be a collective concern given that some amount of that expertise was subsidized by public money via state and federal grant awards.[39]

Pervasive assumptions about the educational and professional developmental benefits of postdoc work fuel the notion that these employees have an exceptional situation to which normal labor standards do not fit. These positions were originally considered training positions and a form of apprenticeship. Yet scholars increasingly contend this is convenient cover for what is essentially an engineered market failure that quietly pays dividends to university management. One vocal advocate, Paula Stephan, was a member of the Committee to Review the State of the Postdoctoral Experience for Scientists and Engineers, a group within the NRC. Their report argues that the narratives of nonpecuniary returns are often flawed, due to the fact that so few ever advance to the tenure track, and to make matters worse, few are provided mentorship and training in any kind of systematic way throughout their stay. She contends that the problem rests with perverse institutional incentives: it is clear that future career prospects of a given postdoc hired for one to three years has no bearing on the institution that hires them. From the university perspective, postdocs are cheap, flexible, short-term, and eager to show diligence and gain experience. It is what some scholars would term a "no-brainer." Nebulous issues like PhD oversupply do nothing to moderate the unqualified multiple benefits to the employer.[40]

As a deeper layer of complication, the majority of postdocs are international workers in the country on temporary visas, which stipulate ongoing employment. Research shows that among US doctoral earners, noncitizens are more likely to seek postdoctoral employment. These visa restrictions can dampen postdocs' willingness to speak out about potentially abusive working conditions.[41]

Because postdoc positions have become so long-term, many national reports have recommended that after a five-year period, postdocs need to be offered some form of promotion opportunities if they continue on. However, there is no systemic way to ensure that this recommendation is implemented. Most institutions do not offer such an option. But the fact that national reports concede five years to be a reasonable length of this role shows how far beyond the original intention for this type of position we have shifted.

Salary

The extremely low salary of postdocs has been brought up in reports and recommendations again and again for many decades. It was not until 1994 that a minimum stipend (of $19,608) was finally established. And it was not until 1999 that the first postdoctoral salaries were over $25,000, a result of recommendations from the National Research Council's report on the national needs for biomedical and behavioral research. Since then, salaries are not adjusted regularly for cost-of-living increases and tend to stay constant for years at a time. Today, the College and University Professional Association for Human Resources (CUPA-HR) pegs the salaries of postdocs at between $40,000 and $55,000 per year, depending on the field. Postdocs in business, management, marketing, and related fields are the highest paid at about $55,000 on average, while postdocs in family and consumer sciences/human sciences are the lowest paid at around $38,000 on average. A 2014 report from the NAS aggressively recommends increasing the starting salary for all postdocs to at least $50,000 per year to bring them out of a pay grade which they consider exploitative given the many years of intense training and forgone earnings required to gain such a post.[42]

Lack of Benefits

Access to benefits is highly uneven among postdoc appointments. The source of funding for the position often determines the amount and type of benefits provided. Research has found that benefit packages very widely among institutions and within a single institution depending on the funding mechanism. Postdoc employment does not guarantee access to benefits. There is no national research available about benefits, but some surveys demonstrate that access to health benefits is most common. One survey found 91 percent of postdocs had health insurance and 88 percent of those received dental insurance. Of course, other traditional benefits that accrue over time and have long-term impact, such as retirement benefits, are not available to postdoctoral candidates. Therefore, the longer a postdoc is in a contingent position, the longer they put off accruing important benefits like retirement savings.

Workload and Ambiguous Job Assignments

Similar to contingent research faculty, postdocs report feeling pressured to work additional hours and take on additional responsibilities, hoping to improve their chances of secure, stable employment. They also frequently report not having clear work responsibilities or contracts. With little to no definition of the obligations for postdocs, they end up working longer hours, unsure whether they are meeting expectations. Institutions have been able to avoid having to pay postdocs because there are no administrative mechanisms that track their hours. And while national reports have repeatedly called for reining in unpaid overtime work, institutions often make the dubious argument that it would be too administratively cumbersome to track the hours of postdocs. Additionally, they suggest this sort of soft standard of expectations is typical to academic culture and that doing professional work often precludes a neat accounting of hours worked. In fact, one study found that less than 3 percent of institutions officially track the hours that postdocs work.[43] As with most other contingent employees within the Gig Academy (instructors, researchers, staff, graduate assistants, etc.), work responsibilities are measured in tasks completed rather than time dedicated. This mode of accountability benefits the employer far more than the worker.

Discrimination

Experiences of discrimination are also found to be widespread among international students. Research by Cantwell and Lee based on interviews with international postdocs, supervising faculty, and key administrators across four large public research universities reveals substantial cultural stereotyping. South and East Asian postdocs in particular, they found, are seen as possessing a natural disposition to hard work and technical diligence, and consequently they end up disproportionately assigned to tedious, limited-skill technical duties while being excluded from broader theoretical and analytical dimensions of the research.[44]

There have been rising reports of women experiencing sexual and other forms of harassment during their postdoctoral positions. A 2017 survey from the National Postdoctoral Association offers a glimpse of the staggering reach of sexual harassment among women postdocs: Nearly one-third of postdocs reported being sexually harassed, with more than 90 percent of those victims electing not to report the incident. Some claimed they did not know how, but the majority (51.5 percent) blamed their workplace for not being helpful or having clear procedures and resources in place to handle such situations.[45]

Postdoc scientists who are women face additional career obstacles. A study by Goulden et al. found that among married postdocs who have children during their appointments, women were more than twice as likely as men (41 percent to 20 percent) to conclude that becoming a tenure-track academic with a research focus was no longer tenable, pushing them to either accept a contingent faculty role or leave the academic workforce altogether. Lee et al. studied this group of women scientists more closely and discovered that nearly 20 percent of respondents (in a sample of 1,000 postdocs) cited negative reactions to their parenthood from their principal investigators, and 40 percent reported that their institution had insufficient maternity leave. A meager 15 percent enjoyed maternity policies with provision for caretaking, and a full 10 percent were altogether denied leave. The authors estimate that the sunk cost for each postdoc pushed out of a STEM pipeline is around half a million dollars, much of which, as we noted earlier, was publicly supported. In recent years the National Science Foundation started offering supplemental parental leave for graduate students and postdocs working on NSF-funded grants, which can assist in covering costs of both the leave and wages for a temporary replacement. However, such programs are generally limited to institutions that already have a policy of formal leave.[46]

Additionally, postdocs complain they can be denied full or fair authorship in publications.[47] The full extent of the issue of this form of abuse is unknown but has certainly been reported by postdocs.

Invisibility, Marginality, and Lack of Change

Reports on the state of postdoc employment have made many of the same critical assessments and recommendations described here for nearly fifty years. The first was released in 1969 by the NRC and was succeeded by new reports in 1980 and 2000. The new reports contained few substantive shifts, only more urgency as the years went on. In 2005, the National Postdoctoral Association was founded and put out parallel calls for postdoc reform. Other studies by the NSF followed suit. The newest and most comprehensive report, published in 2014 by the National Academy of Sciences, cites only extremely limited progress, such as more university offices of postdoctoral affairs and more grant applications requiring applicants to articulate the roles postdocs will specifically play and how they will be mentored. However, the NPA report expresses profound regret at how little has concretely improved in five decades: postdocs by and large remain substantially overworked, underpaid, and deprived of benefits, visibility, and meaningful mentorship, not to mention a voice in the research enterprise. Although these positions are predicated on improving employment prospects, postdocs receive little support in job seeking. No clear data have been collected about postdoc placement to assess whether these positions are actually meeting the goals intended to guide them. Available data remain highly inadequate in terms of the volume and quality of research. This essentially ensures that both the policies addressing the appropriate role of postdocs in research as well as the basis for informed decision-making by prospective postdocs about their future opportunities will continue to be problematic.[48]

The reports that for fifty years have raised serious concerns about the nature of postdoc appointments are staggering in their consistency. As early as 1960, reports indicated that employees were being primarily used as a means to accomplish a task rather than receiving a meaningful position and training that would lead to additional employment. There has always been concern that postdocs are being exploited and that these were not truly training positions but cheap labor to support the growing research desires of institutions. While we focus on the postdoc appointment specifically, an evolving range of titles and positions has emerged that basically translate to some version of employee-in-training, most of which have only superficial differences while sharing many tactics of exclusion from some of the traditional benefits associated with standard employment. This category in itself is problematic, and the proliferation of positions and titles speaks to larger patterns of problems that are likely to deepen over time. For example, the University of Wisconsin human resources system lists all of the following as employees in training: research associates, postdoctoral fellows, postdoctoral trainees, postdoctoral scholars, research interns, postgraduate trainees, non-physician interns, and graduate intern/trainees. These categories also include graduate students, which we describe next.

Graduate Assistants

Graduate assistants (GAs), like other contingent university employees, contribute a tremendous amount of labor that is vital to the daily operations of universities, particularly research institutions. Increasingly, arguments are being made that graduate assistants should be considered employees rather than students. Efforts to unionize, which we will discuss in chapter 5, have often been thwarted by institutions' arguments that GAs are in apprenticeship roles and that a traditional employee status could compromise this role. The share of academic work GAs do has increased substantially in the last few decades. Researchers at the Economic Policy Institute found that in the ten years between 2005 and 2015, the graduate workforce grew 16.7 percent and was eclipsed only by NTT faculty hiring, which grew 21.5 percent. Nationally, the number of graduate research assistants in 2017 was estimated at 136,000. These are triple and quadruple the 4.8-percent rate of tenure-track faculty growth in the same period. The report adds that the supply of doctoral students rose at twice the rate of new full-time faculty openings—including those off the tenure track.

Combined, GAs and NTT faculty made up slightly less than three-quarters (73.2 percent) of the academic workforce in 2015.[49]

The work of GAs can vary widely, but primarily they serve as teaching assistants and/or research assistants. The US Department of Labor defines a graduate teaching assistant as someone enrolled in a graduate program, who is employed to "assist faculty or other instructional staff in postsecondary institutions by performing teaching or teaching-related duties, such as teaching lower-level courses, developing teaching materials, preparing and giving examinations, and grading examinations or papers." Research assistants, however, are not encompassed by a singular definition for the Bureau of Labor Statistics but are rather grouped by field or discipline. They can generally assist with every aspect of research, including applying for grants and for ethics review board approval, gathering and analyzing data, preparing manuscripts for submission and publication, presenting at conferences, and otherwise producing or disseminating knowledge in ways that garner institutional prestige. Though most GAs work in teaching and research, they can also be found in campus libraries, museums, communications, marketing, and media offices, and other technical or clerical positions. Fifty-seven percent of all doctoral students work as GAs. On average they are thirty-one years old and five years removed from college.[50]

Salary

For all this work and added value to the institutional bottom line, graduate work has long been plagued by undercompensation. It is easy to grasp, from a management perspective, the benefits of using graduate students, rather than permanent faculty, as instructional and research labor: the former are incredibly cost-effective. Bureau of Labor Statistics data reveal that graduate assistants made a median wage of $32,460 as of May 2017. At first glance this may seem like reasonable pay for what is billed as only half-time employment. But as any graduate worker will readily attest, and as survey data discussed later reinforce, half-time designation amounts to little more than a bureaucratic ruse. Graduate assistants (like other workers in the Gig Academy) have task-based rather than truly time-based accountability structures, which quietly extract the maximum amount of time and effort possible from each individual without the need to make any explicit demand for it. If their work on a research project and class preparation take 35 hours, they have little recourse but to work the 35 hours even though they are being paid for 20 hours work a week. But more importantly, as we noted with other contingent instructors and researchers, GAs do highly professional work that would command a much higher price in the hands of permanent faculty.

In many places where research universities are located, particularly urban environments, $35K per year does not constitute a living wage, much less a professional salary commensurate with work at such a high skill level. It is roughly half the salary of entering tenure-track faculty and only a third of what professors with tenure typically earn. GA pay does vary somewhat by discipline, with full-time GAs in STEM fields earning as much $45,000 annually while those in the humanities and social sciences are likely to make less than $20,000 per year. Regionally speaking, very few GAs in 2016 were paid a sum that approached a living wage, particularly in large urban centers, where the vast majority live, work, and study. For instance, the Economic Policy Institute calculates that in the New York City region, average GA compensation is half of what someone would need to live stably. Doctoral degrees are not only expensive, they significantly delay entrance to the workforce. The negative impact of subsistence wages paid to graduate workers is thus compounded over the long term because of earning potential sacrificed to years of training. As PhDs' career plans get continually waylaid in short-term or insecure academic work, whether as postdocs, adjuncts, or contract researchers, they feel increasing pressure to advance economically in the face of a nearly impenetrable academic job market.[51]

Benefits and Workload

The benefits made available to graduate assistants can vary wildly by institution and across discipline. STEM fields generating the most lucrative research may offer much better health coverage than what is offered to GAs toiling just as hard in a humanities field.

As for other contingent employees, graduate assistants' work responsibilities are often ill defined, so that they find themselves open to exploitation and working well over their 50-percent designated time.

Graduate students often report pressures to publish, present, and take on any opportunities presented to them, knowing how competitive the job market is. Therefore, they assume much unpaid work in hopes of building their vitae.

Contingency

Graduate working conditions can barely be distinguished from most other forms of postsecondary employment we review, consisting in short-term contracts with no benefits, vulnerability to arbitrary termination, no minimum wage (much less a living one), and no overtime protection. As Bousquet argues, graduate education is far more effective at preserving administrative access to cheap teaching and research labor than it is at preparing future faculty. This is entirely by design and a clear reflection of university priorities. Given the paucity of PhDs hired into tenure-track appointments, doctoral degree holders, he reasons, should be seen less as a "product" of graduate employment/training than as a "by-product."[52]

The adjunct crisis we discuss in earlier sections is not the result of conventional market failure, in which the supply of availability of skills happens to exceed demand for them in ways that the market cannot correct. If anything, the demand for academic research and instructional skills has risen steadily over the last few decades, demonstrated by the aggregate growth in the academic workforce. The central problem, as Bousquet cogently explains, rests with what he calls the "fictive" nature of the academic labor market. By this he means it is barely a market at all, for the simple reason that university managers have outsize power to regulate both supply and demand, creating a situation in which the so-called market works perpetually in the favor of institutions, at the expense of individual students, the academic workforce, and society at large—insofar as taxes underwrite a great deal of specialized training that is ultimately destined to become wasted public investment. Furthermore, the incentives to keep the number of PhDs high and the number of tenure-track openings low make sense at the level of individual institutions; thus, to admit that academic managers have engineered a fictive job market as an intentional means of exploiting GAs and contingent faculty is not to suggest that some kind of centralized coordinating effort is needed. Graduate school is merely the first stage of a long victimization process that leverages fear of sunk costs to keep highly trained scholars trapped in a casual labor market that was actively and not accidentally built.[53]

Unprofessional and Unsafe Environments

Since GAs typically lack formal collegial protections and (at least for the nonunionized majority) recourse to due process, they often struggle around issues of professional respect and fair treatment in the workplace. Research has long shown environments that lack or impede collegiality, GA exclusion from departmental communities, poor mentoring, high pressure to publish, and climates of hyper-competition, all of which degrade the graduate experience and strongly contribute to doctoral attrition.[54]

These issues take on additional layers of complication as they get refracted through multiple lenses of racial, ethnic, and gender identity. GAs who are women and/or students of color face a great deal more bias, harassment, and lack of support in their doctoral training. A landmark study on doctoral completion rates by Sowell et al. showed that roughly half of all PhD students are lost to attrition within a decade (figure 2), though there is considerable variation across discipline and between genders. It is important to note that attrition is caused by a variety of factors, but two major areas are bias and lack of support. Women in PhDs have a

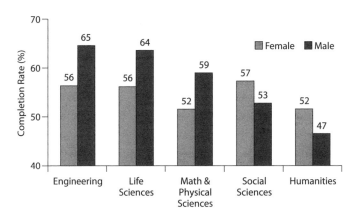

Figure 2   Ten-year completion rates by broad field and gender.
R. Sowell, T. Zhang, K. Redd, and M. King, *PhD Completion and Attrition: Analysis of Baseline Program Data from the PhD Completion Project* (Washington, DC: Council of Graduate Schools, 2008)

slight edge in completion rates over men in social sciences and humanities programs—the areas that, it is worth noting, pay the lowest wages and have the fewest job openings. Meanwhile, science and technical fields show huge gaps in completion with men possessing a clear advantage.[55]

In addition to attrition caused by substantial stress and mental duress (discussed next), gender bias and sexual harassment in the workplace appear to play a major role in keeping women out of STEM fields. According to a 2014 study by Williams et al. examining bias in science fields against women of color, one in three women scientists in academia experiences sexual harassment at work, and 100 percent of the sixty participants interviewed had encountered at least one instance of gender bias.[56]

Concealed Anguish

Both working conditions and financial struggles are important influences over the health and well-being of graduate students. Research shows mental health struggles are much more common among doctoral students than among the general population, with one recent study showing a likelihood that is six times higher. And conditions such as depression and anxiety linked to work relations and expectations disproportionately occur in women, both in graduate school and the general workforce. In a 2018 study by Posselt addressing mental health issues in graduate school, participants who struggled financially were two to three times more likely to exhibit anxiety or depression than those who did not. A recent self-study by the graduate assembly at UC Berkeley found nearly half of its graduate students scored high enough on a depression scale to qualify for a clinical diagnosis, with proportions significantly higher among students of color as well as older and low-income students. In a new study by researchers in Belgium, half of PhD students were found to have experienced psychological duress, and a third were considered at risk for a psychiatric disorder.[57]

It is a well-established fact that prolonged exposure to poor working conditions can degrade mental health. By pursuing a path of optimal efficiency and maximum extraction, universities not only undervalue graduate work but often demand so much of students that GAs feel perpetually overloaded. The toxic culture and working conditions in many graduate programs can take a serious psychological toll. In the most recent National College Health Assessment, an annual survey of graduate mental health issues administered by the American College Health Association (ACHA), researchers analyzed data from more than 14,000 students at sixty-seven US institutions and reported that in the previous year:

- 83 percent felt overwhelmed by their responsibilities,
- 81 percent felt exhausted,
- 57 percent felt overwhelming anxiety (though only 20 percent received any professional treatment for anxiety),
- 55 percent felt severe loneliness,
- 44 percent felt a sense of hopelessness,
- 35 percent felt so depressed it was difficult to function (though only 15 percent received any professional treatment for depression), and
- 6 percent had seriously considered suicide.

Additionally, they report percentages that experienced trauma related to:

- Academics: 40 percent
- Career issues: 35 percent
- Finances: 29 percent

A further 25 percent had experienced trauma from sleeping difficulties. In fact, according to the assessment, only 65 percent of graduate students sleep enough to feel rested the next day at least three times per week. This is also an emerging trend with NTT faculty and staff, but little research has been conducted to date.[58]

Magnified Disparity

The extractive nature of graduate work generates longer-term consequences as well. Earning a doctoral degree takes a long time and can be costly; tuition remission typically lasts four or five years, though the median length of time spent finishing a doctorate is seven to eight years. This postponed entry to career not only means years of potentially forfeited income but extended interest accumulation on student debt, whether from undergraduate or graduate education. These debt burdens are highly disproportionate by race, as much recent research has shown. An analysis by the Brookings Institute determined that African Americans' debt loads on average are almost twice their white counterparts' four years after college graduation, which is when most graduate students begin their studies. Under such conditions, graduate education can only be poised to exacerbate, not mitigate, racial wealth disparities.[59]

Professionals and Administration

The professional/administration workforce within higher education encompasses a growing sector with a dizzying array of jobs and income levels. In order to keep the discussion comprehensible and manageable, we adopt a typology used by CUPA-HR, which gathers annual salary data sector-wide and classifies nonfaculty work into three broad categories:

1. Staff—lower-to-middle–income office and clerical workers, technical and paraprofessionals, skilled crafts workers, and service and maintenance workers, plus a smattering of miscellaneous nonsupervisory employees (191 distinct positions).

2. Professionals—a range of middle-to-upper–income positions in areas such as information technology (IT), staff supervision, legal work, finance and accounting, and student/academic affairs (353 distinct positions).

3. Administrators—the uppermost income level consisting of senior or executive members of administration, such as presidents, provosts, deans, and other chief officers (149 distinct positions).[60]

Above, we described how staff have experienced declines in wages and benefits, increased contingency, and deprofessionalization. These trends apply primarily to the first (and lowest-paid) category of staff. We now move onto to describe professionals and administrators, as they have also had their roles altered in the Gig Academy.

New Professionals

We now shift to the area where employment is decidedly growing and experiencing positive, not negative, working conditions—new professionals and administrators. We start with the new professionals that are part of category 2 above in the list of employment types. CUPA-HR identified almost 600,000 workers in 353 distinct positions within this growing area of employment on campus, a group that largely did not exist a few decades ago. Their de facto function in the Gig Academy is arguably to maintain a thick buffer between the executive or senior administration and the "rank-and-file" instructors and staff members. This is a major distinction between the Gig Academy and the gig economy. For firms in the latter category, it is not a large managerial force creating this buffer but the technology used to distribute labor and execute transactions. As Slee and others have noted, Uber drivers do not have middle-management supervisors. Their supervisor is the app itself, which uses digital surveillance and an advanced algorithm to replace the substantial overhead that traditional organizations must typically cover for midlevel management. By confining middle management to an algorithm, gig economy firms both save on costs and minimize the capacity for workers to seek redress if they have a complaint. The Gig Academy, has not yet evolved to replace its human managers with digital ones, but to the extent that distance learning and online program management software are proliferating, such a future is not inconceivable.[61]

Growing Numbers

Professional employees—such as business analysts, human resources staff, admissions staff, computer administrators, counselors, athletic staff, and health workers—are the largest group of noninstructional staff on campus. Typically these positions either support the business functions of colleges and universities or provide noninstructional services to students. Professional positions grew astronomically and twice as fast as executive and managerial positions at public nonresearch institutions between 2000 and 2012, outpacing enrollment growth. Professional positions increased, on average, by 2.5 to 5 percent per year between 2000 and 2012. Across most types of four-year institutions, the number of new professional jobs was second only to the number of new part-time faculty positions added during the previous decade. The average number of faculty and staff per administrator declined by roughly 40 percent in most types of four-year colleges and universities between 1990 and 2012 and now averages 2.5 or fewer faculty and staff per administrator. Managers are outpacing hiring in any other category. As noted in other sections, there is a gap in research about how these trends play out across different institutional types.[62]

Anthropologist David Graeber has another theory to explain the boom in professionals in the academy: "managerial feudalism," which he argues has led to the proliferation of what he glibly calls "bullshit jobs." As he describes,

> Rich and powerful people have always surrounded themselves with flashy entourages; you can't be really magnificent without one. Even at the height of industrial capitalism, CEOs and high-ranking executives would surround themselves with a certain number of secretaries (who often did most of their actual work), along with a variety of flunkies and yes men (who often did very little). In the contemporary corporation, the accumulation of the equivalent of feudal retainers often becomes the main principle of organization. The power and prestige of managers tend to be measured by the number of people they have working under them—in fact, in my research, I found that efficiency experts complained that it's well-nigh impossible to get most executives, for all their "lean and mean" rhetoric, to trim the fat in their own corporations (apart from blue-collar workers, who are ruthlessly exploited).[63]

Admittedly this is a playful framing, and his research methodologies have been questioned for their lack of rigor. Nevertheless, many in academia would be hard pressed to refute his claim in light of the outsize growth in professional managerial roles over the last few decades—240 percent between 1985 and 2005, according to Ginsberg, which is what Graber cites, compared to just a 40-percent rise in the number of students.[64]

There is also a connection between the unbundling of faculty roles, which separates out the teaching, advising/mentoring, and research functions so that these can be conducted by cheaper means—contingent faculty, staff, or through technology. But having been separated from the professional faculty with expertise, the task requires management by the new professionals to ensure quality and accountability and hence the growth of new professionals. New professionals take on much of the work once performed by faculty and staff but can be more directly controlled by management.

Salary

Professionals' salaries can vary significantly by job type, but the most recent available data from CUPA-HR suggests that compensation rates are, at a minimum, uniformly a living wage: none of the 353 positions cited in the report make less than $40,000 per year, the average salary is near $80,000, and many approach the six-figure range. Furthermore, the best estimates available show that professionals at this middle level receive on average annual salary raises of around 4 percent per year.[65]

Shifting Costs

Graeber's ideas may be brash, but he is undeniably responding to real organizational changes in terms of cost-shifting. In exploring whether the change to a contingent faculty and more part-time and outsourced staff was saving institutions money, Hurlburt and McGarrah identified a shifting of money to professionals and administration rather than any cost saving. Money allocated for instruction and faculty did decline significantly between 2002 and 2013, but overall expenditures were not reduced.[66]

Public four-year institutions used savings associated with part-time contingent faculty to increase expenditures on administration and maintenance. At private four-year institutions with large shifts to part-time contingent faculty, total compensation costs per full-time equivalent (FTE) employee declined, but at a slower rate than declines in instructional compensation per FTE faculty member. The savings were offset by non-faculty-related costs—in particular, costs related to benefits for all employees. Many commentators have noted that the obligation to pay defined benefits retirement packages for all employees has driven up costs.[67]

Overall, the public and private nonprofit higher education workforce grew by 28 percent between 2000 and 2010, more than 50 percent faster than during the 1990s (due to the growth of professional managers). However, the proportion of staff to students at public institutions grew more slowly in the 2000s than in the 1990s, just as the millennial generation was entering college. By 2012, a few years after the Great Recession, public research universities and community colleges had fallen significantly behind their private counterparts, employing 16 fewer staff per 1,000 FTE students than they had 12 years earlier, whereas private institutions managed to hire 15–26 additional staff per 1,000 FTE students over the same period.[68]

Administrators

While faculty, graduate students, postdocs and staff continue to struggle with subsistence wages, declining or no benefits, and job insecurity, administrators on college campuses are growing in number, making more money than ever before with regular salary increases, and have enhanced benefit packages with merit and bonus clauses. Administrators, using the CUPA-HR definition, include senior or executive members of administration, such as presidents, provosts, deans, and other chief officers. We preface this section by noting that administrators are subject to external pressures from boards, legislators, and alumni, many of whom are deeply influenced by the neoliberal and gig economy logics. Administrators experience and are subject to these forces, including declining public funding, demands for greater accountability, and calls for cost-cutting.

Increasing Numbers

While there is increasing rhetoric about productivity and the need to lay off staff workers to stay lean, administrative jobs have grown substantially in the last two decades. As noted in the last section, executives are hiring new professional managers, creating an entire new workforce to oversee. And executive positions are also growing at a rapid pace. Executive and managerial positions grew by 2.5 percent in public institutions; growth was faster in the private sector but still lower than for professional positions. Professional positions increased, on average, by 2.5 to 5 percent per year between 2000 and 2012.[69]

For decades, administrative positions have been growing while faculty jobs become more contingent and less money is available for instruction. There were at least three FTE faculty and staff for every administrator in

1990. By 2012, this figure had declined by roughly 40 percent, to an average of 2.2 to 2.5 faculty and staff per administrator at public institutions, and two or fewer faculty and staff positions per administrator at private institutions.[70] The shifting balance among these positions has played out steadily over time in favor of administrator both in terms of number of jobs and share of budget. Whether this administrative growth constitutes unnecessary bloat or is justified as part of the complexities involved in running a modern-day university remains up for debate.

Salary

While administrative salaries vary, they are much higher than those of faculty and staff, generally ranging from $70,000 to $300,000. And of course, many senior executives far exceed the salary range. The 2018 *Chronicle of Higher Education* report on executive compensation listed eight presidents at public universities and fifty-eight presidents at private ones who earned more than $1 million in annual salary packages in 2017.[71] Each year the *Chronicle* reports these figures, which highlight the widening gaps between the vast majority of faculty and staff, whose employment becomes more and more precarious, and executive administrators, whose salaries approach meteoric heights.

Looking back over decades of data, studies of executive salaries in higher education show that they are consistently higher than faculty and staff earnings and tend to increase more than other employees wages, in terms of both percentage and absolute amount. As noted earlier, administrators at the middle level are also receiving annual salary raises of approximately 4 percent each year. These disparities were profiled in a recent *NEA Almanac* in which Rosser compares the extremely low wages of staff to the growing share of executive administrators earning salaries over six figures. For instance, as Bauman et al. report for the *Chronicle*, the highest-paid executive in higher education in 2015 was the president of Wake Forest University in North Carolina, whose salary exceeded $4 million. The authors helpfully note this sum is equivalent to the tuition of 84 undergraduates and additionally is 27 times the salary of a full professor (approximately $150,000) and 135 times the current annual salary of a full-time admissions counselor, as recorded on Glassdoor (approximately $30,000 as of May 2017).[72]

Change in Background of Administrators

Administrators are increasingly coming from outside higher education, with a background in other sectors, and generally lack an understanding of the unique features of colleges and universities. In the past, administrators largely came out of the faculty and had an understanding of the classroom experience and what is required to create a quality learning environment. However, they may have lacked experience with important administrative activities such as budget management and strategic planning. Today's academic leaders are hired for their skills in budget and strategy and with much less regard for the importance of understanding the mission of the institution and how to support it. Twenty percent of US college presidents in 2012 came from fields outside academia, up from 13 percent six years earlier. Those numbers actually went down in recent years to 15 percent. Years of criticism about administrators from outside higher education being able to handle challenges of academic institutions may finally be impacting hiring decisions. One of the major cases that received much visibility was the firing of Tim Wolfe from the University of Missouri, who had a business background and was seen by many as unable to manage race relations at the university. Another example is Simon Newman, a former president of Mount St. Mary's University who had been a business executive and consultant. He failed to understand the institution and created significant problems before being forced out. Many books and articles describe how the shift to a set of professional administrators with very limited experience in higher education and a mindset more aligned with the business world has amplified neoliberal trends in the academy.[73]

Bloat at All Levels

In addition to administrative bloat at the campus level, system offices have also grown in their staffing, taking away needed money for faculty and staff who work with students. While there is no breakdown about how much central-system offices contribute to the cost of running universities, one survey in 2010–2011 by the National Center for Higher Education Management Systems put the average at $484 per full-time student. The highest per-student cost rang in at $3,336.[74] This continued growth has happened at a time when states have collectively cut their higher education spending by 18 percent, forcing hikes in tuition. The University of Maine System central office is among those that grew the most. It ballooned by 26 percent, despite an enrollment decline and budget cuts resulting in the termination of at least five academic programs and 51 faculty members—among what a spokesman said were 902 jobs eliminated.

For-Profit Institutions

Thirteen percent of the higher education sector is now made up of for-profit institutions. These are even more aligned with neoliberal philosophies than traditional higher education because they are unencumbered by most public and government scrutiny and exist unabashedly to turn a profit, in spite of the fact that most rely almost entirely on publicly subsidized financial aid to operate. In recent years an investigation by the House Oversight Committee revealed that for-profits managed to claim $32 billion in taxpayer money from 2009 to 2010, which amounted to a full quarter of the Department of Education's entire financial aid budget.[75]

Detailed data about employment—such as salaries, benefits, and job security—are largely unavailable within the sector because for-profit institutions are private firms with very few public disclosure requirements. What is known is that they hire faculty almost exclusively on a contingent and part-time basis, provide few if any benefits, and pay generally abysmal wages, with instructors earning a median rate of $1,560 per course, which is nearly half the already low compensation afforded to adjuncts in not-for-profit institutions. Staff—who make up a large majority of the employee base because they do the work of assessment, instructional design, and technology— are also largely underpaid, contingent, and deprofessionalized. Meanwhile, CEOs of publicly traded for-profits took home an average of $7 million in 2009, with some earning as much as $20 million in a single year.[76]

Conclusion

It should be clear after this exhaustive survey of trends that no aspect of higher education has gone untouched by neoliberal restructuring. The magnitude of this transformation is so enormous and totalizing that virtually none of the labor keeping colleges and universities open can be said to resemble the conditions, roles, and functions historically found in these institutions. This is why we must frame them in a new way. Just as careers in the taxi industry—with their unions, regulations, and opportunities for modest security—have been swallowed by the metastasized market for contingent work under gig economy firms, so too the market for contingent labor in higher education has completely absorbed a wide range of once dignified and stable career options.

THREE

Disintegrating Relationships
and the Demise of Community

Academic capitalism and the Gig Academy are built on the concepts of privatization, corporatization and managerialism, entrepreneurialism and micro-entrepreneurship, marketization, atomization, and automation, which all work to dismantle community and collective action. This is particularly problematic in academia, which was previously organized around intellectual exploration and the pursuit of knowledge for the development and sustenance of community, democracy, and the public good. In chapter 2, we described changes in labor practices on college campuses; here we note how these changes specifically reshape relationships and break down communities.

The growing division between managers and employees described in the last chapter also exacerbates this breakdown of community. We explore this attack on community not only through the logics of academic capitalism and the gig economy but also through trends in empirical data that reflect this breakdown of relationships. For example, we review the demise of shared governance, tension between unions and corporate administration, gaps in communication, declining morale, lowered satisfaction, decreased engagement, and increasing staff and faculty turnover. We examine the relationships between various groups on campus and how these relationships have shifted over time, creating a greater gulf between administrators and faculty/staff, between faculty, between staff, and between departments that we argue is detrimental to learning.

We will examine the ramifications of these changes to community in subsequent chapters. In chapter 4, we will explore how the breakdown of community and social interactions impacts teaching and learning, demonstrating why this loss of community is so important. In short, the Gig Academy restricts deep and substantive interactions in the learning environment, making them rare and difficult. Community and interpersonal interactions are essential conditions for learning in many cultures and have been central to Western higher learning since the time of Socrates and Plato. Current evidence from educational psychology and neuroscience (which we will discuss further in chapter 4) suggests that community and relationships are essential preconditions for learning and student success—the primary mission of higher education institutions. Even beyond the primary mission of learning and student success, the very character of higher education is transforming under the Gig Academy. Community is also essential to collective action, the topic of chapter 5. We see the assault on community as also impairing collective action and will underscore again how employment trends are bringing about a future where any notion of a democratic workplace will become increasingly out of grasp.

While there is very little research on the breakdown of campus community to date, we view reflection on the current state of affairs as essential. This type of forward thinking has been missing from the higher education literature, and as a result the sector is lacking direction for policymaking and practice. We examine the logics employed in structuring the academic workplace and indicate their lack of correspondence with the realities of how teaching and learning take place. In examining some of the unintended consequences of the shift to the Gig Academy, we hope to motivate more intentional practical responses to the structures of work in academia.

Academic Capitalism and Gig Logic

Academic capitalism leaves behind notions of a public or collective good, worker empowerment and participation in decision-making, community among workers, unions and organizing among workers, and public-sector employment relationships, and instead privileges a radical individualism and the privatization of institutional operations.[1] Individualism is achieved by promulgating values of entrepreneurialism so that people see themselves as solely responsible for areas of educational work and as competing with others. Privatization is achieved through market-based values that defund public higher education and encourage a competition for scarce resources, which also reinforces individualism. Inherent in the individualistic logic and the privatizing logic is a move away from collective or community values for organizing higher education.

Furthermore, logics of marketization and entrepreneurialism shift the values of academia away from providing education and conducting research in order to solve problems of public concern. Instead, individual faculty stars are refashioned into entrepreneurs and rewarded for bringing in substantial grants, patents, and licenses, regardless of the focus of the projects. Such faculty are incentivized to bring in large grants by compensation schemes that award bonuses or other forms of discretionary additional compensation, such as buyouts from teaching responsibilities, while their contingent teaching counterparts are paid fractions of that amount based on the number of courses taught. Generating innovations and pursuing their commercial dissemination via technology transfer become the most encouraged and rewarded activities for faculty. Academic capitalism brings an essential shift from a focus on community to a focus on economics, fashioning the university and its subdivisions into a collection of firms. Faculty are encouraged to see themselves not as a community of scholars, as in the past, but as individual entrepreneurs with their own business enterprises.[2]

According to corporate logic, universities are best operated as businesses and through corporate approaches to management. And while many universities and colleges are indeed businesses to some degree, academic capitalism is loath to respect academic traditions, unions, and the value of academic community. Slaughter and Rhoads focused on how corporate and market rationality reshaped the nature of academic work toward entrepreneurial research activities and deemphasized teaching. Ironically, teaching was considered a cost and not seen as generating revenue. Slaughter and Rhoads did not extrapolate how corporate or market logic would refashion the very notion of academic community. But as we can see, over time academic capitalism altered relationships on campus, moving away from interactions among professionals to strict, hierarchical relationships between managers and employees.[3]

Rhoades alludes to the corporate restructuring and increasing deprofessionalization of faculty in *Managed Professionals*.[4] Yet his work did not predict the scale of these changes. Today the corporate logic has shifted all employees into divided groups, casting administrators as managers and all other employees as workers to be monitored, controlled, and accounted for. Over time, more and more managerial approaches have been introduced to the academic workspace, including post-tenure review, productivity and monitoring reports, auditing, and performance funding. College employees across the board are subject to dozens of new performance and accountability systems, which increasingly measure and micromanage their actions within the workplace and reduce their autonomy. These systems create wholly different relationships between administrators and employees by structurally and relationally subordinating the workers to their supervisors, harming relationships and campus community. This entire radical breakdown of community is inherently tied to the academic capitalism logic, where managers are constructed as decision makers and directors of action, the mind of the workplace, while workers are constructed as executors of managerial decisions, the body of the workplace.

As identified in the last chapter, non-tenure-track teaching faculty are hired in droves, mostly as adjuncts whose ability to create or experience a sense of community is limited by their situation working for multiple institutions or in another profession in addition to higher education. Campuses provide few ways for these individuals to be part of a community, with practices that instead send the message that their participation in the academic environment is impermanent, unnecessary, tangential, supplementary—*adjunctive*. For example, last-minute notice of hiring and firing sends the message that their ability to plan their lives is not important. Providing little or no orientation sends the message that their presence on campus is not essential and thus their alignment with the campus is unimportant. Providing no office sends the message that there is no space for them on campus. Stipulating no mentoring or other human contact that might contribute to their growth and development as professionals and as educators sends the message that they do not deserve the investment of institutional effort. Structurally and organizationally, contingent faculty are rendered adrift with no connection to the overall campus. And outsourced and contingent staff have also experienced the same untethering from the organizational core or community. Many staff are no longer housed on campus; they have no orientation to its values and goals, no relationships with faculty, staff, and students, and no regular communication or interaction with faculty or students. The concept of contingency itself works to break down collective connections, structurally and linguistically rendering workers as incidental to the business of the college.

In chapter 2, we discussed how decision-making power has been increasingly concentrated among administrators and academic managers, individuals whose functional roles are separate from teaching and learning and many of whom come into academe from other sectors of the economy. They are thus increasingly separate—both in terms of function and in terms of experience and knowledge base—from the actual processes involved in teaching and learning. Academic capitalism brings about a growing separation between the administration and management of daily operations and the actual realization of the ends of higher education, such that academic managers fall increasingly out of touch with the commitments and values that animate their underpaid staff. The separateness of academic managers from the labor of academia, and the managerial application of logics and ideologies from other economic sectors, leads them to view the work of faculty, the work of "doing education," as a "net cost to the organization, rather than the producer of its value."[5] This alienates academic managers and faculty from one another, as the two groups are effectively speaking different languages. Academic managers are also alienated from students, who are traditionally associated with the end goal of higher education (learning).

Building from academic capitalism, Gig Academy logic further undermines any possibility of community and moves to shift relationships from connected and democratic to disconnected and hierarchical. We review these features next.

Contingency and Fissuring

The extreme uptake of contingency is perhaps the worst offender and culprit in the breakdown of community. With reduced benefits and compensation, Gig Academy workers are increasingly distracted by the need to supplement their meager compensation and benefits from the university with extra work.[6] The anxiety produced by the constant need to hustle reduces their ability to invest in community at the university—many simply don't have the time. Contingent academic workers are too distracted by working to make ends meet to be able to attend to other dimensions of life in the workplace, like community. This forces academic workers to view their relationship to the university from a more utilitarian perspective, which changes the nature of their relationships with their colleagues, supervisors, and students. With staff and faculty having such a tenuous working connection, any sense of community is quite challenging.

The Gig Academy keeps pushing to break down labor and make it more contingent through outsourcing faculty or staff. Outsourcing labor is the worst extreme of Gig Academy employment practices, which fissure the workforce.[7] Employees hired through outside companies report the lowest levels of connection to the campus community. It is not difficult to see why employees who no longer are hired through campuses would lack any sense of community. They undergo no orientation, participate in no collective or community events, receive no communications from the campus, and are managed by outside groups. Their connection is only as a site of work. Academic capitalism is pushed to a further extreme under the Gig Academy where new and further modes of contingency are explored, such as outsourcing faculty and core educational staff and thus making unionization and any collective action close to impossible. The arrangements between universities and subcontracting labor agencies work to separate contingent groups—supporting administrative authority by constraining the ability for various types of staff to organize at a larger scale.

Atomization and Unbundling

Closely related to contingency and the fissuring of the academic workforce is atomization and unbundling of academic work processes. Managerial logics imported from the broader economic environment bring the assumption that a highly specified and controlled production process is the most efficient and easiest to manage. The contemporary university has managed to break down complicated professional roles to displace large portions of work onto contingent hires. Managers are better able to oversee activities if they are atomized, rather than leaving the entire process to be overseen by experienced faculty or staff. Breaking down the activities into component parts also means deprofessionalizing the workers who play a role in each part.

As a result, university work has been reshaped and is no longer conceived in terms of whole or connected processes, such as the notion of a broad liberal arts experience or a holistic education. Instead, this experience is increasingly packed into smaller units that are conceived both as easier to consume and to deliver. Learning and the mission of the institution are modularized into discrete activities. MOOCs are an example of modularized course content. The move to unbundle tenure-track roles that once connected teaching, research, and service is another example of atomization; teaching itself is further unbundled into assessment, advising, and delivery. Staff work areas are also being dissected. For example, advising is seen less holistically and broken into processes like early warning systems, divorced from the advising needed to remedy the warning. Atomization as an organizing principle works against community, as it inherently is invested in disconnecting not just processes but people. An additional effect of atomization is the reduction of the expertise required by individuals holding those positions. They act as agents fulfilling the plan of an academic manager rather than as experts or professionals entrusted to exercise their knowledge and skills in the fulfillment of their roles.

Higher education is also atomized at other levels. For example, departments as well as administrative units are increasingly rendered distinct, reducing their similarity and thus their affinity. As a result, the workers within each unit view themselves as increasingly separate from workers within other units, as they favor the familiar organization of their own unit and find the organization of other units confusing or not desirable. The units themselves are also less able to collaborate, as they have separately developed their own processes and modes of being. Rather than collaborating, units or departments are more likely to seek their own solutions to common issues in house or to develop a formal relationship with an external service provider to purchase the solution to their issue through a market framework. As is discussed in the following section, the atomization of departments also sets up separate departments and administrative units in opposition, as competitors for scarce institutional resources.

Micro-Entrepreneurialism

Entrepreneurialism advocated under academic capitalism takes new forms and is further encouraged under the Gig Academy. Research faculty, like Uber drivers, do not belong to the institution but are largely freelance workers raising their own money for their gigs. The university grants them access to its infrastructure while retaining ownership of the products of their research. As noted in chapter 2, research faculty report the greatest stress and unhappiness. The radical push for faculty to raise the money for their own salaries not only creates stress but decreases community, as they spend all their time trying to identify sources of revenue. This allows them virtually no time to connect with others. And as noted in chapter 1, entrepreneurialism breeds competition that drives wedges between individual workers and among departments and units.

So while entrepreneurialism is built into individual roles, it is also built into how units are divided organizationally. Managers incentivize departments to focus on their own needs and benefits rather than considering a more holistic perspective that views the campus and all the departments within it as a larger organism.[8] Like employees, departments are increasingly atomized and pitted against each other to compete for increasingly scarce funding. This contest can lead to additional dysfunction and chaos within the institutional environment. This can be seen between academic affairs units, between student services units, and between academic affairs and student affairs.

Responsibility-centered budgeting (RCB)—a corporate model of funding increasingly used on campuses—hinders collaboration and creates competition between departments that breaks down working relationships and a sense of community. Responsibility-centered budgeting is a decentralized approach to budgeting that rewards entrepreneurship and asks units to raise their own funds and cover their own costs. Units must expand to create greater financial security, as the overall institution no longer provides buffer funding. Administrators are increasingly utilizing budgeting and accountability techniques that create this kind of division, transforming academic communities into feudal war zones. Proponents of RCB argue that it allows institutions to maximize their strengths and reduce their weaknesses, while critics point out that the way it does so is by contributing to the survival of units that generate growth from their management of revenues and expenditures and killing off those units that do not. This Darwinian method of managing institutional units drives to the root logics of capitalism, which assumes that growth and innovation emerge from the chaotic struggle for organizational survival.[9]

This method also misunderstands the processes whereby organizational learning takes place. Organizational units must be supported in developing the capacity to better serve their goals. Having a lack of administrative support erodes the ability of the members of a unit to invest in community and prevents the unit itself from doing so, as instead their activities must be oriented around restricting expenditures and generating revenue. RCB obscures the real goal of education, which is focused on teaching and learning, and the development of community that is crucial to achieving this goal.

RCB also creates real divisions between differently-situated departments. Certain disciplines, such as biomedical research that results in lucrative technology transfer licensing, are privileged; those with less-defined avenues towards monetizing results, such as the humanities, are hindered.[10] Thus, RCB provides an excellent example of how the micro-entrepreneurial logics of the Gig Academy pit departments against one another, eroding community and sacrificing student learning.

Automation and Technology

As previously noted, universities in the Gig Academy rely on processes of automation to organize work and provide cheaper on-demand labor, reducing the need for paid workers, dividing workers, and inhibiting meaningful interactions necessary for community. Universities use technology in ways that break down community as faculty move increasingly into teaching online and are not as often required to come to the campus to teach or to interact with students. Technology is used to mediate between college employees and students, serving as a first-line monitoring and communication tool that automates the processes of advising with artificial intelligence. Technology is also increasingly being used to farm out academic tasks, like grading, to students themselves, shifting labor costs onto the student and reducing the need for paid faculty.[11]

Using technology as a student-facing monitoring and primary communication tool vastly reduces the complexity of interactions with students. Digital analytics alert the unit tasked with addressing whichever micro-component of the student experience needs to be addressed in a particular scenario. This works when a student simply needs to be reminded to schedule a meeting but is not as helpful if the student is experiencing challenges outside of school that are interfering with their studies. Used in this way, technology can encourage passivity among students, moving them away from interacting with faculty unless prompted by an app. When the app is programmed to tell students what office to visit based on particular circumstances, workers are less informed members of the campus community and have fewer occasions for collaboration.

As work is divided up and fragmented by technology, interdepartmental knowledge and relationships suffer. Under the paradigm of automated processes, workers may be able to quickly find out where they should send a student to address a particular question but have less knowledge of why they are sending the student to that department, who is there to receive the student, or how the student will be received. Technological applications that separate people and reduce labor costs in university spaces are proliferating. Starfish, Packback, Inside Track, BBookx, Perceptiv, and M-Write are a few contemporary examples of tools that are being deployed in this fashion. Starfish offers a set of communication and analytics platforms that serve as a first-line communication tools between university employees, such as faculty or advisors, and students. Packback offers an online discussion platform that uses artificial intelligence to moderate online discussions and coach students. Inside Track is an online coaching tool that automates the advising of prospective and current students. BBookx is an AI-assisted tool for generating textbooks. Perceptiv and M-Write are platforms that facilitate students in peer reviewing and grading each other's work.[12]

Furthermore, the Gig Academy is premised on a manager class that uses technology to deploy contingent labor to meet consumer needs in the least expensive way possible. In chapter 1, we discussed technologies such as the Workday platform that allow managers to hire adjuncts at the last minute to teach courses. This last-minute, just-in-time hiring prevents faculty from being able to interact with others to orient themselves to their work and the campus community. Relationships themselves are unimportant, perhaps suspect, under this logic and are not identified as serving the purposes of profit and revenue generation.

Breakdown of Community Relationships

We next provide empirical evidence about the breakdown of community and relationships by reviewing the documented demise of shared governance, tensions between corporatization and unions, strained relationships between managers and employees, growing middle-level management that creates a gulf in community, declining satisfaction, morale and engagement, rising turnover and difficulty recruiting employees, and growing discrimination.

The Demise of Shared Governance

Gig Academy logic asserts that the managerial class needs to maintain decision-making power to continue to maximize profits and institutional benefits. This comports with the view that academic managers are the institutional strategists who make executive decisions around structuring the work of their departments. Therefore, democratic structures (or public good structures as referred to by Slaughter and Rhoads) have been dismantled so that power can be concentrated at the top of the hierarchy and so that academic capitalism and gig logics can remain dominant in decision-making and operating structures. Relationships among faculty, staff, and administrators needed to be altered to support the authority of the managerial class and disempower the faculty and staff. We can see this logic playing out most significantly in the decline of shared governance.[13]

In prior decades, faculty and administrators made decisions jointly through a system of shared governance. Faculty members' professional expertise was considered important to making decisions about curriculum and the teaching and learning environment. Shared governance helped to facilitate positive relationships and communication between administrators and faculty as they made decisions together about important areas related to academic programs. Yet in the neoliberal Gig Academy, shared governance has gone into decline.[14]

Part of the neoliberal agenda of the Gig Academy is to deprofessionalize faculty members, and this can be accomplished partly by taking away authority. In the last thirty years, most campuses have centralized decision-making among administrators and divested decision-making authority from faculty. Even areas that had enjoyed relatively strong faculty control, such as curriculum planning, are being taken over by central administrations who create online curricula and new programs of study with little or no faculty input. Additionally, faculty are being asked less for their advice on core issues of missions and goals.[15]

This shift in authority over campus decisions is legitimized by neoliberal trends that put administrators in charge of managing the product being offered. Schuster and Finkelstein, in a national study, found that tenure-track faculty participated significantly less in governance and consistently reported feelings of having less influence over important campus matters. Faculty report less influence on issues like campus priorities and budgets while being saddled with more local service responsibilities that underutilize their expertise, such as course scheduling. Decisions of consequence come to rest with the exclusive and largely unchallenged authority of the manager class.[16] This has also fueled the disintegration of relationships described in this chapter.

Perhaps the most foundational and insidious way that governance responsibilities are shifting from faculty to administrators is structural, in the core move to contingency. With three-quarters of faculty off the tenure track, significantly fewer faculty are available to participate in governance activities on campuses, even if participation in shared governance was again made more available to them. The trends have become so alarming that the Association of Governing Boards, representing college and university trustees, published a national report—*Consequential Governance*—calling for a decisive restoration of shared governance and criticizing the concentration of decision-making power in the hands of administrators as a threat to the public mission of higher education and the quality of education. They call for campus leaders to involve boards, faculty (particularly contingent faculty), staff, and students more in governance. When a national association of trustees implores administrators to redistribute power, this should be taken as a clear sign of institutional imbalance.[17]

The centralization of power not only affects faculty but staff as well. University senates that include staff are experiencing less input on decisions and diminishing authority. In addition to these formal structures, staff are also seeing a concentration of authority in managers, and staff input and feedback have declined (see chapter 2).

Tensions between Corporatization and Unions

Partly as a result of the decline of shared governance, which facilitated communication between faculty and administrators, tensions between unions and administrators are at an all-time high. Barrow described these rising tensions between employees and administrators as resulting from administrators' corporatized goals, language, and viewpoint.[18] Union members perceive administrators as focused less on academic goals, teaching, and learning and more on reducing costs, generating revenue, competition, and prestige. On the converse, the Gig Academy lens through which administrators look tends to view unions as power-hungry entities that invade workplaces, appropriate funds, stymie innovation, and interfere with the achievement of the goals of education.

There is also a gulf between academics and administrators related to the role of students. Administrators increasingly position students as customers and commodities in the marketized environment, quite the opposite of the developmental view that academics hold of them—as learners. Willis describes these tensions playing out in at Empire State College in New York, with administrators feeling threatened by unionization and making very concerted efforts to stop it from happening. Lafer noted how administrators used tactics to pressure faculty to side with the administration over graduate students who were trying to unionize. They argued that graduate student unionizing would negatively affect the learning environment, aiming to manipulate faculty based on their commitment to student learning, though the administrators really were focused on preventing graduate students from developing the power to demand better working conditions or otherwise influence the academic environment as a cohesive constituency with power and voice. It has taken years for these manipulative arguments to be reversed. Lafer notes how unions have turned to the external community (local organizations) to combat the abusive and anti-union techniques of university administrators. Similarly, universities seeking to crush unions partner with external organizations to coordinate and execute their union-busting strategies.[19]

Tensions between academic management and unions have increased as working conditions have deteriorated for academic workers and as workers have become more atomized. Whereas unions and university leadership used to have more cooperative management dynamics that contributed to developing desirable solutions for employees, relations between unions and universities have become more combative and hostile. Unionized faculty or staff are often viewed as a cumbersome presence on college campuses because their collective power allows them to influence college governance, which means that administrators cannot make unilateral governance decisions without involvement from faculty.[20]

Growing Middle-Level Administrators

In the last chapter, we described the dramatic growth of a new set of professional staff, middle-level administrators who report to administrators. These new middle-level administrators emerged to buffer the administration from any contact with faculty and staff, ensuring minimal interactions and communications, which are essential for community development. In terms of material conditions, these employees are provided a privileged set of working conditions compared to all other employees to ensure that they monitor staff and faculty. The emphasis on principles of accountability ensures their allegiance is to the administrators who hired them, and they are instructed to work within the logics of academic capitalism and the Gig Academy. Yet in bridging between administrators, academics, professional staff, and external constituencies, these new professionals form a hybrid identity.[21]

Administrators lose contact with faculty and staff as the new middle-level managers increasingly take over that role, which means administrators become less familiar with the working conditions, needs, and experiences of faculty and staff. While their work involves bridging academic, administrative, and market-focused perspectives in interacting with different constituencies, many such workers report that the function of their work is limited to supporting the managerial decisions of their supervisors; they are valued as disseminators of information, as developers of new structures to arrange university work, and as analysts, but not as decision makers. In short, such third-space professionals function more as extensions of the agency of administrators than as agents in their own right. While their perspectives are not considered by administrators, their presence in academia is often viewed with suspicion from academic constituencies, leading to limited opportunities to form community themselves. The hybrid identities of these workers render them able to communicate with the different constituencies working within higher education, while their hybridity often causes others to keep them at a distance.[22] The isolation of administrators through the growth of the middle-level administrators has not served campuses well when it comes to building community and has rather served as a technology to foster greater levels of division.

Poor Morale, Anxiety, Fear, and Strained Supervisory Relationships

Sense of community among Gig Academy workers is hindered by working conditions that reduce morale, foster anxiety and fear about job insecurity, and subject them to abuse by their supervisors. In general, studies of campus employees' view of relationships demonstrate a historical low. Rosser documents how the quality of interpersonal relationships between educational support staff and their supervisors has become increasingly negative over the past few decades. These relationships have been identified as profoundly affecting the job satisfaction and morale of support professionals. In surveys, staff list interpersonal experiences in general and with supervisors as a central matter of concern and believe that they are treated like second-class citizens, that supervisors and administrators do not respect them, and that communication is poor. In short, they experience exclusion in their work environments and strain in relationships on campuses. Magolda, after spending a year with custodial staff in an ethnographic study, qualitatively identified how staff feel marginalized, alienated, disconnected, and increasingly unhappy. His study documents how custodial staff have declining working conditions (discussed throughout earlier chapters) but also less opportunity for mobility than in the past, fear their supervisors, and no longer have collegial relationships they once had with students, other staff, and faculty—as administrators discourage them having relationships. Custodial staff are pressured by accountability regimes and regular audits of their work that create stress. They once felt part of an academic community but now feel discarded and abused by a system that treats people as disposal labor.[23]

Numerous studies have identified how adjuncts feel they are invisible. If they are noticed at all, they are second-class citizens, disrespected, marginalized, and not part of the academic community. Even though adjuncts feel a strong commitment to their role and to students, increasingly there are reports of adjuncts leaving academia altogether as well as of the stress and burden on those that stay. Kezar identified the psychic burden of being an adjunct—driving from institution to institution, rushing late to the classroom, running out of the classroom to the next assignment, carrying all of one's materials in a suitcase, having nowhere to meet with students and no connection to any other faculty members, being completely alone in one's work. Adjuncts believe that tenure-track faculty members look down on them and that administrators exploit them. Numerous studies identify how contingent faculty report feeling exploited and are unsatisfied with their pay, lack of benefits, the climate within their departments, and their lack of input into their courses. Women contingent faculty note feeling especially exploited because they are overrepresented within the ranks of contingents and their job insecurity leaves them open to various forms of gender harassment. Campus climates hostile to racially minoritized faculty, contingent and tenured, contribute to negative experiences that strain their relationships and diminish a sense of community. For racially minoritized contingent faculty, experiences of negative climate may be all the more damaging due to the lack of job security.[24]

As noted earlier, contingent research faculty report the highest degree of alienation and isolation among adjunct faculty and are most likely to leave academia and report that they would not come back.[25] Unlike contingent teaching faculty, they do not even have prior relationships with the administration or other faculty; they have never been a part of the academic community.

Whereas postdocs and graduate students were formerly part of the academic community, they have, over the years, moved from training and mentoring positions to being so overworked and distressed that they find it challenging to maintain the kinds of relationships they formerly had with students, staff, and faculty. Graduate students and postdocs used to work closely with faculty and had time to connect with students. With their increasing workloads and expectations, they find limited time to develop and maintain relationships—even ones that might help them with their career, which is part of their reason for being in these roles. The few remaining tenure-track faculty are stretched across more grant projects and have less time to mentor and support postdocs or graduate students. Postdocs do share some of the experiences of research faculty in that they are often isolated in a lab with few connections to others. Most campuses have a single resource person for postdocs (if they have anyone at all). Very infrequently an office may exist. Campuses often lack any policies or practices related to their employment, and like adjuncts and research faculty, postdocs are often considered invisible. The first major book to be written on postdocs is called *The Postdoc Landscape: The Invisible Scholars,* and it outlines the alienation, lack of institutional support, and difficult relationships with faculty that postdocs experience.[26]

Measuring Declining Satisfaction, Climate, and Engagement

Gallup has conducted surveys of employee engagement across many industries and found that universities and colleges are among the least engaged workplaces in the world. As they note, colleges "are failing to maximize the potential of their biggest asset—their faculty and staff." The survey found that 52 percent of higher education faculty are not engaged in their work, and 14 percent are actively disengaged. Only 34 percent of faculty and staff were found to be engaged in their work. These data uncover a very serious trend that individual campus employee satisfaction surveys may not identify—the mass disengagement, poor morale, and dissatisfaction that result from poor working conditions and relationships on campus. Gallup is capitalizing on decades of research in the business world showing that the kind of disinvestment in employees that has happened in higher education will result in poor organizational performance. The firm advocates for engagement, which essentially builds on decades-old organizational theory about the positive results of creating a humanistic work environment. Engagement is defined as meaningful work, a positive and humanistic work environment, supportive management, opportunities for growth, trust in supervisors, and an environment that is fair. Gallup's is one of the few publicly available sets of data that documents these trends. Gallup also conducted recent surveys of students that identified faculty and staff as central to their success, underscoring again the importance of community and relationships.[27]

Many individual campus survey results can be found online, usually showing declining satisfaction, professional development and advancement, morale, and the like. For example, a 2013 survey from James Madison University found that 72 percent of faculty at the institution were dissatisfied with their salaries; faculty were overall dissatisfied with resources provided for research, scholarly activities, and instruction, with a lack of faculty influence over curriculum, and with a lack of regard demonstrated for faculty input. A 2004 faculty satisfaction survey from the

University of Illinois at Springfield found that administrative leadership was rated lowest among the areas surveyed, with 46 percent rating administrative leadership as "poor" or "very poor" and the overall mean score sitting far below the median score on the satisfaction scale. The majority of respondents to the survey also stated that faculty voices were not adequately acknowledged in campus-wide matters—indicating that they felt unheard by administrators. The University of Washington, Tacoma, conducted a satisfaction survey in 2013–2014 which found that faculty on average were dissatisfied with senior leadership as well as with recognition for their work. Of course, some campuses have positive results to such surveys, but the few national surveys suggest an overall trend toward dissatisfaction with only pockets of satisfaction.[28]

The declining work environment has fostered an entire for-profit market of firms focused on survey deployment so campuses can identify and measure the negative environment that they are creating. Dozens of climate surveys for faculty and staff now exist with questions about working conditions, working relationships with administrators, and other key issues reviewed in this and earlier chapters. Most of the data is proprietary, owned and not shared by the firm that conducted the study or the institution that commissioned it.[29]

In a move to create some social pressure around these poor relationships and working conditions, the *Chronicle of Higher Education* developed an annual survey of "Great Colleges to Work For." This survey is being used to assess faculty and staff satisfaction at institutions of higher education across the United States. It has two parts: an institutional questionnaire, which audits institutional policies and practices, and a "Higher Education Insight Survey" designed to measure faculty and staff satisfaction. This survey profiles campuses that perform particularly well in terms of job satisfaction, professional development, compensation, benefits, work-life balance, quality of facilities, policies and resources, shared governance, supervisor relationships, relationships among faculty, staff, and administrators, communication, collaboration, fairness, respect, appreciation, and pride. The instrument helps campuses to identify areas where they might improve.

The work to uncover these problems is being done by external groups, including Gallup and the *Chronicle,* which put pressure on higher education leaders to re-examine basic employee arrangements and campus work environments. In the past, positive work environments were strengths of colleges and universities; as these surveys are now finding, higher education is now scoring worst compared to all sectors of organizations and businesses that they survey. The poor employee work environment and disengagement should be a major concern to administrators as well as to the board members who oversee them. This clearly shows a failure to create the kind of positive community in which employees are going to thrive and help meet the mission of the institution.

There is a bit of an irony in all of the survey work happening on college campuses to investigate why employees are so disengaged, given that administrators created these working conditions with their choices. Likely, many current administrators were not involved in earlier decisions that created this environment decades ago and may even be unaware of the systemic trends. Even longtime administrators may not be able to identify how choices they made over time led one by one to this systemic problem.

Hiring and Retention Problems—Faculty and Staff Turnover

Perceived exploitation, inadequate working conditions, poor climate, and negative relationships between administrators and employees have resulted in increasing turnover of faculty and staff on college campuses. Increased turnover breaks down community as individuals cycle in and out of the institution. Transient faculty and staff detract from the college community because the development of relationships takes time. Additionally, institutions are facing challenges in recruiting employees due to their low wages, insufficient benefits, and lack of job security. For example, according to 2017 data from the College and University Professional Association for Human Resources, staff median salary is $36,580 and mean salary $37,294 across all positions; adjuncts receive median compensation of $872 per credit hour; and while faculty salaries vary across disciplines, the entry salary for history is $57,000 and $65,000 for physical sciences. While certainly tenured faculty make most out of all groups, the pay in higher education in general is quite low, given that many have degrees and even advanced degrees. Colleges and universities have traditionally paid slightly less than other sectors but compensated with generous benefits packages and job security; this is no longer the case.[30]

Meyer, reporting on a recent survey of college and university faculty and staff, noted that they have significant turnover rates and difficulty recruiting.[31] The survey found that employee recruitment and retention is now a common challenge for colleges and universities. Contributing factors to that challenge include compensation rates, workload, workplace culture, and competition from other sectors. Key findings related to employee recruitment and retention from Meyer's study include

- 61 percent of institutions have difficulty attracting top faculty, and 59 percent struggle to retain top faculty;
- 62 percent have difficulty attracting top staff, and 69 percent struggle to retain top staff;
- 27 percent report above-average turnover rates for faculty;
- 41 percent report above-average turnover rates for staff;
- 71 percent see a correlation between faculty engagement and retention; and
- 80 percent see a correlation between staff engagement and retention.

Data on turnover are not regularly public, making it hard to systematically examine these trends.

Conclusion

These various trends taken together create a very different kind of academic community than has existed at any time in the past. Faculty and staff are turning over in their roles more than ever and are largely unavailable given their contingent and outsourced status. And interactions among faculty and staff are likely to be tainted by their low morale, declining satisfaction, and overall feelings of disengagement. The structures and mechanisms that channel human relationships in the Gig Academy exacerbate the stress experienced by academic workers, contribute to distrust between colleagues, reform formerly collaborative supervisor-employee relationships into antagonistic ones, and push academic workers to spend a far greater proportion of their time and energy strategizing to survive within an increasingly exploitative employment setting. Without long-term and stable faculty and staff to interact with students, there is no viable community for students beyond their peers. Administrators have adopted logics that have dismantled the academic community that is central to a quality learning environment. While we do not necessarily believe that administrators were actively attempting to erode community, they have done so through their choices, fueled by the logics of the Gig Academy.

FOUR

How Employment Practices Negatively Impact Student Learning and Outcomes

In this chapter, we continue to trace the consequences of the Gig Academy's dissolution of community on campuses and describe effects on student learning and outcomes—the primary goal of the academic enterprise. We first review trends associating Gig Academy employment practices with student learning and outcomes. Next, we review two bodies of literature that shed light on why the teaching and learning environment is compromised given these changes in employment trends and working conditions—social learning theories and empirical research on faculty-student interactions. Both are significant bodies of research that help to explain why current trends will continue to compromise quality learning. Social learning theories help illuminate the social dimensions of the learning environment, highlight the role of faculty and staff as key pillars in the learning process, and provide theoretical support to explain the negative student outcomes associated with the Gig Academy. Research on faculty-student interactions provides the empirical evidence that learning outcomes are negatively associated with faculty working under Gig Academy conditions. In short, the combination of theory and evidence demonstrates that quality education is tied to an investment in and support of employees at the college, which then translates into community building and the development of supportive relationships. Gig Academy employment structures limit the ability of college workers to invest in these relationships and community with their colleagues and students. There is a need for additional research on staff, but those studies that exist find staff play a central role in student outcomes, making them feel validated, contributing to a sense of belonging, and serving as role models. The role of staff in supporting student success and learning should not be overlooked.

In this chapter, we focus on the primary mission of higher education institutions—learning and student success. Yet the move to contingent faculty and staff significantly impacts other important objectives of higher education institutions as well. While we do not examine the implications of the move to contingent faculty on knowledge generation and the research function of higher education, we would be remiss not to acknowledge how scholarship, research, and innovation are likely suffering due to the change in workforce. The fact that so many faculty are no longer protected by academic freedom clearly impacts the nature of research produced. There are many cautionary tales of faculty being attacked historically for controversial research. Today, scholars are being attacked for research on climate change, for example, suggesting the importance of academic freedom and tenure for protecting the nature of inquiry. Contingent faculty are not taking the risks that tenure-track faculty once did, and this is reshaping the nature of scholarship. Research faculty on grants (soft money contracts) are constrained in what they can explore. And only topics funded by outside research are generally being pursued within this new environment.[1]

We also do not focus on the important contribution of faculty and staff to their local and regional communities. Gig Academy structures, including the unbundling of faculty roles into teaching and research and the reduction in compensation and other supports, reduce the capacity of faculty to engage in community activities. For example, an adjunct has little time to support a local homeless initiative that is central to her sociology research. Staff members who are outsourced are no longer connected to institutional efforts to support tutoring, address homelessness, or enhance jobs.

While we believe that knowledge generation and community engagement are extremely important, there is less research to date about these trends and their impact on college and university campuses. Thus, we focus on the connection between the Gig Academy employment conditions and the student learning mission of higher education, where there is ample evidence of the impact of the shift. However, we anticipate that future research will demonstrate how the changing employment relationships also impact other important missions, like knowledge generation and community engagement, so that policymakers, leaders, and others who influence the nature of academic work can have a full understanding of the impact of the decisions they are making.

Gig Academy Employment Practices That Shape Student Outcomes

As the numbers of contingent faculty have swelled, various studies have investigated whether and to what extent this shift in faculty employment is associated with a concomitant negative trend in student learning and success. Research into the growth in contingent faculty has documented some negative outcomes for students related to transition, retention, persistence, graduation, transfer, and academic performance, particularly among first-generation, low-income, and racially minoritized students. Collectively, these studies provide a wake-up call for higher education institutions, showing that reliance on contingent faculty is interfering with the educational mission of colleges and universities.

Research by Kezar demonstrates how the accumulation of poor working conditions and lack of any supportive infrastructure has led to a phenomenon called "lack of opportunity to perform," a dynamic in which contingent faculty's working conditions prevent them from educating to their potential. Faculty frequently experience burnout from attempting to compensate for a gross lack of institutional resources and support. Employment factors prevent contingent faculty from investing as much time and effort into developing relationships with their students as they would like to. Contingent faculty typically do not have stable teaching appointments or office hours that permit effective planning and preparation. Design, redesigning, or updating curricula requires time and participation that contingent faculty may not have. Contingent faculty who do not participate in departmental tasks are unable to contribute to the development of course syllabi or structure their courses to fit their personal teaching styles. Hence, contingent faculty may be less likely to make important connections to course content and learning objectives. Their working conditions make it more difficult to develop effective or diverse instructional strategies to meet students' academic needs and to deliver course content clearly.[2]

The lack of resources invested in contingent faculty interferes with their ability to be excellent educators and community members, as performing the behaviors associated with robust community participation and supporting students in a comprehensive way is more costly when they must provide the resources themselves. Contingent faculty often tend to lack opportunities for professional development, orientation, mentoring, feedback, and evaluation.[3] Thus, if contingent faculty wish to become familiar with the campus, they must conduct research themselves. Getting to know the ins and outs of their departments also becomes an exercise in trial and error. Without formal mentoring opportunities, contingent faculty must hope (if they have the time for concerns about growth) to find individuals around them who are willing and able to share insights and invest time in them. Without opportunities for feedback and evaluation, contingent faculty are unable to place their own teaching and scholarship within the context of the work being done at their employing institution or find aspects of their teaching that they should emphasize and others they should limit. Contingent faculty are thus left without a compass in these settings.

The same faculty often lack office space where they can meet with students outside of class to provide support or feedback. They are usually not compensated for office hours, which can limit the amount of time they have available. They may lack school-issued email addresses that help to facilitate communication with students. Additionally, they are often only hired to teach, are excluded from the broader life of their campuses and departments, and may not be invited or encouraged to participate in activities or to serve as advisors or mentors for individual students or student groups, which denies them an additional area for connecting with students in substantive ways. Short-term contracts mean faculty are not there the next semester to write a letter of recommendation or follow up with a student to answer questions about their major or career. Although they may be excellent teachers in the classroom, they simply lack the same opportunities as their full-time peers to be involved in the lives of their students and provide them with similar support outside of class. And while part-time faculty may be able to demonstrate some of the characteristics associated with high-quality faculty-student interaction, such as being approachable, their inaccessibility or lack of engagement outside of class may unintentionally present cues that make them seem distant, unsupportive, or unapproachable.

Student experiences in college are particularly important in their early years, when they often do not yet know what to expect and are looking for signals from faculty and staff to help guide them forward. Yet first-year courses, particularly developmental courses that serve students at the most risk, are increasingly taught by part-time faculty who may not have time for the type of frequent and substantive interaction that can help support students in building their self-confidence. When non-tenure-track faculty do not have the support and ability to spend time with students in these first-year and developmental courses, their students are less likely to seek contact with faculty members later on, regardless of the subsequent instructors' tenure status and ability to spend time working with them outside the classroom. This suggests that the prevalence of part-time faculty leading introductory courses may be an even greater problem than we imagined.

Students look for accessibility cues that signal a professor is available to help. Research shows contingent faculty's working conditions often interfere with their ability to create such cues, inadvertently inhibiting student help-seeking, which can harm their learning. Students may observe their instructor arriving just in time to start formal instruction, rushing off at the end of class to head to their next gig, or lacking familiarity with the textbook and conclude that they are not available to answer student questions or provide other forms of support. Creating conditions where students are comfortable asking questions and ensuring instructors have the resources available to provide appropriate responses to such questions is key to students making important connections among complex concepts and real-world experiences.[4]

Numerous studies highlight the substantial effects of the diminished time and quality of student-faculty interaction caused by Gig Academy employment structures. Contact time and personal interaction between traditional faculty and students has been shown to foster student success. Unsurprisingly, the growing shift towards contingent faculty brings about a reduction in contact time, with scholars arguing that the inaccessibility of part-time faculty to students due to time pressures, limited availability for office hours, and frequent need to hold jobs at multiple locations prevents students from getting advisement and from building rapport, bringing about a proportionally negative association on student outcomes. Instructors are less available to students when they lack time and space for regular office hours or cannot stay after class to answer important student questions.[5]

Thus, we are not only undermining students' chances for faculty-student interaction through our growing reliance on part-time faculty but setting up these instructors to be less accessible and seem less welcoming than they could otherwise be, despite their own best efforts to serve their students well. When part-time faculty members are not provided an institutional email address or office space, students may have difficulty finding opportunities to discuss their interest in course material, receive feedback on assignments, or seek out help. Part-time faculty may only have limited availability for office hours, which could signal inaccessibility to students. Also, because part-time faculty are often paid very little and may have their hours capped by their institutions, many must work on multiple campuses to piece together a salary, which means instructors may be rushing out of class to make it across town for their next course, leaving behind or putting off students seeking help after class. Even when they are making efforts to be involved, they may seem less supportive or approachable.

The Gig Academy working conditions also prevent staff from supporting students in ways they have in the past. Magolda documents how staff on college campuses who work as custodians (and the analogy can be extended to workers in food service, transportation, and groundskeeping) often play the role of family to students, particularly first-generation students, low-income students, and racially minoritized students.[6] They check in on students, offer emotional support, and in general provide social support. But as campuses embrace neoliberalism and the Gig Academy, staff are made part-time and outsourced and are no longer able to provide the emotional support that they have long contributed to their college campuses.

Student Learning and Outcomes Impaired by Gig Academy Practices

Having summarized some of the most relevant working conditions facing contingent faculty and staff, we next move to summarize the research on how taking courses with contingent faculty affects student outcomes. Gig Academy employment conditions are negatively associated with persistence, retention, graduation, academic performance, transfer from two-year to four-year institutions, early-college experiences, and high-quality faculty-student interactions. For a more in-depth consideration of the association between the move to largely contingent faculty employment structures and student learning, see Kezar et al., Kezar and Sam, and Kezar and DePaola.[7]

It is important to note that none of the studies contends that contingent faculty themselves are responsible for lower student outcomes. Until recently we had little direct evidence to understand why these negative outcomes were associated with contingent faculty, particularly part-time adjuncts where the findings are most pronounced. Kezar documents the direct ways that employment policies impact contingent faculty, reducing their opportunities to perform, and she points to policies that need to be changed to improve student success, which will be reviewed later in this section. Several researchers have hypothesized that the poor working conditions of contingent faculty impact student learning conditions.[8] There is mounting research evidence that employment policies and structures affect staff and faculty in higher education, which in turn affects student experiences and shapes their outcomes.

Persistence, Retention, and Graduation

Given the national urgency for increasing graduation rates, the move toward greater employment of adjunct faculty—with their accompanying poor working conditions—should be of particular concern to institutional leaders. Ehrenberg and Zhang and later Jaeger and Eagan found that graduation rates declined as the proportions of contingent faculty increased. Increases in part-time faculty have an even more pronounced negative association with graduation rates and retention. Bettinger and Long found that contingent faculty were associated with reduced first-year student persistence into the second year.[9]

Academic Performance

In a study of college freshmen, Harrington and Schibik found that taking courses with part-time faculty was associated with lower second-semester retention rates, lower GPAs, and fewer attempted credit hours. A recent study by Ran and Xu with a statewide data set and perhaps one of the most ambitious designs to date demonstrated that taking courses with adjuncts, particularly those on short-term contracts with tenuous links to the departments where they teach, is negatively associated with student performance in future courses, continuation into the major in which they took courses with adjuncts, and persistence in both two-year and four-year institutions. Bettinger and Long also found that older contingent faculty were associated with more distinct negative outcomes in terms of student persistence in particular academic subjects, whereas younger contingent faculty were associated with more distinct negative outcomes in terms of student persistence in more professionally oriented subjects.[10]

Transfer from Two-Year to Four-Year Institutions

Another key concern in higher education is the rising imperative to improve transfer from two- to four-year institutions, particularly in connection with the need to graduate more racially minoritized and low-income students, many of whom enter higher education via two-year institutions. Research has found that studying at two-year colleges with a greater proportion of full-time, tenured faculty was associated with a greater likelihood of transferring to four-year institutions, while studying at two-year institutions with greater proportions of part-time and contingent faculty was associated with a lower likelihood of transfer to four-year institutions. Similarly, Gross and Goldhaber found that a 10-percent increase in the proportion of tenured faculty predicted a 4-percent increase in transfers to four-year institutions. Eagan and Jaeger also found that taking an increased number of classes with contingent faculty was associated with lower transfer rates for students.[11]

Quality of Courses, Pedagogy, and Student Interactions

Faculty working conditions affect their capacity to plan and develop the classroom environment, which are critical to social learning. Planning and preparation are particularly important elements of effective teaching in social learning theory, as getting to know your students is helpful in designing classroom activities that work. Time before and after class to get to know students helps with ongoing planning, as faculty can adjust the instructional tempo, anticipate areas of difficulty for their students, and strategize for future adjustments and activities. Planning time also allows professors to continuously realign to student learning objectives and progression toward their academic goals.[12]

Repeated studies have identified that adjuncts (often with little choice due to lack of time, control over curriculum, and lack of professional development opportunities) are forced to use less engaging and less student-centered pedagogies, spending less time preparing for class. Considering the intense need for Gig Academy instructors to rigidly control their time to manage a greater array of responsibilities and functions, it is not surprising that many adopt faculty-centered pedagogies that correspond to the needs of their employment situation. Other studies have shown that adjuncts use fewer practices that are related to reliably fostering student success and learning, including active and collaborative learning strategies, culturally sustaining pedagogies, and challenging assignments that set high expectations for students while providing adequate levels of support.[13]

The previous sections show empirically that the move to Gig Academy employment structures has interfered with the mission of creating educational environments maximally conducive to student learning and success. In the following section, we will use social learning theories to explain some of the negative associations between student outcomes and the rise of Gig Academy instruction, delving into the nature of social learning to better understand why the shift to the Gig Academy has been so problematic for student learning and success.

Social Learning Theories

Social learning theories suggest learning is inherently grounded in the relationships and interactions between people, which shows why faculty and staff are such key actors in the learning experiences of students. Such theories include situated learning theory, social learning theory, social cognitive theory (SCT), social development theory, and the most recent research from neuroscience.[14] These theories are the most prominent and well-established theories of learning and explain how and why faculty-student as well as staff-student interactions enhance learning. One of the most often-used theories is SCT, and we therefore focus on applying it to provide theoretical support to explain how Gig Academy employment structures and practices interfere with student learning in keeping with the empirical evidence previously outlined. We hope to pave the way for further research to more explicitly test the connection between theory and evidence.

Social Cognitive Theory

SCT conceptualizes the learning process as social, integrated, and interactive, involving cognitive or personal elements, environmental elements, and behavioral elements. Cognitive elements involve things like the student's beliefs and attitudes, environmental elements involve social norms and the treatment of the student in social contexts, and behavioral elements involve the student's actions, like practice and self-efficacy. SCT presents a framework to understand that these three areas mutually influence one another, such that learning cannot be reduced to any one area. Bandura emphasizes that learning takes place in a social context and that learning entails more than merely acquiring knowledge from others. Rather, learning is a complex process of social participation where the personal, environmental, and behavioral are intertwined.[15]

Cognitive features focus on prior knowledge and existing skills that a student brings to campus.[16] Environmental elements encompass interactions among student, faculty, and staff in and out of the classroom. Social cognitive theory suggests the faculty and staff have a significant role in shaping the learning environment and the resultant learning process. Finally, behavior represents the actions and academic tasks students undergo, based on their interactions in the environment created by faculty and staff. The cognitive processes, environment, and behaviors interact in reciprocal and bidirectional relationships. This means that students are less likely to draw on their prior knowledge and existing skills if the environment is not conducive to doing so or if the behaviors of the faculty and staff do not foster the motivation to do so.

Social cognitive theory documents how student experiences in the learning environment are shaped by personal, behavioral, and environmental conditions that have continuous reciprocal effects on one another. Learning is a result of the interactions between what students bring to the classroom and the environment facilitated by their professors. Faculty and staff serve as primary socialization agents that lead the classroom by providing implicit and explicit knowledge that can direct their students toward academic achievement. Social cognitive theory highlights how teacher-student experiences facilitate student learning in the classroom, not only in terms of formal curricular content but also in terms of indirect and subtle lessons that fundamentally shape motivation and influence academic endeavors. Teacher-student interactions and experiences often lead to learning beyond content within the classroom as students observe subtle lessons that influence their academic endeavors.[17]

Social cognitive theory also shows how interactions in the environment are critical for motivation. For example, professors can seek to present content in engaging ways and appeal to culturally relevant everyday experiences. Students' desire and ability to apply what they learn depends on their capacity to find value in the content presented and the relationships built within the classroom setting. Such relationships require that faculty leading the classroom make an effort to get to know their students.

Vicarious Learning

Bandura also notes the importance of vicarious learning to the overall learning process. Vicarious learning results from observation of others and from unstructured opportunities for interaction that may or may not be part of a formal lesson or educational objective. Students learn valuable lessons from their professors or staff vicariously through personal advice or stories. Bandura argued that people learn new information and behaviors by observing other people.[18] He states, "of the many cues that influence behavior, at any point in time, none is more common than the actions of others."[19] Bandura points to how students model an activity better when it is demonstrated versus being described in a book. Although observation is seemingly passive, it impacts learning as learners, teachers, and the environment continuously interact and affect one another. Student-faculty relationships are thus a critical factor in the learning process.[20]

Academic Self-Confidence and Self-Efficacy

Bandura documented that a sense of self-efficacy—when students believe they can learn and perform—is necessary for learning to take place. Learners must have confidence in their capabilities. Students are constantly seeking cues from others in their social environment that shape their self-efficacy, such as feedback on a task or how others react to their performance. Self-efficacy is strongly tied to the overall learning environment created through the mechanism of reciprocal determinism and whether students feel like they are validated and matter (we will further discuss validation and mattering in a subsequent section).

Bandura also emphasizes how individuals process and interpret information based on their own beliefs and background and the environment in which they learn. This process is complex, interactive, and bidirectional. Social modeling and social persuasion are important in developing self-efficacy. Social modeling occurs when people observe others (role models) developing self-efficacy. Social persuasion occurs when students are provided opportunities for attaining realistic but challenging goals. Mentors and role models who get to know their students can aid them in avoiding both easy successes, which can create a false sense of ability, and overwhelming failures, which can deter the development of self-efficacy. Thus, it is essential for students to have access to mentors who are knowledgeable and have the time and abilities to construct effective learning experiences.[21]

Researchers have found that encouraging, supportive faculty-student interactions significantly increase self-efficacy and the student's sense of value and worth as they relate to schoolwork. This is an important finding, since students who lack confidence in their ability to succeed may also lack willingness to engage in their courses. Feelings of intimidation and inadequacy may prohibit students from fully participating in class, particularly when these feelings are tied to a lack of understanding of course content. Faculty can help to mitigate these risks and increase self-confidence through positive interactions with students.[22]

Validation, Mattering, and Sense of Belonging

Over the years, social cognitive theory was extended by other researchers exploring, in particular, success among low-income, first-generation and underserved minority students. This research shows even more significantly the importance of quality relationships to learning for this growing demographic in higher education. Three new concepts are associated with this extension of SCT: validation, mattering and sense of belonging. Like SCT, these focus on the relationship between student outcomes and the relational and social dimensions of student experience. These theories also posit that achieving desired student outcomes is predicated on students having positive social experiences, especially with faculty and staff, in the educational environment. While validation, mattering, and sense of belonging are all related, we will briefly describe them separately below.

Validation

Rendon's validation theory focuses on more clearly articulating the kinds of social environments that are needed within college and university settings to encourage the most development and learning among first-generation, low-income, and racially minoritized students. The theory emphasizes the importance of "enabling, confirming and supportive" interpersonal experiences with institutional agents like faculty, staff, and peer mentors in helping students succeed. Student validation occurs when institutional agents, such as faculty and staff (and in some cases peers) take an initiative to identify students as capable learners, as part of the learning community, and as creators of knowledge while fostering students' social adjustment as well. Validation encompasses two forms: academic and interpersonal. Academic validation includes actions *by institutional agents* that foster academic development. For example, providing feedback, encouraging participation and learning behavior, and valuing student contributions. Interpersonal validation consists of actions that foster the students' social adjustment to the institution. Examples of interpersonal validation include recognizing students' achievement and encouraging their involvement in campus activities. Both forms of validation can occur in and out of the classroom. Rendon identified that the most important aspect for the success of low-income and first-generation college students is feeling validated as learners by faculty and staff on college campuses. Validation occurs as faculty and staff acknowledge students as capable and see their assets. Many studies conducted using Rendon's validation theory have identified the pivotal role faculty and staff play in student success, particularly for racially minoritized students, first-generation students, and low-income students.[23]

Mattering

Mattering is defined as a feeling that the student counts and makes a difference due to the social roles they fulfill or their position in a community—that they matter because others depend on them. Mattering is this closely related to perceived self-worth and can contribute to psychosocial and psychological well-being. Rosenberg and McCullough defined mattering as consisting of three distinct elements: (a) awareness that the individual commands the interest or notice of others; (b) the belief that others take what he or she has to do or say as important; and (c) the notion that others depend on the individual. Students can be cued to feel like they matter when institutional agents and peers take notice of them and affirm their actions and presence.[24]

Crombie and others found that students who sensed that their instructors cared about them demonstrated increased levels of engagement in their courses, which resulted in student success and higher rates of retention. Faculty demonstrate caring by showing respect for students, giving personalized attention, valuing student contributions, and encouraging participation and inquiry in the classroom. West and Pearson showed how when instructors affirm students' responses to questions, they also increase students' willingness to participate and engage in class.[25] Validation and mattering both stress the influential role institutional agents play in students' development, learning, and outcomes by influencing how students perceive their role in the social or community environment of the college campus.

Sense of Belonging

Sense of belonging is another concept associated with student experiences that has been demonstrated to increase student success and observed to increase retention and graduation. Faculty and staff are pivotal agents in fostering a sense of belonging through interactions. Sense of belonging is a pervasive human motivation that is relational, drives people toward relationship-building, and shapes their perceptions. Cultivating and maintaining a sense of belonging is an essential prerequisite for students to learn and persist in the college environment.[26]

Sense of belonging is subjective and can manifest with the student's perception of social support, mattering, feeling valued and respected, a sense of connectedness and importance, or indispensability.[27] Interactions with faculty contribute significantly to sense of belonging, which again suggests that current Gig Academy employment structures detract from student outcomes by interfering with the ability of faculty to be present and to show up for students in a meaningful way. Ultimately, students are more likely to depart from college if they are not supported in developing a sense of belonging. These three areas that extend Bandura's social cognitive theory show that relationships are even more important for supporting today's college students, who increasingly are the first in their families to attend college and are questioning whether they belong.

Social cognitive theory provides a framework for understanding the mechanisms of learning that are relevant to our consideration of faculty working conditions and student outcomes. The concepts of validation, mattering, and sense of belonging provide further evidence of how students' interactions with college employees influence their motivation and shape their educational outcomes. These mechanisms help illuminate the ways that faculty and staff are inhibited by Gig Academy working conditions from being able to interact with students at the frequency and quality required to foster learning. In the next section, we review the research on faculty-student interactions to show that positive student outcomes are attainable when faculty are supported with appropriate working conditions.

Faculty-Student Interactions as Empirical Base for Learning Theories

Interactions between faculty members and students have long been documented as one of the main educational practices affecting the attainment of positive student outcomes and their educational experiences.[28] Research on faculty-student interactions provides empirical evidence that social interactions are important to various student outcomes, including how these relationships contribute to students' aspirations, promote student engagement, increase motivation to learn, boost academic self-confidence (self-efficacy), provide validation for students, contribute to students' sense of mattering, build student sense of belonging, increased persistence and completion rates, yield higher GPAs and standardized test scores, and develop leadership, critical thinking, sense of worth, career and graduate school aspirations, and self-confidence. As Cox and others note: "No shortage exists of empirical studies of the nature, quality, and frequency of faculty-student contact and their educational consequences for students."[29]

In a study examining historical findings about faculty-student interactions between 1990 and 2000, Kuh and Hu found that positive outcomes were associated with frequent and high-quality contact between students and their professors, establishing that faculty-student interactions remain relevant even as campus conditions and student demographics have changed over time. In one of the earliest studies to examine the ways colleges influence students, Jacob found that institutions where faculty-student interactions were "normal and frequent and students find teachers receptive to unhurried and relaxed conversations out of the class" showed better student outcomes and learning. Hundreds of subsequent quantitative and qualitative studies have probed the educational outcomes of faculty-student interactions and found generally positive associations or relationships.[30]

Studies correlate higher learning outcomes with more frequent and high-quality interactions with faculty members in a variety of ways, ranging from being a guest in a professor's home to working on a research project with a faculty member, talking with instructors outside of class, and serving on committees or through campus organizations with faculty. Informal interactions outside the classroom have been found to improve learning and academic performance. Numerous researchers have found that informal student-faculty interactions outside the classroom that include academic advisement also contribute to significant positive academic outcomes. Informal interactions outside the classroom may revolve around academic progress, upcoming assignments, career plans, or future aspirations about degree attainment. Common interests may lead to additional intellectual discussions or deeper conversations about personal well-being. Students can vicariously learn and benefit from professors and staff who share their academic challenges or successes as well as broader life lessons. These types of relationships may develop into short-term or long-term mentorships that have been found to lead to academic, personal, and professional development for students. In fact, Kuh and others conclude: "In general, for most students most of the time, the more interaction with faculty the better. Both substantive in-class and social out-of-class contacts with faculty members appear to positively influence (though indirectly) what students get from their college experience, their views of the college environment (especially the quality of personal relations), and their satisfaction."[31]

Persistence, GPA, and Graduation

One of the strongest outcomes in research has been the relationship between faculty-student interactions and persistence toward degree completion, which, as described at the beginning of this chapter, has been a perennial concern among the public and policymakers. One of the factors that we know decreases dropout rates and increases persistence is the amount of time that students spend with faculty and the quality of these relationships. Studies have also associated frequent and high-quality interactions with other common measures of student success, such as students' grade point averages and performance on standardized tests. These interactions have been found to have a more pronounced positive influence for students with lower SAT scores. Persistence and academic performance both contribute to graduation rates.[32]

Student Aspirations, Major Selection, and Transfer

Various studies have found that faculty have a major part in increasing students' aspirations on a range of issues. Examples of these aspirations include the desire to major in a certain area, forming a deeper commitment to complete a degree, and increasing the desire to transfer from a two- to four-year institution or attend graduate school. For example, in a recent study of students' aspirations for and success in STEM disciplines, faculty-student interactions were found to be the most important factor in whether students decided to persist in their majors. Faculty can also help to encourage students to pursue certain careers that match their interests and skills; studies examining students' later career choices find that faculty strongly influence these decisions.[33]

Studies have found that faculty also positively influence students' engagement with course material, which affects persistence. Some of this has been attributed to a connection between faculty members' passion for their fields of study and student interest and engagement; students find faculty passion and interest to be a source of encouragement. There is also an association between faculty-student interaction and students' engagement outside the classroom. Kuh and Hu noted that the frequency of faculty-student interactions had a significant and positive influence on the amount of time students spent engaging in other cocurricular and extracurricular educational activities, which increased their access to other important sources of support in college. Aspiration, engagement, and passion for learning are also associated with motivation, one of the most significant factors in retention, student success, and degree completion. Researchers have found a strong relationship between faculty-student interaction and students' motivation to work on course material or continue their studies.[34]

Importance of Interactions for Racially Minoritized Students, First-Generation Students, and Low-Income Students

Although interactions and relationships with faculty members are strong predictors of success among all groups of students, they have been found to be strongest for racially minoritized students, low-income students, and first-generation college students. No other factor plays as strong a role for racially minoritized students, making this a particularly important finding for colleges and universities, which are serving increasingly diverse student bodies and are responsible for creating conditions more conducive to the success of racially minoritized students. Studies looking at faculty interactions among racially minoritized students find that faculty-student interactions encourage racially minoritized students to engage more with learning, try harder, and meet high academic expectations. Faculty-student interactions vary significantly based on setting, quality, purpose, and other factors. While studies find generally that having a greater number of faculty-student interactions tends to be associated with positive student outcomes, in the following section we proceed to address some of the nuances regarding faculty-student interactions.[35]

The Importance of Faculty-Student Interactions in the First Year of College

We know that the most vulnerable time for students is their first year of college. Faculty-student interaction has been found to have a significant role in determining the success of students during this transition period. In various studies, relationships with faculty predicted the development of academic competence among new students in the first year of college and helped facilitate sophomore-year success as measured by GPA and satisfaction. Additionally, studies importantly find that students' earliest interactions with faculty shape their future relationships with professors and whether they even seek them out. When these initial contacts are successful, students will be more likely to pursue subsequent interactions later on; when they are unsuccessful, students will be less likely to pursue interactions later on.[36]

Depth and Quality of Faculty Interactions

Earlier studies focused on the number of contact incidents between faculty and students and found more frequent interactions to be related to more positive outcomes for students. But in more recent years, studies have found that the depth and quality of relationships is more important than frequency of contact incidents. Studies of students' development of higher-order cognitive skills also suggest that the purpose and quality of faculty-student interactions may be more important than their frequency. When examining the type of relationships that are related to positive outcomes for students (including motivation, aspiration, persistence, and achievement), Arredondo found that deeper and more meaningful interactions—such as working with a faculty member on a research project, spending time with a faculty member outside of class in a social situation, or having a conversation about careers and the students' future—were most important. Various programs that are identified with student success often build in this type of faculty mentoring through undergraduate research programs, course-connected internships, or having faculty members serve as advisors for student clubs. Other studies have demonstrated that more tutorial-style classrooms, where faculty meet with students individually and interact with them each week, are associated with greater student learning.[37]

Interactions with a substantive focus appear to have a greater impact on knowledge acquisition and skill development, for example, than do more casual, less-focused contacts.[38] However, studies have still found informal and infrequent contact to be associated with persistence, increased graduation rates, and improved student development. These lesser types of interaction include talking after class about academic or personal issues, contact through occasional greetings, and receiving advice about a major or job. While deeper interactions lead to greater outcomes, any positive interactions lead to learning and student outcomes like persistence. In general, research helps us understand what constitutes a high-quality faculty interaction or relationship and whether these come from formal or informal contacts. Studies have specifically identified four characteristics as most important: faculty members are approachable and personable; faculty members have enthusiasm and passion for their work; faculty members care about students personally; and faculty members serve as role models and mentors.[39]

The most recent confirmation of the importance of relationships (and faculty-student interactions) to learning and having a positive experience in college is a book by Chambliss and Takacs, *How College Works*. They followed a hundred randomly selected students for ten years and identified that "Time after time, in descriptions of a wide variety of situations, students told us of how encounters with the right person could make a decisive difference in their college careers."[40] In the end, their longitudinal study confirmed that interactions with faculty, staff, and peers were the most important factor in the experience of students, either positively or negatively. Further, they found that positive interactions have results that go far beyond the effort. Their study confirms data from various learning theories that suggest that satisfactory interpersonal relationships are a prerequisite for learning and that personal connections are central to daily motivation around learning and experience. They highlight how the single most significant aspect of college is relationships (both with faculty and staff), which points to the importance of colleges maintaining the priority of gathering a group of people in service of creating an environment supportive of student learning and success.

A recent quantitative study—The Gallup-Purdue Index—is a comprehensive, nationally representative study of nearly 30,000 US adults who had completed at least a bachelor's degree.[41] The study identified support from faculty and staff and positive relationships in college as having a stronger association with long-term outcomes than the type of institution they attended, its selectivity, curricula studied by students, or other elements of the college process. Relationships were pivotal to long-term outcomes. For example, if graduates recalled having a professor who cared about them as a person, made them excited about learning, and encouraged them to pursue their dreams, their odds of being engaged in their work roles after college more than doubled, as did their odds of thriving in all aspects of their well-being.

Staff-Student Relationships as Key to Social Learning

As noted in the introduction of this book and earlier in this chapter, while there have been few studies focused on the role of staff to student success and learning, those that have been conducted demonstrate their critical role to student engagement, motivation, feelings of support, and validation, all mirroring the key type of interactions that relate to learning and student success associated with faculty-student interaction.[42] But staff also provide an independent source of observational learning about professional demeanor, office skills, and issues like time management. Staff work with students in varying ways to accomplish these outcomes. Sometimes students work directly with staff in work-study roles, sometimes they are role models, and sometimes they serve as informal mentors or interact in ways that lead to more vicarious learning.

One study that identified the role of staff for student success is by Kuh et al., *Student Success in College: Creating Conditions that Matter*. The study, known as Project Documented Effective Educational Practices (DEEP), focused on twenty institutions that ranked highly in student engagement and graduation rates. One of the key findings is that these campuses had a shared responsibility for student success, education, and learning among staff of all types and faculty of all types. Education was seen as central to all individuals' roles. The studies highlighted stories of groundskeepers, residence hall staff, cafeteria workers, custodians, bus drivers, and various staff as being noted by students as contributing to the educational process. Not only do students identify these individuals as critical to their developments, but these institutions provided support for their staff to support student learning. This included attention to professional development, opportunities for promotion, and recognition. The study did not explicitly explore the contracts, salary, and benefits offered by these institutions, but it is likely that they provided other types of supports for them as well. Their research identifies how collaboration of the whole campus and bringing together myriad personal resources can create an environment in which students excel and are able to develop and succeed.

A study focused directly on support staff documented how they train, mentor, support, and advise students. First, in terms of training, staff provided a variety of office skills and input on professional demeanor, typically when the students are on work-study assignments.[43] The study also highlighted the importance of navigational support, as students often did not know how to speak with faculty or how a process (such as registration) should occur. Staff were knowledgeable about how the institution operated and able to mentor and support students in navigating the campus and administrative environment. Most often staff were noted as important support to speak with around challenges in classes, how to approach a faculty member, time management, and maintaining balance. Students noted the emotional support they received from staff, whether it be a kind word, someone to chat with, a needed smile, or a shoulder to cry on. Staff provided critical support that helped students to be motivated and persist in their learning. Ash identified how students felt staff constituted the heart and soul of different units, making them places where students felt cared for and a part of something larger so they were less isolated.

Conclusion

In this chapter, we present how faculty and staff are central determinants of student success. A very important driver of learning within psychological theories is motivation to learn. Individuals in the social environment are absolutely critical to fostering that motivation. As described in social cognitive theory and its extensions, human interactions in the learning environments create the foundational mechanism by which all learning stems. Bandura found that motivation was complex and multifaceted but was deeply tied to the social environment. Motivation can come from professors who get to know students personally, who make material engaging and active, or who make curricula culturally relevant or sustaining.

As we document with studies about faculty and student interactions, the degree of passion and enthusiasm that a faculty member has for a particular topic can be an extremely motivating factor within the learning environment. Staff, while less documented, are also critical to students' motivation and positive sense of self. But just as easily as a faculty member can create motivation, negative interactions with faculty or the absence of interaction can demotivate. Therefore, the shift to a higher education environment in which students have less and less interaction with faculty and staff is very likely to decrease students' motivation to learn.

Taken collectively, the sections of this chapter present a picture of American higher education where faculty, staff, and other college workers are continually hindered from being able to comport themselves toward students and toward the educational environment in ways most associated with student success. The employment structures and practices associated with the Gig Academy contribute to a situation where the human connections that form the foundation of student learning are being eradicated, albeit inadvertently. Students and workers alike are becoming disconnected from one another in ways that have dire consequences for student outcomes and for the viability of higher learning.

Gig Academy employment practices have also brought about another outcome—increasing unionization on campuses. Unionization on college campuses in response to Gig Academy conditions is the subject of chapter 5.

FIVE

The Growth of Unions and
New Broad-Based Organizing Strategies

....

Given the declining working conditions brought on by massive structural changes in higher education employment, it is perhaps not surprising that unionization is on the rise. In addition to the profound sense of despair among contingent faculty, staff, graduate students and postdocs, there have also been forces pushing these groups toward unionization. Recent changes in policy from the National Labor Relations Board (NLRB) have allowed unionization not only among contingent faculty but notably also with graduate students and many staff workers, even some who have rarely unionized in the past, such as residence hall directors. As detailed in earlier chapters, contingent faculty, staff, graduate students, and post-docs increasingly share a common experience of being exploited in the workplace. These common hardships are supporting greater unionization and possibly the emergence of new forms of solidarity that help break down occupational interest silos and increase the negotiating power of contingent campus workers as a whole.

This chapter will review data about the contemporary growth of unions, the motivations and strategies behind current union drives, and the concrete goals sought by today's unions. Additionally, it will review the outcomes or impacts of unionization thus far by looking at early comparative analyses of recent union and nonunion bargaining agreements. We discuss the influence of emergent technologies and shifts in competitive messaging as both sides vie to be seen as the guardians of students and their learning. Finally, we explore some of the context that distinguishes today's academic labor movement from its mid-twentieth-century predecessor, such as the increasing focus on social justice unionism, largely due to the leadership of graduate organizers, which goes beyond narrow issues like wages and benefits to include critical feminist and antiracist priorities, and a focus on broad-based organizing strategies and direct action that brings multiple university constituencies together. The chapter concludes by discussing the implications of these conditions amid a time of uncertainty in the American labor movement.

Contemporary Growth of Unions

In 2017, 15.7 percent of all workers at colleges and universities were covered by a collective bargaining agreement, according to Current Population Survey data. This compares to only 11.9 percent among all US workers, according to Hirsch and MacPherson, or 12 percent, according to the US Bureau of Labor Statistics.[1]

While postsecondary researchers have traditionally paid very little attention to union resurgence, especially among private institutions, unionization campaigns are proliferating in the academy. Historically, college faculty have not unionized like other sectors. Faculty apprehension toward unionization in the model of trade unions and collective bargaining was due to the fact that they considered themselves *professionals,* not laborers, which made them wary of affiliation with unions and slow to embrace their organizing and bargaining tactics. However, the postwar higher education boom caused the number of professors at public two- and four-year colleges to swell considerably throughout the 1950s and 1960s, over which time faculty attitudes on the question of unions increasingly varied by institutional type. Professors at large research universities and prestigious liberal arts colleges (sometimes members of the American Association of University Professors, AAUP) tended to eschew unions, while those at public community colleges and regional universities (more often members of American Federation of Teachers, AFT, or National Education Association, NEA) tended to embrace union-style organizing and bargaining. While AFT and NEA experimented with collective bargaining in the 1950s and 1960s (with mixed results and varying degrees of ambivalence), AAUP maintained firmer restrictions on collective bargaining and prohibited striking until the late 1960s, when they began to soften their position on unions, ultimately affirming their support of unionization by the 1970s.[2]

Staff often followed suit and were less likely to unionize than other sectors, although some unionization efforts did occur over the years. But the new classes of employees (e.g., contingent faculty, postdocs, graduate students, and staff) we have described throughout this book are bucking these longtime traditions of sidelining unionization. Adjunct faculty and staff have been unionizing steadily over the last decade, joined by graduate students and now postdocs. While national numbers are not available for all areas of higher education, data from the National Center for the Study of Collective Bargaining in Higher Education and the profession identified that faculty and graduate students are organizing more and more.[3]

Faculty Unionization

Forty years ago, very few staff or faculty were unionized. In the 1970s, as community colleges grew as a sector, many of these campuses unionized. According to Cain, in 1974, 92,300 faculty at 331 institutions had bargaining agents.[4] That figure increased to 427 agents by 1980 and then only to 460 by 1990, though all of that growth was at two-year institutions; the number at four-year institutions actually shrank during the same decade.

In 2012, 390,000 faculty were in collective bargaining units, a 14-percent spike from 2006. Roughly 27 percent of all higher education faculty members were unionized as of 2012, and the AAUP, the AFT, and the NEA individually or collectively represent nearly 80 percent of unionized faculty.[5] In 2016, 20.3 percent of postsecondary teachers were covered by a collective bargaining agreement.[6] The percentage of unionized faculty is particularly high at public institutions, with a third of the public sector represented by collective bargaining. About 42 percent of public two-year college faculty are represented by collective bargaining agreements, the largest percentage of any sector within postsecondary education. In recent years, community colleges have seen growth in union activity, with new agreements covering part-time faculty, a 14-percent increase in collective bargaining agreements, and the addition of 50,000 unionized members since 2006.[7] These contracts cover a total of 160,062 full- and part-time faculty and professional staff.

The majority of new collective bargaining has come in the private sector. Twenty-two non-tenure-track (NTT) faculty collective bargaining units at private-sector higher education institutions were newly certified in 2016 (versus three at public-sector institutions). Public institutions only experienced a 2-percent increase in collective bargaining since 2012.[8] The relatively low level of recent growth in the public sector is attributable to various factors: the scope of pre-existing union density, the limited number of states with laws permitting bargaining on campus, and the erosion of collective bargaining rights in certain states. In 2016, the Service Employees International Union (SEIU) filed a public-sector representation petition seeking to represent a combined statutorily defined unit at the University of Minnesota of approximately 3,000 tenured, tenure-track, and non-tenure-track faculty. This petition was shot down in 2017 by an appellate court, which ruled that NTT faculty could not join the faculty unit because they lacked academic "rank" and instead would have to bargain with a different unit representing administrative and professional staff.[9]

The largest area of recent union growth in higher education has been NTT faculty.[10] Trends of lower pay and precarious employment among such a massive number of employees provided an opportunity for collective action. In many ways, the shift is analogous to the fissured workplaces in other industries.[11] Between 2006 and 2012, twenty-two new NTT bargaining units were certified in the private sector, with an aggregate of 3,700 faculty members. Sixty-eight percent of the new units included both full-time and part-time NTT faculty. Only five units were composed solely of part-time NTT faculty, and two consisted of only full-time NTT faculty. These newly created units represent a remarkable 28.5-percent increase over the number of private-sector units found in the National Center's 2012 survey.[12] In the public sector in 2016, three new NTT units were created, composed of part-time faculty, with an aggregate of 1,546 faculty members. This compares to nine new tenure-track public sector faculty units, with a combined total of 2,060 faculty members. The increase in public sector faculty bargaining units represented only a 2.1-percent increase over the number of such units in 2012.

Staff Unionizing

Staff organizing has been idiosyncratic and inconsistent. There have been efforts to unionize staff going back as far as 100 years. Union efforts have emerged and then declined in fits and starts. There were some successes, including Illinois janitors in the 1910s, Harvard cafeteria workers in the 1930s, Howard staff in the 1940s, and Duke staff in the late 1960s. Among clerical workers specifically, the majority of union activity has taken place since the 1970s. Yale non-faculty workers won recognition in 1984, Columbia in 1985, and Harvard in 1988. As universities reduced compensation for staff amid financial pressures in the 1980s, union activity among university staff also increased. Unionization among clerical workers in higher education presented some examples of organizing successes in the wake of declining working conditions, but not all examples have been well documented.[13]

University staff unionize for many of the same reasons other workers seek to unionize—to combat a sense of disenfranchisement by building independent collective power to ensure a fair relationship with the university.[14] In the 1990s, as staff salaries declined and many were making less than a living wage, unionization among staff grew. The issue of low staff wages was brought to the forefront in 2001 at Harvard University, when the institution decided to set up a committee to examine wages and increase salaries after twenty-one days of protest by students and faculty. Another protest over extremely low staff wages followed at the University of Connecticut. Over the coming decade, 100 protests about low wages occurred. Most recently, the clerical, technical, and other professional staff at Emerson College voted to unionize with SEIU in the spring of 2018 and within a few months had unanimously approved a first contract with significantly improved benefits, including 14.5-percent raises across the board for the life of the contract, additional benefits for commuters, "just cause" protections against arbitrary dismissal, creation of a sick leave bank for catastrophic illnesses that exhaust individual allotments, and expanded parental leave.

Historic data show that 23 percent of white-collar staff and 42 percent of blue-collar staff on college campuses are unionized. This brings the overall number of unionized staff to approximately 28 percent, or a million white-collar and 300,000 blue-collar workers.[15] While there has been little research on staff organizing in higher education, research shows that unionization of academic librarians is associated with higher salaries and that union members in general benefit from union membership. As with other university workers, academic librarian unionization has increased as working conditions have continued to decline.[16] Research also shows that unionization has benefitted academic advisors, bringing about the establishment of grievance policies and procedures, retrenchment policies, and contracts that clarify workloads and have freed them from additional work tasks not associated with their roles.[17]

Graduate Student Unions

Graduate student unionization, too, is on the rise. Graduate students have a long history of union activism, and while they have sometimes been included in faculty unions, their numbers are difficult to ascertain. The first appeared in 1969 at the University of Wisconsin–Madison. As labor market prospects for the growing PhD population began to stagnate in the 1970s and graduate indebtedness began to swell from the 1980s onward, graduate unionization grew in popularity, though organizing attempts were not always successful. In the 1990s graduate students deployed as part-time instructors increased dramatically and this coincided with a doubling of the number of unionized campuses from the mid-90s to the mid-00s.[18]

Graduate students at private universities, since they are subject to the rules of the National Labor Relations Act (NLRA), have generally had more challenges trying to unionize.[19] However anyone working in private nonprofit higher education has likely noticed a recent intensification of graduate organizing since 2016. That summer the NLRB issued a landmark decision against Columbia University reestablishing the legal right of these employees to collectively bargain, which had previously been possible only for a brief period between 2000 and 2004.[20] Additionally, the board sought to end the longstanding debate leading to multiple ruling reversals on this issue in the first place—over whether GAs were primarily students or primarily employees. This time, instead of simply overturning the last ruling once again, the majority opinion reinstated graduate employee status by arguing that the so-called "primary relationship" question is irrelevant. Academic and employment relationships are not in any way mutually exclusive, they reasoned, citing a complete lack of evidence to support universities' longstanding contentions that graduate unions hinder learning and mentorship and destabilize institutional budgets.

A 2012 National Center analysis of survey data found more than 64,000 graduate student employees in bargaining units at public institutions.[21] Since then, new units were established at Portland State University, the University of Connecticut, and Montana State University. By 2015, over 64,000 graduate students would collectively bargain over working conditions.[22]

Currently the number of recognized graduate unions in the United States is over forty and growing. In the wake of the NLRB decision, the 2016–2017 academic year alone yielded NLRB election certifications for American University, Brandeis, Columbia, Grinnell, The New School, Portland State, and Tufts, totaling about 7,400 employees across seven bargaining units.[23] In addition, at least twenty other universities have graduate unions that continue to go unrecognized by their universities or are still in the process of organizing, including most of the so-called Ivy League. While some graduate workers (mostly in the public sector) are represented by traditional academic unions such as the AAUP and AFT, in recent years more and more are choosing to be represented by organizations historically associated with the industrial and service sectors, such as SEIU and United Auto Workers (UAW), in part because the latter category were the first to dedicate organizing efforts to contingent academic workers. Recent GA union developments at private universities follow:

- **American:** Unionized April 2017 (SIEU). Administration agreed to bargain. Negotiations ongoing.
- **Boston College:** Election success. Bosses refused to bargain. Withdrew petition to preserve national employee status.
- **Brandeis:** Unionized May 2017 (SEIU). Contract agreement reached in August 2018. Poised to make the second graduate collective bargaining agreement in the nation at a private university.
- **Cornell:** Failed unionization vote February 2017. NLRB ruled illegal interference by administration in May 2018.
- **Chicago:** Election success, but met with administrative refusal to bargain. Ultimately withdrew petition in favor of voluntary recognition strategy.
- **Columbia:** Administrative refusal to bargain despite orders by the NLRB. In May 2018, around 2,000 GAs struck during the week of finals.

- **Duke:** Failed election in March 2017. Pursuing voluntary recognition strategy.
- **Georgetown:** After initially refusing, administration pledged in April 2018 to allow election to proceed uninhibited and to bargain in good faith if affirmed.
- **George Washington:** Still organizing. Hostile administration.
- **Harvard:** Unionized April 2018 (UAW). Administration agreed to bargain. Negotiations ongoing. 5,000 TAs/RAs represented.
- **Loyola Chicago:** Unionized February 2017 (SEIU). Administration agreed to bargain but then reneged in October 2017, refusing negotiations but conceding slightly higher stipends and better healthcare.
- **New School:** Unionized May 2017 (UAW). Administration agreed to bargain. Negotiations ongoing. Frustrated GAs strike May 2018.
- **Northwestern:** Still organizing, but already successfully pressured school of music into restructuring continuation fees. SEIU and AFT competing.
- **Penn:** Still organizing. Hostile administration.
- **Tufts:** Unionized May 2017 (SEIU). Administration agreed to bargain. Negotiations ongoing.
- **USC:** Still organizing. Hostile administration.
- **Yale:** Eight microunit election successes. Refusal to bargain. Month-long hunger strike in 2017. Petition ultimately withdrawn.

Postdoctoral Unionization

As we describe in chapter 2, postdocs fulfill a growing share of the research labor of universities, for which they receive substantially lower compensation than secure faculty. Though less frequently than GAs, postdocs have also begun to organize with national unions such as the UAW, AFT, and the AAUP. In 2005 the National Postdoctoral Association first released an official position statement on the question of unionization, asserting its support for "standards of compensation and benefits that reflect [postdocs'] high levels of skill, education and expertise . . . [and]

recognizes the rights of postdocs to bargain collectively with their employers under the National Labor Relations Act."[24]

There have been just six examples of postdocs forming a union in the United States. The largest and most prominent of these is the postdoctoral union at the University of California (UC), which has more than 6,500 members system-wide, according to the UAW, which also represents student-workers at UC. They were certified in 2010 after a five-year unionization campaign, which Camacho and Rhoads note was a rather swift victory compared to the graduate employee union, which organized for sixty-one years before finally attaining recognition. Prior to unionizing, UC postdocs were paid on a scale with a minimum of $25,000 per year, which the first contract negotiation increased to $38,000 annually. Health coverage, which had been highly uneven before, was restructured to provide universal minimum benefits, including a new mandate to cover spouses and children as well. Additionally, they negotiated no-cost life insurance, accidental death and dismemberment, and short-term disability insurance, none of which had been standard before. Further, the current contract entitles UC postdocs to a minimum twenty-four days of annual personal time, whereas the prior *maximum* was twenty. There is also today a strong "just cause" provision for dismissal, with a required layoff notice of thirty days, where before postdocs could simply be fired at-will.[25]

Other existing postdoctoral unions are almost entirely in the public sector, at the Universities of Massachusetts, Connecticut, Alaska, and most recently, the University of Washington. The last example is the only postdoc union to vote to form their own distinct bargaining unit. Unions have been slower to appear at private institutions, with the only current example being postdocs at Rutgers University, which formed in 2009. This may be changing, though. Nearly 2,000 postdoctoral researchers at Columbia recently formed a union with UAW but are currently locked in the same battle with administration that graduate workers are also fighting. United Auto Workers is the leading organization, counting almost 75,000 dues-paying postdocs among their members.[26]

Camacho and Rhoads argue that postdoc unions have been able to move from campaign to contract more quickly than other unions because many postdocs already developed experience organizing and working with labor organizations as graduate workers. Under pressure from workers and advocates, the Department of Labor in 2015 more than doubled the Fair Labor Standards Act exemption annual salary level from $23,660 to $50,440. The Future of Research Institute has been monitoring university compliance in the years since. College and university lobbying organizations have argued for a delay, and one federal judge did declare an injunction. They also argued for a longer timeline to implement changes, proposed a lower salary level of approximately $30,000, and modified the language to exempt postdocs based on their status as trainees. Keeping postdocs in trainee status, similar to medical residents, would mean they are not entitled the protection of full employees. There continues to be activism among postdocs to address the low pay, which would affect colleges' and universities' incentive to continue postdoctoral positions for longer and longer periods of time. Still, it remains an open question whether postdoc union campaigns will proliferate.[27]

Motivations and Strategies Behind Current Union Drives

Unions have expanded their reach and adopted new approaches in recent years. They began to target several new groups (such as part-time contingents, graduate students, postdocs, and employees at private institutions). They have likewise adopted new approaches (such as metro-level campaigns and microunits) and arguments (regarding the impact of working conditions on student learning and on local and regional communities) that have helped expand their presence in postsecondary organized labor. In this section, we review some of these promising trends, which suggest higher education might be one of the few sectors where unions will have great success in coming years, based partly on the exploitative environment described in chapter 2 and the promising strategies advanced by unions.

Organizing New Groups and Institutions amid Legal Shifts

First, as noted earlier, adjunct faculty unionization is where some of the greatest growth in unionizing has occurred. The NLRB's modified rules for processing cases assisted with union efforts of adjuncts. The modified rules were aimed at expediting the resolution of questions of who is eligible to unionize and whether contingent faculty are management or not. Unions argued that contingent faculty are not management, upending a longstanding precedent that prevented unionization of faculty at four-year institutions, in particular, where shared governance was argued to make faculty part of management as they had some decision-making authority. In their 2015 ruling concerning *Pacific Lutheran v. Service Employees International Union Local 925*, the NLRB increased the burden of proof for asserting that faculty hold managerial status.[28] Under the new standards, specific proof must be presented demonstrating that faculty actually exercise managerial decisions or "make effective recommendations" concerning five specific areas: academic programs, enrollment management, finances, academic policy, and personnel policy and decisions. Another strategy leading to the increase in contingent faculty unionization has been the coordinated activism of organizations like the New Faculty Majority and the Coalition of Contingent Academic Labor, faculty organizing campaigns such as SEIU's Faculty Forward, and organizing by other unions including AFT, NEA, and AAUP.

The recent uptick in graduate and postdoc union campaigns signify a shift by unions toward groups that have not historically unionized but are increasingly understood to be workers within higher education contexts. Executive administrators have long argued that because graduate students and postdoctoral employees are in training positions, they are exempt from traditional policies relating to employees. By 2001, 27 GSE unions had won recognition.[29] This was in part thanks to new developments in the graduate union movement that emerged in 2000, when the NLRB's landmark decision against New York University overturned its own prior precedent and rejected the "primarily educational" test, citing the changing economic structure of higher education and the critical role of GSEs in carrying out the functions of the university.[30] Unfortunately, just four years later the NLRB reinstated its previous position of deeming the GSE's relationship to the university as being "primarily educational," thus stymying new union efforts. Despite the setback to organizing efforts posed by the Brown decision, organizing efforts continued to progress.[31] In 2013, New York University became the first private institution to voluntarily (re-)recognize its GSE union, the Graduate Student Organizing Committee–United Auto Workers Local 2110 101 (GSOC-UAW), after eight years of unrelenting pressure from student workers.[32] Until recently, NYU had the only recognized GSE union at a private university in the United States, but since the 2016 Columbia ruling several more have begun to emerge, as the prior list in this chapter shows. Currently, no comprehensive list of GSE unions in the United States exists. A website hosted by the Coalition of Graduate Employee Unions had been tracking them until it went offline in 2018. At that time there were a total of 33 recognized unions across public and private institutions, and though recent developments clearly indicate that number is growing, the exact figure remains elusive.[33]

The legal doctrines from *Yeshiva* and *Catholic Bishop* that have long stymied growth in private-sector faculty unionization are being dismantled through current union strategizing.[34] Starting in 1980, *Yeshiva* obstructed unionization among private-sector tenured and tenure-track faculty.[35] For years, only the most militant faculty at private four-year institutions attempted to form unions, with rates of unionization at 3 percent and 8 percent for full-time and part-time faculty respectively. But in 2015 the ruling against *Pacific Lutheran* revised many of those restrictions, clearing the way for a new wave of faculty organizing. Only a few months later another ruling opened a major door to more organizing on private campuses, as graduate student instructors were legally declared employees of their institutions and thus entitled to form unions. As Herbert reported, the rate of newly certified units at private colleges and universities in 2016 far outpaced new units in the public sector: a 25.9-percent private-sector increase compared to 2012, versus 2.1 percent in the public sector over the same time period.[36]

New Unions and New Approaches to Unionization

In recent years, historically nonacademic unions have entered the space of higher education to organize groups that traditional academic unions had not actively recruited, including adjuncts, graduate students, and some staff workers. More and more employees in higher education are choosing to be represented by organizations that were originally tied to the manufacturing and service sectors, such as SEIU, UAW, United Electric, and United Steel, in part because unlike AAUP and NEA the they were the first to dedicate resources to organizing campaigns for contingent academic workers exclusively. SEIU has been particularly supportive in organizing faculty off the tenure track, but prior to that they were also highly active among non-teaching staff on college campuses. For instance, in the 1990s their "Justice for Janitors" campaign at the University of Southern California garnered SEIU notable fame and brought together a broad array of campus and community groups in that fight, though its achievements were ultimately mixed.[37]

New approaches to unionization are also being developed for these new groups who have contingent and Gig Academy employment arrangements. SEIU's Faculty Forward initiative (also referred to as the metropolitan strategy) works to unionize multiple institutions across a regional area, which is supportive of adjunct faculty who work at multiple institutions. Already they have achieved notable success in Washington, DC, Boston, Los Angeles, Oakland, St. Louis, and Seattle. As of 2018, SEIU locals have unionized more than 54,000 contingent faculty and graduate workers on sixty campuses as part of the Faculty Forward campaign, and SEIU represents around 120,000 public and private higher education workers. Rhoades' analysis of SEIU's negotiated contracts indicates a trend of stronger language of protection relative those negotiated by the AAUP, AFT, and NEA. Further, according to SEIU's self-reported calculations, the average pay of its members is 25 percent higher per course than nonunion instructors.[38] SEIU's ultimate goal is to achieve a critical mass of members that will force institutions to go through the local union chapter if they seek to hire any contingent faculty, creating conditions to equalize minimum levels of compensation and rights to due process. Similar adjunct actions are occurring through the steelworkers' union in Pittsburgh and the AFT in Philadelphia. This strategy disrupts management's efforts to break collective bargaining and to fragment work.

Another strategy is organizing and bargaining for specific demands such as substantial increases in salary that would make contingent roles less attractive or even disadvantageous for institutions. Currently, professional employees put in many unpaid hours, providing universities additional productivity at no cost. But as professionals unionize they will no longer conduct work for free for the institution. And the SEIU strategies of organizing contingent faculty and graduate students around a universal $15,000 minimum in total compensation per course taught, and institutional caps on the proportion of faculty permitted to be hired for part-time instruction, are two approaches aimed at stemming contingency. The focus on issues like pay and benefits make contingency less attractive, with unions working to secure more full-time and secure positions.

Academic unions are increasingly drawing on strategies from other sectors and seeing themselves less as unique entities needing distinct collective bargaining strategies. This is providing them with more tools to leverage changes within the academic workplace. For example, Julius discusses how the Yale University union effort pursued a microunit strategy (in which workers unionize in smaller groupings, e.g., by department) modeled on unionization efforts in other sectors. As Horowitz, a multidecade officer for a regional NLRB, shows, microunit strategies are being sought more and more as union organizers look for creative ways to secure worker protections, including at Yale. Julius also argues that borrowing strategies from unions in other sectors will benefit college and university employees' efforts to organize. He predicts academic employees will increasingly use strategies from other sectors that share their concerns over the effects of neoliberalism and the gig economy on labor.[39]

Unions are now organizing around public or broader interests (e.g., student learning, changing demographics, diversity and equity, social and community development, and democratic and civic engagement) to support collective bargaining efforts. There is a history of unions tying their efforts to broader public issues. This strategy has waned in recent years with the takeover of academic gig logics but is experiencing a re-emergence. For example, faculty unions are beginning to echo their primary and secondary school counterparts in advancing the logic that faculty and staff working conditions are student learning conditions, advocating for pay equity for contingent faculty. The California Faculty Association (CFA) has used this argument and won significant advances in salary, entitlements, and job security. That logic has been used through several rounds of collective bargaining. The same argument can be used for graduate students, who likewise face subpar working conditions.[40]

Unions are also drawing a connection between diversity/equity and declining support for public sector employees as faculty and staff at colleges and universities. In a report by the CFA, they attack the declining budget for the California system as well as its faculty and staff as part of a large disinvestment from institutions that support students of color. They also equate growing contingency and lower pay with the increased presence of women and faculty of color on college campuses. Rhoades argues for unions' role in supporting public purposes such as research, community development, and civic engagement and connecting to communities, government, businesses, and student interest as a way to gain greater support. Given that higher education is a values-driven enterprise, college and university faculty and staff have gravitated toward this approach, which connects to supporting the public good. In one example of how a union has intervened on issues of racial equity, last fall the graduate union at the University of Michigan negotiated the first contract ever to include additional protections for workers who engage in diversity work. This is a considerable gain considering the substantial labor that students and faculty who are tapped to serve on diversity and inclusion committees or task forces are typically expected to provide free of compensation.[41]

Building on gains related to public good and diversity-based union strategies, unions are uniting around social justice issues as well. Graduate student unions have taken major leadership in this area. For example, at Yale, the Graduate Employees and Student Organization successfully campaigned to force the university to divest from its investments in private prisons. They have fought and won battles to improve the diversity of faculty hires and filed grievances stating that the lack of more professors of color denies students of color important sources of mentorship.[42] Similarly, graduate unions have battled pervasive sexual harassment and assault, such as the Harvard GSU, which has set up its own sexual assault committee, and continue to be among the most vocal advocates for undocumented students and community members. The graduate union at the University of Washington, for instance, in addition to better working conditions (including a $7,302 raise and 92-percent increase in summer pay), was instrumental in helping to pass the Washington DREAM Act, eliminating a cruel surcharge on international students and eliminating all fees for 50 percent of international student workers, and continues to fight efforts to restrict student visas.[43]

The Coalition of Graduate Employee Organizations passed a resolution on "taking an active anti-racist stand in our unions and supporting the Movement for Black Lives" in which they decry rampant police violence and assert that "these forces manifest themselves directly through campus policing and on the bodies of Black, Latinx, and indigenous students and employees." In the same year they passed additional resolutions to "address the inequitable treatment of international graduate student workers, who are "often preyed upon due to their legal and economic vulnerability, lack of familiarity with the legal system and limited local support networks," while also being "frequently subject to intimidating xenophobia."[44]

Work issues and social justice issues are not distinct, though—a point that is emphasized by more and more graduate unions. Graduate workers at UC Berkeley, for instance, recently made an explicit shift in strategy from what is often called "business unionism," which focuses on narrow economic demands, to a social justice unionism approach, focused on "anti-oppression demands" and direct action instead of "closed-door negotiations with management." These authors make a point to show that this shift has paid off in terms of their contracts. Under their previous contract (2011–2013), they were only able to negotiate a 6-percent wage increase over three years, which is less than the rate of inflation, and slight increases in childcare reimbursement. But after shifting to a more social movement strategy prior to negotiating the current contract (2014–2018), they won a 16-percent wage increase over four years, more teaching opportunities for undocumented students, all-gender bathrooms, reduced class sizes, and more family leave.[45]

Concrete Goals Sought by Today's Unions and Outcomes of Unionization

In addition to the traditional goals that unions have pursued of job security, increased wages, opportunities for advancement, professional development, and resources to appropriately conduct one's work, unions are increasingly examining important new areas that support workers in the neoliberal and Gig Academy environment. It should be noted that studies examining these traditional union issues (salary and benefits) identify that unions are successful; unionized employees do obtain higher salaries and benefits than their counterparts on nonunionized campuses. The earlier reported study by CAW illustrated that unionized contingent faculty had better working conditions with access to professional development, staffing and resource support, benefits, shared governance, appropriate evaluation, and other important advantages. These results are detailed below. Academic employees, often leery of unionization, should be aware that unions have historically succeeded in their objectives.[46]

With the Gig Academy comes a host of new issues that have led to a significant shift in the way unions approach bargaining. As noted in chapter 1 and described in detail in chapter 2, gig employees face contingency, deprofessionalization, outsourcing, unbundling, offloading costs, auditing and control, and issues around automation and technology—all conditions that unions have taken head on.

Address Contingency and Flexibility

In terms of new areas for bargaining among Gig Academy employees, unions have secured greater job security through multiyear contracts for non-tenure-track faculty.[47] For contingent faculty, multiyear contracts are particularly important to create greater job security and are a major area for collective bargaining. A recent analysis of 35 new collective bargaining agreements by Edwards and Tolley found that a full 97 percent of new agreements made between 2010 and 2016 secured multiyear contract guarantees for contingent instructors.[48] Unions have also had success with obtaining payment for courses that are canceled. This is a significant issue, as currently many adjuncts spend dozens of hours preparing for courses and receive no compensation when classes are cancelled. This is a form of employee exploitation.[49] Another area where adjuncts have been exploited in terms of working but not being paid is office hours or service. Contracts routinely do not speak to office hours or service on committees, and employees are not paid for these activities but are nonetheless expected to perform them. Unions are bargaining for much more precision in contracts in terms of role and pay for specific expected activities. Also, unions have obtained access to a group benefit pool, even for institutions that do not provide benefits. This is advantageous for contingent employees, who at least have access to affordable benefits, even if they are not subsidized by the institution.[50]

The move toward part-time and contingent labor has deeply affected staff, and they are looking for protections to maintain full-time employment. Given that staff have borne the brunt of declining employment trends, many are seeking clauses to ensure they will not be laid off, and unions are occasionally successful in obtaining these. It is through union struggles that they have achieved the most success, particularly on issues of job descriptions and performance evaluations, due process, promotions, transparent hiring, career mobility, job security, part-time and contingent labor overreliance, hours and overtime protections, layoffs, and clear contracts.[51]

Reprofessionalize

A defining hallmark of a professional is both professional development and advancement. Because professional development was bundled a professional role, as unbundling has occurred faculty are arguing they should be paid for professional development and to attend conferences, as required to keep up to date with their discipline and to keep courses current. Unions are also attempting to reprofessionalize faculty by bargaining for promotional tracks and advancement for faculty on contingent appoints with merit increases for obtaining benchmarks. Another feature of being a professional is participation in governance, and unions are increasingly bargaining for access to decision-making among contingent employees. Access to governance by contingent faculty is extremely important; Kezar and Sam demonstrate that campuses that include contingent faculty in shard governance have better working conditions for NTT faculty.[52]

Issues around advancement remain critical to staff who have low salaries and want some opportunity for mobility over time. Unions have been able to bargain for clear job descriptions, performance evaluations that might lead to promotion, and more transparent hiring processes for full-time positions. Staff are often expected to work overtime without compensation even though they are not exempt employees—especially if they want to be considered for promotion. As a result, unions have been arguing for ensuring staff are paid for hours worked and overtime. Many staff work at colleges so that their children might obtain free tuition. Thus, efforts to protect tuition benefits are increasingly being advanced.[53]

Protect from Manager Control and Power

As noted earlier, due to staff and faculty fearing retribution if they report wrongdoing in their workplaces, unions are increasingly striving to obtain contract language about protecting whistleblowers. Additionally, unions are bargaining around grievance procedures due to the pressures that employees feel from managers in the top-down, neoliberal environment. Nascent efforts are emerging to stem the growth of managerial audits and to provide rationale for the frequency and approach to auditing.[54]

End Outsourcing

Outsourcing is on the rise in higher education despite a lack of clear empirical evidence demonstrating its efficiency. Unions are trying to incorporate more language in contracts to prevent outsourcing, including provisions that require institutions to justify outsourcing and limit its usage.[55]

In 2018, Eastern Michigan University released a long-awaited ruling by an arbitrator as part of an AAUP-filed grievance. The union had accused the university of betraying its obligation to solicit full faculty input in key areas related to curriculum development, personnel, and instruction when it made a 2016 deal with Academic Partnerships, an online program management firm. Faculty union members fought the arrangement and deployed an advertising campaign and online petition to call for a moratorium on the contract, fearing that the administration would turn important faculty decisions over to a for-profit subcontractor. The arbitrator ultimately ruled in favor of the university.[56] As more universities turn to online programs, outsourcing is likely to grow in importance as an issue for future academic union struggles.

After the governor of Tennessee sought in 2015 to cut the state budget with a plan to outsource all facilities management and service staff member throughout the state university system, United Campus Workers, which included 1,800 dues-paying members across the state, waged a successful campaign to prevent its implementation. This was a notable victory in part because Tennessee is a so-called "right-to-work" state where public employees are banned from collective bargaining, plus it had elected Republican supermajorities in both houses of the legislature. United Campus Workers is an almost two-decades-old union that includes a wide range of campus workers and students. It has won many concessions over the years, including overturned terminations, base pay increases, expanded healthcare, and better safety protections, through the sheer power of disciplined rank-and-file organizing, solidarity from other unions, and creative collective actions. Organizers recruited the owners of university-contracted local businesses to participate, waged aggressive letter writing, phone banking, and press campaigns, rallied greater numbers of campus workers to stand together, and even occupied the statehouse entrance. Eventually the state government caved to pressure to include an opt-out clause, and after the plan passed, every University of Tennessee campus took advantage of it.[57]

Combat Technology and Automation

Technology and automation are increasingly areas of focus for bargaining as employees examine the implications of new technologies. Unions are bargaining for compensation to be trained for new technologies. Faculty contracts have argued for intellectual property rights as teaching and curricula move online.[58]

While no national data exist on the number of contracts that include these new areas of bargaining, NEA and AFT occasionally provide trend data showing that these areas are being bargained for and also obtained through new contracts. These represent important trends that if successfully argued for will offer important employee protections.

Noble describes how the faculty union at Florida Gulf Coast University, for instance, fought successfully against a rapid and undemocratic scale-up of an online distance learning program that rested on hiring short-term, NTT faculty and was to be the university's pedagogical foundation moving forward. Florida Gulf Coast University faculty and others, such as those at the California State University system, the University of Washington, the University of Kansas, and Penn State, have fought similar campaigns, which often involved exposing the administration's intentions to share instruction and learning data with proprietary third parties and attempting to institute draconian surveillance processes over digital classroom spaces.[59]

Impact

Studies generally show that unionization improves the working conditions of various employee categories on campus. More studies have been conducted of faculty unionization (though we report on staff studies we could find), given that such efforts have existed since early 1970s and been more widespread than for other categories of campus workers. Furthermore, in general, there is a greater amount of research on faculty as an employee category. Few national studies or data exist on the impact of unions; studies tend to examine and compare a set of institutions that are unionized and nonunionized but with similar characteristics. Studies are also increasingly exploring factors (such as public vs. private, state, or region) that shape organizing outcomes.[60]

Ehrenberg found in 2004 that unionized campuses had much higher salaries for staff across all categories, particularly for skilled workers, but that unions did not increase salaries significantly for graduate students. It would be interesting to conduct the study again with more graduate students having unionized and the movement being farther along. He concluded that unions were particularly important for staff, who had low wages, poor benefits, and job insecurity, and that they may not be as important for graduate students, at least in terms of salary. But as several CBAs can testify, this is not entirely true. UC Berkeley's graduate union was able to negotiate a 16-percent wage hike over four years in their most recent contract, plus expansion of a number of other benefits (discussed more below). GEU-UAW at the University of Connecticut, as part of their first contract negotiations in 2014–2015, won contractually guaranteed annual stipend increases of at least 3 percent, $900 in additional fee waivers, restoration of state employee health benefits with drastically reduced out-of-pocket costs, childcare subsidies, guaranteed paid family and sick leave, and a host of other protections—none of which they enjoyed prior to unionizing.[61]

The impact on faculty salaries is complex. The following studies include tenure-track faculty; future studies conducted of adjuncts likely will show an even larger impact, given their low salary levels. Wassell et al. demonstrated that unions increased salaries but the impact was uneven, with those in lower salary ranges obtaining an increase but those in higher salary ranges not obtaining the same benefit. Kastinas et al. found that unionized faculty generally received higher salaries—full-time faculty at rural, suburban, and urban regional universities with collective bargaining received on average $92,407, $116,353, and $108,399 in total monetary compensation in 2011; this compared to averages of $82,722, $84,813, and $86,594 at rural, suburban, and urban regional universities without. There are differences by discipline and region that shape salary outcomes as well. Kastina et al. also identified that unionized campuses received better benefits in terms of healthcare and sick and vacation pay. As noted earlier, most earlier studies of unions have only focused on salary and benefits as outcomes. The Coalition on the Academic Workforce found that the presence of a union on campus also appears to have a positive impact on wages for faculty members employed part-time. The median pay per course at institutions where part-time faculty respondents were not represented by a union was $2,475, as compared with $3,100 at institutions with union representation.[62]

There are a few large-scale comparative studies examining the bargaining issues relevant to gig economy employees to date. For example, CAW respondents who reported the presence of a union on at least one of the campuses where they teach were consistently more likely to receive resources and support for instructional activities. Respondents with a union present on at least one campus where they taught indicated the following levels of support:

- 17.9 percent indicated they are paid for class cancellations, as opposed to only 9.9 percent of respondents without a union present.
- 9.7 percent indicated being paid for attending departmental meetings, as opposed to only 5.4 percent of respondents without a union present.
- 14.5 percent indicated being paid for office hours, as opposed to only 3.8 percent of respondents without a union present.
- 33.9 percent indicated receiving regular salary increases, as opposed to only 12.1 percent of respondents without a union present.
- 19.4 percent indicated having job security, as opposed to only 3.9 percent of respondents without a union present.

Support for professional development activities was also reported more frequently by respondents teaching on at least one campus where a union was present (21 percent versus 15 percent). Respondents teaching on at least one campus where a union was present reported greater access to various kinds of administrative support as well, but the difference between unionized and nonunionized settings was not as great as with other forms of workplace support. Cross identified that on unionized campuses, contingent faculty were more likely to have multiyear contracts, grievance procedures, and standardized evaluation procedures. Cain identified how union contracts resulted in greater support for seniority, standardized evaluation, money for professional development, improved communication, and compensation if assigned courses are canceled. All of these items represent potential new or emerging areas for union bargaining.[63]

Cassell and Halaseh's study presents results of a cross-sectional time series analysis and a cross-sectional analysis of higher education performance using data from the Department of Education's Integrated Post-Secondary Data System spanning more than two decades and over 430 public universities and colleges. The authors find support that unionization improves organizational efficiency and effectiveness. They note that beyond supporting individual employees, unions actually improve overall campus functioning. As was alluded to in earlier chapters, employee morale on campus is low and disengagement is very high; this is associated with worse employee outcomes and leads to absenteeism, poor work performance, and other negative outcomes. That unions increase effectiveness and efficiency is therefore not surprising. Kitchen notes, for example, that graduate unions can preemptively diffuse tensions that might otherwise erupt between GAs and their advisors over unclear or unfair expectations by having responsibilities clearly delineated in a bargained contract, thus conserving more productive time and energy for academic inquiry—the reason they are there. Higher education stakeholders—boards, policymakers, governments, and state systems—should be concerned that employment trends are degrading campuses' organizational efficiency and effectiveness and work to stem the current employment trends. Administrative actions need to be reversed and rectified.[64]

Few rigorous comparative studies exist of the impact of graduate student organizing efforts. But in the five decades graduate unions have been bargaining, the empirical research on organizational impacts has been largely positive. Schenk, Jr., analyzed available national data to estimate the economic benefits of unionizing and at the time found a positive effect on the stipends of teaching assistants, though not research assistants. Rogers et al. surveyed unionized graduate assistants and found, regardless of position, reports of better pay, more support, and greater satisfaction in their personal and professional lives. Hewitt's earlier survey of faculty working with unionized graduate students found the overwhelming majority felt such an arrangement did not disrupt their ability to advise, instruct, or mentor their advisees. As much as more research would be useful, as the NLRB pointed out in 2016, there is still a complete dearth of evidence that would legitimize university reservations about unionization.[65]

Conclusion

Debates over academic unionism can often stoke strong feelings and antagonisms among supporters and detractors. It is important to remember, however, that at bottom, a union is nothing but a word that describes workers who come together to act in concert. By stripping away the many connotations and misperceptions that get applied to unions and examining the positive results, we see there has been virtually no evidence that unions on college campuses are deleterious to a university's relational ecosystem or university missions. In fact, the exact opposite is reported: studies show that unions enhance campus effectiveness and efficiency. It becomes clear that collective actions coordinated through a union model can be a powerful tool for democratizing higher education and better serving postsecondary students and workers of all types. Though the future of legally enshrined workers' rights is uncertain, some sectors are rediscovering the economic, political, and social possibilities that unions can offer, bolstered by a growing number of concrete victories that prove what can be achieved when workers decide to leverage their shared interests against forms of exploitation no longer seen as necessary or inevitable.

SIX

Whither the Struggle

Future Trends, Policies, and Actions

....

All trends outlined in previous chapters together suggest a growing tension between Gig Academy imperatives, which call for more cheap, contingent workers, and a rebounding academic labor movement across the postsecondary workforce, which aims to ensure decent working conditions and ultimately student learning and success. This chapter explores possible futures as institutions struggle to reconcile the rising appetite for collective bargaining with ever- deepening pressures to embrace the neoliberal priorities of policymakers, trustees, and other stakeholders. We examine the implications of earlier chapters for policy and practice and consider ways to address the growing chasm between workers and administrators. If trends continue unabated, if organizing efforts (union or otherwise) dwindle or fail to reach a critical mass, and if public boards, policymakers, and community interest groups do not enter the fray to help rebalance institutional power, academic inquiry could see itself wholly subsumed by neoliberal and Gig Academy ambitions that reduce democratic missions and goals into desiccated husks of rhetoric.

To be clear, we do not suggest that most administrators consciously seek the kind of bleak future we sketch. As we have tried to emphasize throughout, the Gig Academy reflects neoliberalism's own drives, which reframe and reorient the ethics of institutional action toward its own ends. The structure of administrative work encourages inattention to how ongoing microdecisions have cumulatively produced a sea change in higher education. No doubt many administrators genuinely believe institutions and students are best served when colleges and universities are treated just like any business trying to thrive in the world of on-demand service providers and new economy tech startups. Our moral judgment on this way of thinking should not be misinterpreted as judgment on every person in a position of leadership.

As we discuss ways of organizing toward a redistribution of power and authority in the academy that centers educational missions and goals, we encourage administrative leaders who see their work as serving noble aims not to dismiss us out of hand. We strive to disabuse the notion that such noble aims can ever be fulfilled within a set of organizational relations built on exploitation, refuting the characterization of this as the only realistic choice available to postindustrial society.

Future Trends

In this section we extrapolate from current conditions to lay out what we see happening unless major changes occur based on union pressure, faculty/student/staff organizing, administrative concessions, or external state and federal policymaking. We take heart from the efforts of faculty to push back on massive open online courses (MOOCs) by questioning their educational value and uncovering their weaknesses as instructional tools and experiences. The faculty at Cal State San Jose are one notable example of workers using data to interrogate the destructive logic of the Gig Academy on student outcomes. It was only a few years ago that these platforms were heralded as the dawn of a new era from which there would be no going back. Thankfully, such predictions have been revealed as naïve, at least in part because academic researchers applied time-tested tools of empirical evidence to scrutinize the substance beneath the high-tech veneer. Among other things, the faculty produced and disseminated studies demonstrating that first-generation, low-income, and nontraditional-age students fare poorly in mass digital instruction, and that their structural flaws prove they are no basis on which to educate a broad citizenry or workforce without incurring severe social and economic costs. These revelations have led many colleges and universities to reconsider investing in these types of programs among mainstream student populations.

We hope that increased clarity around Gig Academy trends will inspire action among faculty and staff to combat these trends and collectively hold administrators accountable for decisions that undermine student learning and institutional missions. Our analysis below addresses contingency, outsourcing, full labor replacement through technology, unbundling, deprofessionalization, and entrepreneurialism as the culmination of the Gig Academy. History demonstrates that trends like these can take hold quite rapidly. When faculty were first becoming contingent, everyone predicted that such a trend would not overtake the academy, and yet we saw that employment category explode. We hope to incite the kind of pushback that happened with MOOCs but on a much bigger scale, to begin to reverse contingency and build a more democratic academy.

Continued Outsourcing

We foresee greater trends in outsourcing that over time will encompass more and more staff positions across a broader array of staff categories. We have already seen the expansion of outsourcing among staff, beginning with more select groups of workers less connected to the central educational mission and then gradually expanding to those operating in closer proximity to the core functions of the institution. Without mass intervention from the workers themselves, outsourcing of instruction is likely to continue its precipitous rise, particularly in the areas of developmental and introductory mathematics as well as language and composition. Certain types of professional and credential programs viewed as easy revenue will increasingly be offered through outsourced mediums, utilizing low-cost online coursework in pedagogically questionable ways. And as these professional and credential programs begin to be perceived as a mainstream way of delivering education, outsourcing of more traditional types of programs will likely occur.

Outsourcing will become a primary means to continue the move toward the Gig Academy until colleges and universities no longer need employed staff to conduct their work. Contingency will become fully normalized among faculty and staff employees. One of the reasons outsourcing will increase is that courts will find that current contingent workers are misclassified. Institutions will respond by outsourcing to preempt regulations. Outsourcing is a major problem in the Gig Academy, but it is an important area that connects postsecondary workers to the broader scourge of gig economy trends across the American (and global) economy writ large.

Increased Reliance on Labor-Eliminating Technologies

As technology usage grows, there has long been an argument that products aimed at instruction or instructional support should complement the work of faculty and staff. Uninhibited, these technologies will become rationalized as forms of instruction and student support (e.g., advising and feedback) in themselves. We see these trends already with remedial courses being offered completely online without any human instructor for any portion of the course. Faculty will be increasingly recruited by technology firms to design learning modules that can then be sold back to institutions for the purpose of additional labor savings, effectively engaging academics in the project of furthering their own obsolescence. Additionally, we are seeing new waves of artificial intelligence in adaptive software like Packback. With intrusive advising systems becoming more mainstream, they will soon be entrenched as a substitute for dedicated counselors and advisers. Increasingly, administrators will begin to see faculty and staff as obsolete and automate as many of their functions as possible, fulfilling the Gig Academy's drive toward a minimally labor-intensive enterprise.

Higher Entrepreneurial Expectations

As noted throughout this volume, faculty who continue to hold full-time jobs are those who raise money to pay their own salaries and benefits or otherwise prove their "value" to the "enterprise." These trends will continue with increasing reliance on research faculty and postdocs for the research function of the university. Instructional faculty will need to become entrepreneurs to raise money to supplement their salaries from their part-time teaching. Increasingly we hear about opportunities to do freelance editing or writing and other kinds of positions that academics should use to supplement their instructional salaries. Profs and Pubs, a new venture, pays faculty to provide lectures in bars; the general public pays an entry fee to hear academics make presentations on their areas of research. These types of entrepreneurial initiatives will increasingly provide a market for their part-time skills, offering ways for them to supplement their salaries from colleges and universities. Entrepreneurship will become an even more powerful idea in the move to deprofessionalize faculty and perhaps even staff.

Further Unbundling, Deprofessionalization,
and "New" Gig Professionalism

As the shift toward outsourcing and entrepreneurship accelerates, the prospect of reversing deprofessionalization will grow more remote. As labor is displaced from the campus, there is less opportunity for involvement in governance and sway over faculty working conditions. Professional development and pathways for career advancement will wither. The for-profit sector exemplifies the type of unbundling that is likely to occur in not-for-profit higher education. In for-profit institutions, the teaching function has been unbundled into microfacets, mirroring the gig economy paradigm. Faculty and staff will be encouraged to see themselves as part of the expanding Gig Academy that draws employment not just from the academic sector but blends in contingent jobs from business, industry, and government. They will have little choice but to embrace entrepreneurialism and operate as freelance academics and entrepreneurs. It will be passé to think about academe as a site of careers. Whether obtaining jobs through outsourcing organizations, temporary agencies, or just as independent consultants, work will not be defined by sector, since unbundled expertise can be freely tapped by employers in any sector for short-term intervals. This will be marketed as "freeing" academics to channel their expertise across more spheres and not be trapped in the ivory tower.

As entrepreneurs, academics are framed as free to be more creative and unconstrained by academic conventions, rules, and polices. Believers in the value of tenure-track policies will be further derided for stifling innovation and advocating conformity. Working across global problems, in global spheres of work, will be touted as superior to long-term ties to an institution and its local politics and demands. Fully contracted, short-term, and piecemeal work will be falsely cast as freedom from institutional control.

Increased Demand for Employees to Provide Work Resources

Just as Uber drivers must be financially responsible for their car, insurance, gas, and maintenance while shouldering depreciation costs to their job equipment, increasingly faculty will be responsible for supplying the means to conduct their work. Already, adjuncts are usually expected to obtain their own computers, printers, paper, and other resources needed for classroom pedagogy that can add up substantially over time. As institutions become much more reliant on sophisticated technologies to facilitate various aspects of in-class and out-of-class learning, they are likely to continue offloading costs onto faculty, asking them to buy software, software updates, or perhaps licenses for software necessary to conduct their teaching.

This is true, for example, in other freelance areas like digital media production, where sound and video editors are forced by industry-dominant software companies like Apple and Adobe to continually purchase the most up-to-date versions of software like Photoshop and Pro Tools, which can run thousands of dollars annually, if they hope to ever find paying work. It is not unrealistic that faculty, too, will be increasingly compelled, if not outright required, to keep their instructional technology licenses up to date to be in sync with the latest versions of technologies the campuses are using, thus imposing further individual baseline costs for instructors to work. While it is difficult to predict all of the increasing areas of cost, it is likely that technology costs in particular will be shifted to faculty. Contingent staff will also increasingly work remotely, and we see the same kind of shift of costs to staff employees (e.g., computers, communications technologies, smartphones with high-cost data plans, and broadband access at home) to conduct clerical and administrative support, advising, or other types of on-call student support. In fact, many teleworkers are already generally responsible for providing their own offices and equipment as well as being on call and responding in a timely fashion.

In the not-so-distant future there may be little to distinguish not just the material constraints (sub-living wages, lack of security) but the actual lived experiences of the vast majority of American workers, inside and outside academe, engaged in perpetual forms of hyper-competition and self-branding.

Envisioning an Alternative: Workplace Democracy

One question that is seriously worth asking: If these trends continue unabated, would there be an academy left that anyone would actually want to work in—particularly among highly trained experts in their fields carrying sizable amounts of student debt? Is it possible that the public good function of the university will be fully and irreversibly subordinated to corporate growth models? Most importantly, who will stand in the way of this eventuality—the ever-dwindling tenured minority? Wealthy tech firm CEOs? Corporate-beholden politicians?

A recent essay by Eidlin and Uetricht raises an interesting and relevant point: Despite our strong collective belief in the rights afforded by democratic rule—rights to due process and elected representation, free expression, press, and assembly—Americans have never been united on the question of whether democratic rights also belong in our places of work.[1] We see ourselves as citizens with rights that are (at least in theory) sacrosanct in our homes and on the street, yet every day we blithely submit ourselves to the broader authority of employers without a moment's pause. It is odd given that most of us spend at least half of our waking life in these places, as the authors point out:

> Employers can limit what people can and cannot say at work, or where and when they assemble . . . With few exceptions, employers are under no compulsion to guarantee due process to those they employ. They can largely hire, fire, and discipline workers at will. To the extent that employers treat their workers well, it is entirely at their discretion, as revocable and subject to change without notice as a king's writ. Even for the 10 percent of US workers who have a union, their scope of activity is usually restricted by a more or less expansive "management's rights clause." Today's unions may guarantee certain basic civil liberties in the workplace, but do little to challenge management's sovereignty in the workplace.[2]

Academe has traditionally been considered one of the few workplaces in which this is not entirely a given. Tenure, academic freedom, and shared governance supposedly guarantee that, if nothing else, the work of intellectual and scientific inquiry remain under a collective purview rather than being guided by the private interest of whoever happens to be in charge or provide a sizable donation. This is decidedly *not* to claim that this ideal has ever been truly actualized and call for a "return" to some romanticized time in our history. It is only to point out that higher education is one of the few sectors where the belief that some degree of democratic control over the workplace may be structurally necessary was not a radical or unusual position either for the people employed there or the general public to hold. Since the dawn of academic capitalism this idea is no longer taken for granted.

Some measure of workplace democracy is arguably important everywhere—hence the persistence (however anemic) of some kind of labor movement—but it has additional importance in academic systems that produce knowledge-power and exert enormous influence over the broad regulation of our collective economic, social, and political life. As the business model of the gig economy spreads, the use of cheap, isolated, and disposable labor is infecting previously unimaginable sectors and deepening economic inequality and workforce segmentation. Academia's gradual embrace of contingency is contributing significantly to the contemporary dissolution of whatever trace of dignity or stability remains in career pursuit for much of the labor force, by normalizing these arrangements even in highly skilled knowledge-work. If professors with PhDs and a decade of expertise can be compelled to work for less than minimum wage, anyone can, no matter how skilled. It is easy to forget that long-term work without any legal protections or a safety net was not always considered typical, much less culturally glorified as bootstrapping self-reliance. A century ago, activists sacrificed their lives for universal rights such as a minimum wage, a forty-hour work week, sick days, vacation time, and due process protections.

This brings us back to workplace democracy. Essentially this notion involves applying democratic techniques to the functioning of workplaces including voting systems, debates, democratic structuring, systems of input, due process, and systems of appeal. It has also been seen as central to collective bargaining and organized labor as a means to achieve greater equity both on the job and in society. As Eidlin and Uetricht note, the labor movement did not always see the bare right to collectively bargain as its endgame.[3] Organized labor was seen as the path to sovereignty in the workplace, where the production process itself could be democratically controlled—supporting a democratic economy that is coterminous with the democratic state. Through history there have been different levels of engagement with this idea. The political theorist Jean-Jacques Rousseau certainly believed democratic activity was not only the province of the formal state but more diffusely necessary to preserve the social contract. Socialist movements historically placed a great deal of emphasis on workers "seizing the means of production," which suggests a forceful takeover of resources. But there are other less divisive paradigms as well, including employee ownership models and cooperatives in which workers collectively take part in decisions about organization and growth, and share in the benefits of its prosperity, or participatory management structures in which decisions are made through various consensus-based approaches.[4]

In higher education, a democratically controlled workplace would need a more equitable distribution of power than what is afforded through limited shared governance such as a faculty senate. One noteworthy experiment (and perhaps the only one of its kind) comes from College of the Mainland, a working-class community college deep in the conservative oil country of Texas City. In 1993, they instituted a new management structure that effectively dissolved the hierarchical chain of authority and replaced it with a system of democratically organized self-managing teams that administered nearly every aspect of operations—from instruction and academic affairs to student services. Team leaders were elected, and decisions were made efficiently by consensus and occasionally majority votes. David Michael Smith, the faculty union president at the time, describes an environment with high levels of academic freedom, in which faculty, staff, students, trustees, and community members worked in close collaboration, leading to drastically improved employee engagement and diminished alienation. For more than a decade this system functioned with relative efficiency.[5]

While this example was prompted by institutional leaders, collective action (through unions, alliances, or other collective efforts) is by far the most efficacious political tool that equity-oriented workers wield in pushing for greater workplace democracy. We may yet rediscover its potency and utility in advancing a more equitable postsecondary system. But with what vision and agenda? How in fact *do* we democratize the academic workplace, and what could that mean for society at large?

Recommendations

In this section, we propose areas of focus to move us beyond the worst extremes of the Gig Academy and toward greater collective ownership of our workplaces. While we are unlikely to quickly dispatch with problematic trends, we can provide policy and action directions that promote positive developments and can be expanded over time. From earlier chapters, we have established that the stakes are already staggeringly high—student learning, educational quality, academic community, employee morale, satisfaction, and performance as well as overall organizational performance and efficiency have all sustained heavy damage. In the years prior to *Janus v. AFSCME* in 2018, we have already seen some crucial groups awakening to the shortcomings of a narrowly conceived union strategy. With *Janus*, courts ruled that employees cannot be compelled to pay union dues and can opt out of paying for collective bargaining fees if their campus unionizes, which can significantly compromise unions' effort to obtain membership and fees that sustain unionization efforts. Unions need to find ways to make membership more attractive to potential members, especially with changing demographics and different concerns and interests. But with the new reality of a national public sector "right to work" finally upon us, there is no longer time to waste—we must mobilize broadly to demand concrete policy changes.

In addition to more basic electoral responsibilities, like voting for candidates at all levels of public office that categorically support workers' rights, we must commit to organizing our colleagues in a disciplined, substantive way. Unionization can no longer be conceived in simplistic terms of getting 50 percent-plus-one to agree to union representation. If there is any chance of improving conditions, defending diversity, and asserting our rights to academic freedom, we must broaden our understanding of unions far beyond the legalistic formalisms of contract negotiations, engaging in *praxis*-based organizing and strategizing for an equitable academy. Though we may be armed only with collective power and decisive action, it is worth remembering that the most significant labor rights victories in our history were achieved with little else.

More Collectivist Forms of Organizing and Bargaining

Wall-to-wall organizing and sectoral bargaining are two approaches that expand our collectivity beyond the narrower, often role-specific groups that traditionally delineate collective bargaining units. Wall-to-wall organizing includes all the workers at a particular workplace (e.g., a particular campus), and sectoral bargaining includes all workers within a particular sector (e.g., higher education). Both strategies offer a path to strengthen bonds and meaningfully build power between groups who have traditionally been viewed as divided due to their different roles (e.g., faculty viewed as distinct from classified staff) and would generate a wider range of negotiating tactics available to workers, radically altering power dynamics on campus. It could be particularly effective in higher education should we push for goals that span multiple types of contingent work, such as statewide living wage floors. United in solidarity, professional staff, classified staff, faculty, graduate students, and postdocs could work across groups to develop institutional plans where all employees feel adequately supported in maintaining a quality educational environment that is conducive to student success.

For too long in higher education, different worker groups have conceived of themselves as separated by distinct, even competing interests and priorities.[6] The divided structure of bargaining units has resulted in ineffective or nonexistent communication across groups on campus, which keeps them isolated and unaware of their common issues and concerns. Existing unions can play a crucial part in breaking down these silos by creating spaces of conversation across historically separated groups of workers and those who have been less interested in unionization. Helping groups perceive their aligned interests and actively support one another will create much more pressure on administrations. Campus representatives weaken groups by restricting information and reducing transparency so they can make isolated deals between separated and stratified groups.

Unions can contribute to building greater institutional power by sharing data, collaborating on strategies, and intensifying pressure for specific changes. This can transfer institutional power to those whose work and passion have the most direct impact on the quality of higher education and the environments in which learning takes place.[7]

Interest-Based Bargaining

Additionally, today's environment might encourage more positional bargaining than in any other time, given the great chasm that we describe between administrators and employees on college campuses. Position-based bargaining suggests that the two groups have very little common interest and need to argue for their particular interests. And while intuitively it may seem that today's environment calls for this position-based bargaining, research demonstrates that interest-based bargaining might better support changes in higher education. Administrators and campus employees do have a shared interest in student learning and success. Beyond that, this interest is one that local, regional, and state communities and political interests also support. Rhoades has argued that unions that focus on positional bargaining will lose community support, as they have in other sectors. By focusing on interest-based bargaining, faculty, staff, postdocs, and graduate students can align with public interest and leverage it against administrators. The Cal State Faculty Association has been very successful in garnering support from local communities when they have had to threaten or go on strike, as has Campus Workers United in Tennessee, as described in the previous chapter.[8]

In many states such as Tennessee, West Virginia, Arizona, and Oklahoma—all "right-to-work" states—there are very few labor protections in place. For public-sector workers, striking is a crime. Yet despite the aggressive efforts of many conservative lawmakers and commentators to demonize those who recently participated in statewide teachers strikes as prioritizing their own enrichment over students, communities in these states overwhelmingly sided with their children's teachers, largely due to being well *organized*. The strong, organic relationships these educators had formed over time with local parents and other community groups served to immunize the movement against concerted attempts to discredit their moral character and portray them as indifferent to children and families who would be affected by lost school days.

It is entirely feasible that unions can strengthen their efforts within colleges and universities through interest-based bargaining and by emphasizing greater outreach to local, regional, and state constituents that share their interest in supporting students and keeping the power of corporate university leaders in check. Building external support for collective bargaining is one of the few ways that employees can apply pressure to halt current trends. We encourage both employees as well as the unions representing them to integrate into their campaigns evidence about the impacts of these employment trends on the mission of the institution and on students and their learning, since it is harder for administrators to deny bargaining rights based on interests they themselves are supposed to share.[9]

Social Justice or Movement Unionism

As noted in chapter 5, social movement organizing among unions is a growing trend that has potential to coalesce the more collectivist collective bargaining strategy we noted above. Social justice/movement organizing focuses on public or broader interests (e.g., student learning, changing demographics, diversity/equity, social and community development, and democratic and civic engagement) to support collective bargaining efforts. We provided many current examples of this strategy in chapter 5, including the California Faculty Association's link between declining funds for public higher education as students in California became more diverse and the University of Michigan negotiating protections for those who engage in diversity work. We noted how the new generation of graduate students, in particular, seems to be engaging in social movement bargaining and brought up Harvard GSU, which has set up its own sexual assault committee, and the work of the graduate union at the University of Washington to pass the Washington DREAM Act.[10]

Broad-Based National Alliances for Research, Organizing, and Action

While unions provide a key vehicle for workers to come together to address problematic working conditions, as we noted, many colleges and universities are in states that prohibit collective bargaining or striking—traditionally the main tools for pressuring managers for changes in working conditions. There are increasingly groups emerging that support workers outside of the narrow scope of collective bargaining and are taking political action to enhance the lives of workers on college campuses. Faculty and staff participating in these types of collective efforts can support overall changes in their working conditions. An example of this type of collective advocacy is the New Faculty Majority (NFM), whose mission is to improve the quality of higher education by advancing professional equity and securing academic freedom for all contingent faculty. For almost a decade this organization has worked to improve the material lives of contingent instructors, including through

- Better compensation and benefits packages,
- Participation in governance processes and professional development,

- Securing unemployment protections,
- Better insurance coverage under the Affordable Care Act, and
- Stronger state oversight over institutions that misclassify workers to avoid providing employment benefits.

While much of their work has been at the federal level, they have also collaborated with workers on individual campuses when they have experienced exploitation. But their scope and resources are limited.

NFM's support does not extend to postsecondary staff, who are no less in need of collective advocacy but lack such a platform. Student activist networks have been among the strongest advocates fighting for better staff wages and benefits. As mentioned in earlier chapters, student protests on dozens of campuses have resulted in improved wages for staff. If faculty partnered more with staff and students in their efforts to improve working conditions, this could amplify their influence. Students in the Gig Academy are construed as a kind of currency, where enrolling more of them means more resources, but they are also largely viewed as *customers*, which gives them some power to make administrators prioritize their needs and desires. And of course, students can also benefit from a critical education about the effects that institutional changes are having on their own learning and success based on the quality of instruction their professors are empowered to deliver.

Chapter 4 provides an important set of data to be shared with students who have connections to powerful parent groups and wider communities (which can and should also be educated about how changes are reshaping the educational landscape). Consider how the Parent Teachers Association became advocates for better working conditions for all academic workers from kindergarten through college. Given that students today are more separated from faculty and staff than they have been in the past, stoking such activism comes with greater challenges. It can be hard to understand the impact of an experience one has not lived; many of today's students never get the chance to develop close relationships with faculty and staff. However daunting it may be, student and parent activism is a critical source of latent power in the Gig Academy that can be better harnessed with disciplined organizing.

Typically, "shared governance" does not include NTT faculty and staff in meaningful decision-making. Workers of all types need to push for more involvement in campus decision-making and governance through organizing. This does not mean advocating superficial fixes, such as permitting a few adjuncts to vote in curriculum committee meetings. We are talking about a fundamental redistribution of power within the academy. Current trends to reinstate shared governance provide opportunities for faculty and staff to reconstitute decision-making power they have lost on many campuses. Work by the Association for Governing Boards (AGB) defends the need for contingent faculty, in particular, to be included in campus decision-making and to revive shared governance; this demonstrates concern, even among board members themselves, that institutions are not necessarily headed in a direction consistent with their missions. The AGB has pressed the point that administrators need more input from faculty, who are responsible for creating a quality educational environment and have knowledge that needs to inform decision-making. Accreditors are another powerful and underutilized group that has long supported shared governance as central to educational quality. They can be stronger allies if pressured to leverage their power in the course of initial accreditation and reaccreditation processes.[11]

Additionally, the AGB made clear that as contingent faculty are included in campus decision-making, changes must be made to campus policies and practices that facilitate this process. AGB, along with some unions, are arguing for multiyear contracts and a higher threshold for full-time appointments that would make faculty participation in decision-making structures more meaningful. As we noted earlier, Kezar and Sam have showed how when contingent faculty are included in governance, campuses are more likely to create policies and practices that support their work.[12]

Many administrators are likely to begrudge conceding the power that they have diligently amassed over the last several decades. It will take an alliance of internal groups like faculty and staff working with external groups like AGB, accreditors, and parents to reclaim the decision-making power that faculty once had and to finally extend such decision-making power to staff.

Disassembling the Gig Academy

There are several areas in which the Gig Academy may be vulnerable to organic challenge from within. One thing is clear: All strategies for resisting the many deleterious conditions that have become normalized and building a vision of authentic workplace democracy will necessarily involve disciplined, inclusive, sustained organizing. This is not just about securing a living wage or fair benefits and protections—though these are obviously important—but about the way the academic production process itself is carried out. But to what specific ends should these tactics be applied? Where are some of the clear pressure points that could potentially allow educators to take control of education again? In this section we discuss several areas that may prove to be productive for workplace democracy-focused organizers to develop actions and agendas around.

Embrace Intersectional Struggle Fully and Unapologetically

If our basic goal is to build power through organizing, such power must be equitably and broadly distributed or invariably it will falter. The postsecondary workforce and student body alike routinely face concrete manifestations of racism, sexism, classism, ableism, jingoism, and many other forms of structural discrimination. Moving beyond managerial talk about diversity will require offering real spaces of inclusion that stand in contrast with the institutional status quo. Cardozo writes extensively on how under neoliberalism, tacit expectations around feminized care work in higher education compound the many challenges already imposed by faculty contingency and empty diversity rhetoric.[13] And outside instruction, it is no coincidence that the staff jobs that are most vulnerable to outsourcing are those that primarily employ people of color at low wages. There is space for all of these concerns to come together in a meaningful way.

Another locus of attention is inequitable hiring practices. Women are overrepresented among contingent faculty. It seems possible that many colleges and universities could be violating not only labor laws but civil rights laws as well. Contingent hiring typically follows no affirmative action processes and is informal. These practices leave people vulnerable not just to job precarity but to abuse and violence as well—as the many scandals that have surfaced on college campuses in the wake of the #MeToo movement amply testify. Workers who band together and take these issues head on will be better able to protect one another from abuses of power and bring national attention to issues of predation that have long been endemic to a white, patriarchal academy. Intersectional struggle is an important part of what unites the Gig Academy and provides a critical basis of cross-sectoral solidarity that can be carried into bigger and broader political struggles.

Demand a Democratic Approach to Technology Integration

While technological advancements may have clear value in supporting educational processes, the conveniences and downsides of "ed-tech" need to be deliberated carefully and collectively rather than be left to administrators uncritically enamored with the potential to slash overhead costs through automation or provide "objective" instruments for measuring teaching and learning that leave much to be desired. In overlooking the importance of people and community to learning, administrators have lost focus of what is needed to create a quality teaching and learning environment. And they are supported by powerful foundations and groups that may not understand (or care) how their actions reinforce Gig Academy predilections.

Instead of rushing to adopt new forms of technology, institutions should carefully evaluate their educational value. In a recent article, the Senior Vice President of Student Services (who, for the record, also happens to be a professor) at Georgia State University—one of the most diverse public research institutions in the nation, with a student body that is two-thirds nonwhite and nearly as many who are eligible for Pell—recounts tremendous strides made in improving student success using predictive analytics. The secret: his office "participating in, no joke, an estimated 10,000 meetings with faculty, staff, vendors, and others" to determine exactly what would be useful to academic and financial aid advisers who work directly with students. They prioritized the needs and expertise of these workers over the preferences of executives and contracted with a company willing to build a platform from the ground up to fit these needs, rather than adopt a cheap, one-size-fits-all software package. Instead of replacing human labor, artificial intelligence was used to enhance their work; administrators deferred to educators and support staff on the ground at every stage, thus ensuring wide buy-in and smooth implementation, and quickly recouped the extra investment costs with significant gains in retention and completion.[14]

Technology platforms that are imposed from the top down, used to pare back labor, and contracted without meaningful participation by their functional users allow the Gig Academy to calcify in ways that few besides a small slice of managers and corporate actors benefit from. That the administrator in the anecdote above is also a real faculty member is unusual and may partly account for GSU's unusually inclusive approach. Most institutions do not appoint traditional faculty in these roles; student advocates should not count on such critical reflection and generosity and take matters into their own hands until there can be more democratic mechanisms to govern the adoption of ed-tech—that is, until we leverage our collectivity to insist that naked profits become subordinate to the professional judgments of committed educators.

Refuse to Abide Worker Misclassification

Adjunct faculty are often misclassified in order to strategically reduce the employer's obligation to them. While gig economy workers are often misclassified as independent contractors, which denies them entitlement to critical protections and benefits like unemployment compensation, overtime pay, and eligibility for public student loan forgiveness, adjunct faculty are often misclassified as exempt workers, which denies them the same benefits (as well as others) based on different legal reasons. Legal sleights-of-hand still abound when it comes to the rights and protections accorded to those paid through a salary versus an hourly wage, much of which has to do with institutions trying to narrowly satisfy conditions of the Affordable Care Act while sidestepping other protections that should rightfully be available.[15]

For example, many adjuncts had workloads that exceeded thirty hours a week but were still considered part-time workers. In response to new regulations in the Affordable Care Act, some campuses began to decrease the number of courses assigned to each faculty member, so they would remain ineligible for the healthcare benefits the new law would have entitled them to. Yet many part-time faculty actually do work full-time and are fully dependent on their employer for their livelihood. Similarly, staff who do the basic work of running campuses, like administrative support, groundskeeping, and maintenance are also employees that will always be in demand as their functions are central to the day-to-day functioning of the campus. Unions and other advocacy groups have a strong foundation to argue in court that many contingent employees in higher education have been misclassified and should be designated as regular employees.

As mentioned earlier, employers are likely to seek increased outsourcing of instructional labor, and we may yet see more moves toward the use of subcontractors, temporary agencies, labor brokers, franchising, licensing, and third-party management in attempts to forge a legal way around this designation. Further research and advocacy related to the classification of contingent workers is needed, including documenting the ways that higher education workers are misclassified and advocating to the Department of Labor.

Connecting Labor to Broader Issues: Taxes and Debt

Two of our recommendations connect to broader political issues and affect academic labor—student debt and public funding for higher education. We believe organizing and collective action are needed to bolster progressive political action at the state and national levels in order to better address the economic vulnerability built into faculty and student lives through student debt, which carries over into their work is important in coming years. It is no secret that the student debt burden among college graduates today is a scourge, particularly among millennials; this disproportionately hurts the working class and people of color, denying them a path to social mobility.

New longitudinal data from the National Student Loan Data System, Beginning Postsecondary Student (BPS) survey reveal less than half of all borrowers entering college in 1995–96 managed to pay off their loan balances within twenty years of their first semester, with default rates continually rising even twelve to twenty years later. Further analysis of these data by the Brookings Institute suggests that among those who began college in 2003–04, as many as 40 percent of borrowers could default by the year 2023. The highest default rates are not among those with the most student debt but rather among those with the least, who carry these balances without having finished their degree. The vast majority of student loan defaults occur with borrowers who initially owe less than $10,000 but then see these balances balloon over time—overwhelmingly people of color.[16] According to another study by Scott-Clayton and Li, Black college graduates owe an average of $7,400 more than white equivalents ($23,400 vs. $16,000, including non-borrowers). Over a short period of time, this gap in Black-white debt more than triples to a difference of approximately $25,000. According to the authors, rates of interest accrual and graduate school borrowing ultimately mean that Black graduates have on average almost $53,000 in student debt just four years after graduation, which means significantly fewer Black degree-holders can afford the risks of an academic career path.[17] Of the millions of low-income people of color forced into default from a much lower debt threshold, precious few will ever gain the education needed to even consider academic employment at all, perpetuating a predominantly white academy in spite of the preponderance of institutional overtures to diversity and inclusion.

Organizing around solutions for student debt is necessary to address labor issues. A new report from the Levy Economics Institute at Bard College argues this is not only feasible but prudent economics. The total of $1.4 trillion collectively owed by 44 million people creates a drag on the entire economy, not just on individual borrowers or even particular racial and socioeconomic categories. The authors of the report estimate that to simply cancel all of it would lead to an increase in GDP of at least $86 billion and add up to 1.5 million jobs *annually*. Of course, to be more than a temporary fix, this solution would also need to be paired with a plan to make higher education affordable again and free for low income students, something equally achievable with sufficient organization.[18]

Increasing public funding for education is critical for ameliorating faculty and staff working conditions, addressing student debt, making public higher education affordable, and other means to advancing equity. Christopher Newfield, the Center for Budget and Policy Priorities, and others have argued for the need to increase public support and funding, so we do not repeat this argument here but note its importance for advancing our argument of improving labor conditions in higher educational institutions.[19] But additional funding, given today's neoliberal logic, will not lead to change unless higher education moves more toward workplace democracy. Increasing education funding does nothing but support conservative criticism when the new funds are simply handed over to decisionmakers who are not accountable to the communities they serve. As we showed in earlier chapters, money saved by moving to contingent labor did not go to support lower tuition but to hire more professional administrators. One hopeful example can be found in Arizona, where the Invest in Education campaign recently succeeded in getting a ballot measure in place for the 2018 midterm elections that would add almost $700 million (the amount needed to restore public education funding to pre-recession levels) to the budget through a new tax on the income of the state's highest earners. The group staged massive statewide walkouts to march on the capitol under the banner #RedForEd and submitted their petition with double the required signatures (almost 270,000) as a way to assert their power and deep level of organizing.[20] After winning over $400 million in new educational investment (from a sales tax increase), #RedForEd now faces state retaliation. Not only did the Arizona Supreme Court questionably revoke their ballot initiative before the 2018 elections, some state legislators have proposed bills that would prohibit organizing by labeling it as "harassment," fine individual teachers up to $5,000 for causing a nonemergency school closure, and compel state attorneys to investigate any public educator suspected of breaking state law. Yet even these draconian prospects do not appear to be deterring educators from escalating their efforts in 2019.[21]

State and national political strategies can only deliver on their goals if they have broad-based organization to support the equitable implementation of new resources. If state university systems begin to see budgetary gains won through political pressure campaigns, the fight will have only just begun. To work so hard to secure such gains only to relinquish the power of appropriations to corporate university managers would be self-defeating. But a broad movement toward workplace democracy in higher education would ensure that the public can follow through materially on victories won in the political arena.

Making Do in the Gig Academy: Harm Reduction Strategies in the Interim

While we are hopeful that collective action aimed at workplace democracy can check neoliberal tendencies, we also recognize that before major changes occur, workers might try to at least reduce the most negative impacts of the Gig Academy. We offer a few of these type of solutions for workers to consider.

Increase Salaries to Make Contingency Unattractive

One strategy in the interim that Gig Academy resistance can take is working to create and enforce disincentives to contingent workforce dependency. For example, unions as well as advocacy groups like the New Faculty Majority have been looking for strategies that challenge the Gig Academy philosophy and dynamics. One way to make contingency less attractive is if contingent employees are paid significantly more. There has been a push for advancing significant salary increases—including the "Fight for $15," as with fast-food workers, where SEIU argued that faculty should be paid $15,000 per course—meaning a professor with three courses per semester would earn $90,000 annually. While this is an aspirational goal, it advances the argument that part-time workers should receive equal pay as full-time workers for the particular type of work that they do. If this were to change, then part-time and contingent appointments would be much less attractive. Staff also can be bolstered by advocating for more market-level salaries. While market-based strategies may also be problematic, as they can reinforce inequalities in the marketplace, this strategy used judiciously has been successful for gaining the attention of those driven by and making policy within the Gig Academy.

Alternative Hiring Practices

Consortial hiring practices across public state systems or consortia of private colleges could be another way to move from contingent to full-time positions, with costs borne across multiple institutions. Some states, particularly in the Northeast, are experiencing enrollment declines and are forced to lay off faculty and staff. However, some state systems and consortia have been able to avoid deep cuts by sharing employees across institutions rather than moving to outsourcing arrangements. We suggest that campus leaders and employees consider cost sharing arrangements that would provide full-time employment and benefits to faculty and staff, increasing job security and stability and without creating hardship for the individual campuses.

An example of such a system is the Five Colleges Consortium in New England, which hires full-time tenure-track and non-tenure-track faculty across multiple neighboring institutions, rather than each hiring its own on a part-time basis.[22] Budget constraints limited the capabilities of each individual institution to hire new faculty, so the consortium combined resources to hire a group of professors they would share. Although the colleges started out by exchanging professors from their existing faculties, they are now jointly hiring full-time faculty members. Those with non-tenure-track appointments receive three-year contracts and the possibility of transitioning into tenure-track appointments. Faculty members can access facilities and resources at each of the institutions where they teach; when they are away from their home institution, they utilize shared office space to work and meet with students, as needed. Similar kinds of arrangements have been used with staff, particularly technology staff that a single institution may not be able to support.

Portable Benefits Systems

If the Gig Academy and contingency prevail, trying to make long-term contingent employment less precarious is another avenue to consider. Some contingent workers, including many academics, find the increased flexibility that independent contracting can offer attractive. There may be a way to preserve the benefits of flexibility while increasing stability and security. Some scholars, activists, and policymakers have endorsed the creation of a national portable benefits system that would allow workers to move beyond the volatility of nontraditional employment.

Among the more substantive visions of such a system is one promoted by David Rolf, the international vice president of SEIU, and several of his colleagues. A recent report by Rolf et al. describes a model resembling social security—that is, a benefits structure which is *portable, universal,* and *pro-rated.* Independent workers of all types, along with those who hire them, pay into a central account that follows them from job to job, allowing them to accrue and maintain essential benefits over time, such as health insurance, worker's compensation, unemployment insurance, sick days, and even vacation time. In order for this to work fairly, contributions would need to be universally mandatory for contractor and contracting agent alike. Contributions from employers would be determined pro-rata, based on either amount paid or time worked. A central digital hub could allow workers to track and manage all of these benefits over time. Adjuncts working at multiple institutions part-time could do so without stigma and retain a measure of security. They could feel more valued, like the professionals they are.[23]

Such a model could be combined with other strategies already discussed. Unions could play an important role in negotiating minimum contributions from employers that would apply to all workers, which would be especially effective in conjunction with a whole-sector bargaining or metro campaign strategy. In fact, in the absence of strong underlying organizing efforts and union advocacy, the benefits accrued could end up being inadequate. And after all, the point is to ensure that gig workers of all types, and not only those caught in the machinery of the Gig Academy, are able to live and work with adequate protection and stability without sacrificing flexibility.

Adapt Existing Professional Employment Models

One of this book's authors, Kezar, has extensively published models of faculty work that restore professionalism and provide possible alternatives to part-time contingency. Some of the models modify the tenure structure, such as teaching-intensive tenure-track positions, while others are non-tenure-track but with long-term appointments and many tenure-track supports.[24] Versions of this are already in use at institutions like Evergreen State College and some medical schools.[25] These long-term positions are created with the flexibility to hone roles based on faculty interests and institutional needs. Similar "reprofessionalized" employment models could be used to guide higher education more broadly and offer a basis for collective advocacy around empirically proven alternative approaches.[26]

Concluding Thoughts

Some may view higher education as having entered another dark age for labor in the wake of the *Janus* ruling. But in the long run this could be the movement's saving grace, and an opportunity for all of us to rediscover a simple but profound truth: that protecting rights always requires an effective mass politics. The struggle that workers face to reclaim these rights will no doubt be tough, but to win under these conditions means that gains will be more durable and no longer depend on friendly political administrations, backroom deals by undemocratic union leaders, or formal but precarious legal protections.

Several recent examples of collective action described in this book give us hope for the future, including social justice organizing efforts particularly among graduate students: Invest in Education, United Campus Workers of Tennessee, and the faculty at Cal State San Jose, to name a few. Missouri voters recently overturned a right-to-work law that would have barred public unionization in that state. Forces of change are afoot. We see the promise of collective action working in real time. The Parkland students—teenagers with seemingly little power—mobilized on the strength of their shared passions and commitment, using both basic and novel organizing skills to advance concrete policy changes. Political change becomes more attainable as the excesses of power become obvious to enough people in their day-to day-experience. And while we focus on collective action, individuals can also act to make a difference. They can vote for different candidates or insist that current representatives respond to crisis. Perhaps they can read and share this book with others. For further examples of individuals who mobilized and changed higher education, see Kezar and Lester's *Enhancing Campuses Capacity for Leadership: An Examination of Grassroots Leaders in Higher Education.*[27]

We began this book with a set of real and inauspicious headlines about the changing postsecondary workplace. We are hopeful that in the coming years we will begin to see new sorts of headlines that reflect shared gains achieved through deliberate action agendas focused on democratic workplace goals:

- Graduate students, staff, faculty, state community agencies, parent-teacher organizations, and local businesses join together across the state of Oklahoma to obtain a significant increase in salary, benefits, and job security.
- Based on several years of policy advocacy by faculty and staff groups, the North Carolina legislature sets up a policy to allow portable benefits for faculty and staff working in higher education. They become a model for other states and regions.

- Based on encouragement from four different unions representing multiple employee groups, six regional accrediting organizations team with the Association for Governing Boards to create a national task force made up of faculty, staff, postdocs, undergraduates, and graduate students to examine new guidelines for shared governance in higher education.
- The California Faculty Association crafts a proposal for debt forgiveness for individuals who take positions in K–12 schools or the higher education system that is passed and made law in the California state legislature.
- Graduate student workers and postdocs organize nationally and form a union, then establish national standards for graduate student stipends and postdoc salaries.
- Faculty and staff at for-profit institutions unionize and push for more ethical recruitment of students and reform of student debt.
- Faculty, staff, and graduate students at colleges and universities around Los Angeles organize and strike to argue that universities buying up real estate to rent to students around the city must provide some affordable housing to combat the displacement of indigenous communities.

With headlines like these, colleges and universities will become more equitable institutions that return to their public good roots, becoming democratic workplaces and supplanting the logics of the Gig Academy. This is the future that we hope you will join in creating.

Notes

···

Introduction

1. Sheila Slaughter and Larry L. Leslie, *Academic Capitalism: Politics, Policies, and the Entrepreneurial University* (Baltimore: Johns Hopkins University Press, 1999); Sheila Slaughter and Gary Rhoades, *Academic Capitalism and the New Economy: Markets, State, and Higher Education* (Baltimore: Johns Hopkins University Press, 2004).

2. Albert Bandura, *Social Foundations of Thought and Action: A Social Cognitive Theory* (Englewood Cliffs, NJ: Prentice-Hall, 1986); Laura Rendon, "Beyond Involvement: Creating Validating Academic and Social Communities in the Community College," 1994, https://eric.ed.gov/?id=ED374728.

3. Daniel F. Chambliss and Christopher G. Takacs, *How College Works* (Cambridge, MA: Harvard University Press, 2014), https://doi.org/10.4159/harvard.9780674726093; Gallup, "Great Jobs Great Lives: The 2014 Gallup-Purdue Index Report" (Gallup, 2014).

4. George D. Kuh, Jillian Kinzie, John H. Schuh, and Elizabeth J. Whitt, *Student Success in College: Creating Conditions That Matter* (San Francisco: Jossey-Bass, 2010).

5. For further information about non-tenure-track faculty, please see The Delphi Project on the Changing Faculty and Student Success (www.thechangingfaculty.org); Adrianna Kezar, "Departmental Cultures and Non-Tenure-Track Faculty: Willingness, Capacity, and Opportunity to Perform at Four-Year Institutions," *The Journal of Higher Education* 84, no. 2 (March 2013): 153–88, https://doi.org/10.1080/00221546.2013.11777284; and Adrianna Kezar and Cecelia Sam, "Understanding the New Majority of Non-Tenure-Track Faculty in Higher Education—Demographics, Experiences, and Plans of Action," Association for the Study of Higher Education, 2010, http://doi.wiley.com/10.1002/aehe.3604. On new faculty models, see Adrianna Kezar and Daniel Maxey, *Adapting by Design*, 2nd ed.

(Los Angeles: The Delphi Project, 2015), https://pullias.usc.edu/wp-content/uploads/2015/06/DELPHI-PROJECT_ADAPTING-BY-DESIGN_2ED.pdf.

6. The Delphi Project on the Changing Faculty and Student Success, www.thechangingfaculty.org.

One: Putting the Gig Academy in Context

1. From here on "gig economy" will drop quotation marks and remain lowercase, since it is a widely used general term in popular culture. Gig Academy is capitalized both because it is our neologism and as a helpful visual distinction for the reader.

2. Wendy Brown, *Undoing the Demos: Neoliberalism's Stealth Revolution* (Cambridge, MA: MIT Press, 2015).

3. David Harvey, *Spaces of Neoliberalization: Towards a Theory of Uneven Geographical Development* (Stuttgart: Franz Steiner Verlag, 2005); Jamie Peck, *Constructions of Neoliberal Reason* (Oxford: Oxford University Press, 2010).

4. Sheila Slaughter and Larry L. Leslie, *Academic Capitalism: Politics, Policies, and the Entrepreneurial University* (Baltimore: Johns Hopkins University Press, 1999); Sheila Slaughter and Gary Rhoades, *Academic Capitalism and the New Economy: Markets, State, and Higher Education* (Baltimore: Johns Hopkins University Press, 2004).

5. The Bayh-Dole Act authorizes the US Department of Commerce to create standard patent rights clauses to be included in federal funding agreements with nonprofits, including universities, and small businesses. This allowed and encouraged higher education to profit from its research activities in ways it had not in the past.

6. Roger G. Baldwin and Jay L. Chronister, *Teaching without Tenure: Policies and Practices for a New Era* (Baltimore: Johns Hopkins University Press, 2001), http://ebookcentral.proquest.com/lib/socal/detail.action?docID=3318123l; John G. Cross and Edie N. Goldenberg, *Off-Track Profs: Nontenured Teachers in Higher Education* (Cambridge, MA: MIT Press, 2009); Jack H. Schuster and Martin J. Finkelstein, *The American Faculty: The Restructuring of Academic Work and Careers* (Baltimore: Johns Hopkins University Press, 2006); American Association of University Professors, "Visualizing Change: Report on the Economic Status of the Profession," *Academe* (2017).

7. Mary Ellen Flannery, "The Homeless Professor Who Lives in Her Car," *NEA Today*, November 1, 2017, http://neatoday.org/2017/11/01/homeless-professor; Caroline Fredrickson, "There Is No Excuse for How Universities Treat Adjuncts," *The Atlantic*, September 15, 2015, www.theatlantic.com/business/archive/2015/09/higher-education-college-adjunct-professor-salary/404461/;

Alastair Gee, "Facing Poverty, Academics Turn to Sex Work and Sleeping in Cars," US news, *The Guardian*, September 28, 2017, www.theguardian.com/us-news/2017/sep/28/adjunct-professors-homeless-sex-work-academia-poverty; Ken Jacobs, Ian Perry, and Jenifer MacGillvary, "The High Public Cost of Low Wages," *Center for Labor Research and Education*, April 13, 2015, http://laborcenter.berkeley.edu/the-high-public-cost-of-low-wages.

8. Jake Rosenfeld, *What Unions No Longer Do* (Cambridge, MA: Harvard University Press, 2014), https://doi.org/10.4159/harvard.9780674726215; Lawrence F. Katz and Alan B. Krueger, "The Rise and Nature of Alternative Work Arrangements in the United States, 1995–2015," Working Paper, National Bureau of Economic Research, September 2016, https://doi.org/10.3386/w22667; Louis Hyman, "Where Are All the Uber Drivers? Not in These Government Statistics," *Los Angeles Times*, July 27, 2018, www.latimes.com/opinion/op-ed/la-oe-hyman-contingent-temp-workers-20180729-story.html; Patrick Gillespie, "Intuit: Gig Economy Is 34% of US Workforce," *CNNMoney*, May 24, 2017, https://money.cnn.com/2017/05/24/news/economy/gig-economy-intuit/index.html.

9. While there are many problematic trends associated with the gig economy, there are also genuine arguments for its advantages for workers who, for various reasons, cannot work regularly or full-time. For example, a parent with multiple children may find traditional work arrangements not feasible and instead make money by renting out part of her house on Airbnb.

10. Marc Bousquet, *How the University Works: Higher Education and the Low-Wage Nation* (New York: New York University Press, 2008); Ursula Huws, *Labor in the Global Digital Economy: The Cybertariat Comes of Age* (New York: Monthly Review Press, 2014); Tom Slee, *What's Yours Is Mine: Against the Sharing Economy* (London: Scribe UK, 2015).

11. Arne L. Kalleberg and Michael Dunn, "Good Jobs, Bad Jobs in the Gig Economy," *Perspectives on Work* 20 (2016): 10–14; Upwork, "Freelancing in America: 2017 Survey," 2017, www.upwork.com/i/freelancing-in-america/2017/.

12. Gianpiero Petriglieri, Susan J. Ashford, and Amy Wrzesniewski, "Agony and Ecstasy in the Gig Economy: Cultivating Holding Environments for Precarious and Personalized Work Identities," *Administrative Science Quarterly* (February 6, 2018), https://doi.org/10.1177/0001839218759646.

13. Slaughter and Rhoades, *Academic Capitalism and the New Economy*.

14. William Davies, "The Sharing Economy Comes to Campus," *The Chronicle of Higher Education*, January 29, 2017, www.chronicle.com/article/The-Sharing-Economy-Comes-to-/238992; David Goldberg, "The Dangers of the Uberization of Higher Education," *Inside Higher Ed*, 2016, www.insidehighered.com/views/2016/08/12/dangers-uberization-higher-education-essay; Jeffrey R. Young, "Here Comes

Professor Everybody," *The Chronicle of Higher Education*, February 2, 2015, www.chronicle.com/article/Here-Comes-Professor-Everybody/151445.

15. Gary Hall, *The Uberification of the University* (Minneapolis, MN: University of Minnesota Press, 2016); Michel Foucault, *The Birth of Biopolitics: Lectures at the Collège de France, 1978–79*, edited by Michel Senellart (New York: Palgrave Macmillan, 2008); Michel Foucault, *Discipline and Punish: The Birth of the Prison*, 2nd ed., trans. Alan Sheridan (New York: Vintage Books, 1995); Slaughter and Rhoades, *Academic Capitalism and the New Economy*; Bousquet, *How the University Works*; Brown, *Undoing the Demos*.

16. Michelle Miller and Eric Harris Bernstein, *New Frontiers of Worker Power: Challenges and Opportunities in the Modern Economy*. New York: Roosevelt Institute, 2017, http://rooseveltinstitute.org/new-frontiers-worker-power/; Deloitte, *Deloitte's 2016 Global Outsourcing Survey* (London: Deloitte Consulting, 2016); Hyman, "Where Are All the Uber Drivers?" The Wagner Act is another name for the National Labor Relations Act of 1935 (NLRA), the cornerstone of US labor law, which guarantees the rights of private-sector workers to form unions, bargain collectively for better working conditions, and undertake collective actions—such as strikes—to protest unfair treatment. It also created the National Labor Relations Board to independently oversee union elections and certify votes to unionize.

17. David Weil, *The Fissured Workplace* (Cambridge, MA: Harvard University Press, 2014).

18. Benjamin Kreider, "Risk Shift and the Gig Economy," Economic Policy Institute, 2015, www.epi.org/blog/risk-shift-and-the-gig-economy; David Weil, "Lots of Employees Get Misclassified as Contractors. Here's Why It Matters," *Harvard Business Review*, July 5, 2017, https://hbr.org/2017/07/lots-of-employees-get-misclassified-as-contractors-heres-why-it-matters.

19. Francois Carre, "(In)Dependent Contractor Misclassification," Economic Policy Institute, 2015, www.epi.org/publication/independent-contractor-misclassification; DPE Research Department, "The Misclassification of Employees as Independent Contractors," AFL-CIO, 2016.

20. Philo A. Hutcheson, *A Professional Professoriate: Unionization, Bureaucratization, and the AAUP*, 1st ed., Vanderbilt Issues in Higher Education (Nashville, TN: Vanderbilt University Press, 2000).

21. Huws, *Labor in the Global Digital Economy*.

22. Sean Gehrke and Adrianna Kezar, "Unbundling the Faculty Role in Higher Education: Utilizing Historical, Theoretical, and Empirical Frameworks to Inform Future Research," in *Higher Education: Handbook of Theory and Research*, edited by Michael B. Paulsen, vol. 30 (Cham, Switzerland: Springer International Publishing, 2015), 93–150.

23. Gehrke and Kezar, "Unbundling the Faculty Role in Higher Education."

24. Robert S. Gold, *A Jazz Lexicon*, 1st ed. (New York: A. A. Knopf, 1964).

25. Bousquet, *How the University Works*, 63.

26. Slaughter and Rhoades, *Academic Capitalism and the New Economy*; Foucault, *Discipline and Punish*; A. C. Brown, "The Impact of Interest-Based Bargaining on Community College Faculty and Administrative Relationships," Northern Arizona University, 2015.

27. John Hoerr, *We Can't Eat Prestige: The Women Who Organized Harvard* (Philadelphia: Temple University Press, 2001).

28. Marc Bousquet, "The Waste Product of Graduate Education: Toward a Dictatorship of the Flexible," *Social Text* 20, no. 1 (March 1, 2002): 81–104; Bousquet, *How the University Works*.

29. Sarah King Head, "MOOCs—The Revolution Has Begun, Says Moody's," *University World News*, September 23, 2012, www.universityworldnews.com /article.php?story=20120920124146236; Young, "Here Comes Professor Everybody"; Marc Bousquet, "Good MOOCs, Bad MOOCs," Brainstorm, *The Chronicle of Higher Education*, July 25, 2012, www.chronicle.com/blogs/brainstorm /good-moocs-bad-moocs/50361.

30. Workday, "Higher Education Financial Mgmt, HR, and Student Software," www.workday.com/en-us/industries/higher-education.html.

31. Albert Bandura, *Social Foundations of Thought and Action: A Social Cognitive Theory* (Englewood Cliffs, NJ: Prentice-Hall, 1986); L. S. Vygotsky and Michael Cole, *Mind in Society: The Development of Higher Psychological Processes* (Cambridge, MA: Harvard University Press, 1978); Veronica Bordes and Patricia Arredondo, "Mentoring and 1st-Year Latina/o College Students," *Journal of Hispanic Higher Education* 4, no. 2 (April 1, 2005): 114–33, https://doi.org/10 .1177/1538192704273855; Laura I. Rendon, "Beyond Involvement: Creating Validating Academic and Social Communities in the Community College," 1994, https://eric.ed.gov/?id=ED374728; Kevin Cokley, "Perceived Faculty Encouragement and Its Influence on College Students," *Journal of College Student Development* 41, no. 3 (2000): 348–52; S. Hurtado, A. Ruiz Alvarado, and C. Guillermo-Wann, "Creating Inclusive Environments: The Mediating Effect of Faculty and Staff Validation on the Relationship of Discrimination/Bias to Students' Sense of Belonging," *Journal Committed to Social Change on Race and Ethnicity* 1, no. 1 (October 13, 2015): 60–80, https://escholarship.org/uc/item/5z7283g0.

32. Anikó Hannák, Claudia Wagner, David Garcia, Alan Mislove, Markus Strohmaier, and Christo Wilson, "Bias in Online Freelance Marketplaces: Evidence from TaskRabbit and Fiverr," *Proceedings of the 2017 ACM Conference on Computer Supported Cooperative Work and Social Computing* (New York: ACM

Press, 2017), 1914–1933, https://doi.org/10.1145/2998181.2998327; Slee, *What's Yours Is Mine.*

33. Brown, "The Impact of Interest-Based Bargaining"; Goldberg, "The Dangers of the Uberization"; Young, "Here Comes Professor Everybody"; Philip Stark and Richard Freishtat, "An Evaluation of Course Evaluations," *ScienceOpen Research,* September 29, 2014, https://doi.org/10.14293/S2199-1006.1.SOR-EDU .AOFRQA.v1; Deborah J. Merritt, "Bias, the Brain, and Student Evaluations of Teaching," *St. John's Law Review* 82 (2008): 235–88; Anne Boring, Kellie Ottoboni, and Philip Stark, "Student Evaluations of Teaching (Mostly) Do Not Measure Teaching Effectiveness," ScienceOpen Research, January 7, 2016, https://doi .org/10.14293/S2199-1006.1.SOR-EDU.AETBZC.v1; Lillian MacNell, Adam Driscoll, and Andrea N. Hunt, "What's in a Name: Exposing Gender Bias in Student Ratings of Teaching," *Innovative Higher Education* 40, no. 4 (August 1, 2015): 291–303, https://doi.org/10.1007/s10755-014-9313-4; Kristina M. W. Mitchell and Jonathan Martin, "Gender Bias in Student Evaluations," *PS: Political Science & Politics* 51, no. 3 (July 2018): 648–52, https://doi.org/10.1017 /S104909651800001X; April Kelly-Woessner and Matthew C. Woessner. "My Professor Is a Partisan Hack: How Perceptions of a Professor's Political Views Affect Student Course Evaluations," *PS: Political Science & Politics* 39, no. 3 (July 2006): 495–501, https://doi.org/10.1017/S104909650606080X; Elaine Nikolakakos, Jennifer L. Reeves, and Sheldon Such, "An Examination of the Causes of Grade Inflation in a Teacher Education Program and Implications for Practice," *College and University* 87, no. 3 (Winter 2012): 2–13; Ad-Hoc Committee on Grade Inflation. "Final Report of the Ad-Hoc Committee on Grade Inflation," American University, 2016.

34. Ryan Mac, "Amazon Releases Diversity Numbers for the First Time and Surprise, It's Mostly Male and White," *Forbes,* October 31, 2014, www.forbes.com /sites/ryanmac/2014/10/31/amazon-releases-diversity-numbers-for-first-time-and -surprise-its-mostly-male-and-white/#3958de8124cf.

35. Jennifer A. Muryn Kaminski and Anne H. Reilly. "Career Development of Women in Information Technology," *SAM Advanced Management Journal* 69, no. 4 (Autumn 2004): 20–30.

36. Tom DePaola and Adrianna Kezar, "The Changing Face of Employment at Research Universities," *New Directions for Institutional Research* 2018, no. 176 (2017): 83–96, https://doi.org/10.1002/ir.20246; National Center for Education Statistics, "Digest of Education Statistics, 2016," 2016, https://nces.ed.gov /programs/digest/d16/tables/dt16_315.10.asp.

37. Gary Rhoades, *Managed Professionals: Unionized Faculty and Restructuring Academic Labor* (Albany: State University of New York Press, 1998); Hutcheson, *A Professional Professoriate.*

38. Davarian L. Baldwin, "When Universities Swallow Cities," *The Chronicle of Higher Education*, July 30, 2017, www.chronicle.com/article/When -Universities-Swallow/240739; Richard Florida, Gary Gates, Brian Knudsen, and Kevin Stolarick, *The University and the Creative Economy* (Pittsburgh, PA: H. J. Heinz III School of Public Policy, Carnegie Mellon University, 2006).

39. We may yet see the emergence of prestige-oriented gig commerce in the business of selling cultural capital as much as its stated service-product. Its beginnings can be glimpsed, for example, in the way Instagram has become a site of accumulation and competition among the aspiring "influencer" class, who essentially perform branding labor free of charge.

40. We acknowledge that states have reduced their allocation to public colleges and universities over the last two decades, and this has contributed to rising costs. Yet private institutions without these pressures have continued to raise tuition even as they hired cheaper labor. And data on public and private colleges demonstrate that they have continued to spent money saved on contingent labor for other costs and not decreased tuition (see discussion of Delta Cost Project in chapter 2).

41. David Platzer and Anne Allison, "Academic Precarity in American Anthropology," *Cultural Anthropology*, February 12, 2018, https://culanth.org /fieldsights/1310-academic-precarity-in-american-anthropology.

42. Slaughter and Rhoades, *Academic Capitalism and the New Economy*.

Two: Employees in the Gig Academy

1. Gary Rhoades, *Managed Professionals: Unionized Faculty and Restructuring Academic Labor* (Albany: State University of New York Press, 1998).

2. Peter M. Magolda, *The Lives of Campus Custodians: Insights into Corporatization and Civic Disengagement in the Academy* (Sterling, VA: Stylus Publishing, 2016). This is not to suggest that custodial staff and others have ever been treated equitably, as they have long had a history of poor pay and benefits; many groups have worked to organize these employees based on their poor working conditions historically.

3. James A. Mello, "In Support of Others: An Examination of Psychological Capital and Job Satisfaction in Academic Staff," *Journal of Academic Administration in Higher Education* 9, no. 2 (2013): 2.

4. "Administrative Jobs," HigherEdJobs, www.higheredjobs.com/admin/.

5. Linda K. Johnsrud, "Higher Education Staff: Bearing the Brunt of Cost Containment," *NEA 2000 Almanac of Higher Education*, 18; Vicki J. Rosser, "Education Support Professionals: Employment Status and Financial Exigency," *NEA 2011 Almanac of Higher Education*, 12.

6. Vicki J. Rosser and Celeste M. Calkins, "ESPs: Employment and Living Wage Update," *NEA 2017 Almanac of Higher Education*, 10.

7. College and University Professionals Association for Human Resources, "The CUPA-HR Staff in Higher Education Salary Survey," 2018, www.cupahr.org /surveys/results/staff-in-higher-education; Rosser, "Education Support Professionals," 126.

8. CUPA-HR, "The CUPA-HR Staff"; Rosser, "Education Support Professionals"; Rosser and Calkins, "ESPs."

9. Rosser, "Education Support Professionals." There are minor variation in pay by staff group. Service and skilled craftsperson salaries range from $14,000 to $20,000 on average with some maintenance roles paying as high as $32,000.

10. Rosser, "Education Support Professionals"; Valerie Martin Conley, "Retirement and Benefits: One Size Does Not Fit All," *NEA 2017 Almanac of Higher Education*, 12.

11. Mary F. Bushman and John E. Dean, "Outsourcing of Non-Mission-Critical Functions: A Solution to the Rising Cost of College Attendance," Collegecosts.info, 2005, 14; CUPA-HR, "The CUPA-HR Staff."

12. Linda K. Johnsrud and Vicki J. Rosser, "Faculty Members' Morale and Their Intention to Leave," *The Journal of Higher Education* 73, no. 4 (July 1, 2002): 518–42, https://doi.org/10.1080/00221546.2002.11777162; Linda K. Johnsrud, "The Worklife Issues of Higher Education Support Personnel," *NEA 1999 Almanac of Higher Education*, 14; Johnsrud, "Higher Education Support Professionals: Demographics and Worklife Issues," *NEA 2004 Almanac of Higher Education*, 22.

13. Vicki J. Rosser, "Support Professionals: The Key Issues Survey," *NEA 2009 Almanac of Higher Education*, 6; Magolda, *The Lives of Campus Custodians*; Rosser, "Education Support Professionals."

14. Rosser, "Support Professionals."

15. Johnsrud and Rosser, "Faculty Members' Morale."

16. Rosser, "Education Support Professionals"; Magolda, *The Lives of Campus Custodians*.

17. American Association of University Professors, "Visualizing Change: Report on the Economic Status of the Profession," *Academe*, 2017; US Government Accountability Office, "Contingent Workforce: Size, Characteristics, Compensation, and Work Experiences of Adjunct and Other Non-Tenure-Track Faculty," November 20, 2017, www.gao.gov/products/GAO-18-49; Steve Street, Maria Maisto, Esther Merves, and Gary Rhoades, "Who Is Professor 'Staff,' And How Can This Person Teach so Many Classes?" Center for the Future of Higher Education Policy, 2012; Roger G. Baldwin and Jay L. Chronister, *Teaching without Tenure: Policies and Practices for a New Era* (Baltimore: Johns Hopkins Univer-

sity Press, 2001); Gary Rhoades and Christine Maitland, "Bargaining for Full-Time, Non-Tenure Track Faculty: Best Practices," *NEA 2008 Almanac of Higher Education*, 7; Adrianna Kezar and Cecelia Sam, "Understanding the New Majority of Non-Tenure-Track Faculty in Higher Education—Demographics, Experiences, and Plans of Action," Association for the Study of Higher Education, 2010, http://doi.wiley.com/10.1002/aehe.3604; New Faculty Majority, "Can Adjuncts Collect Unemployment Compensation between Terms?," 2017, www.new facultymajority.info/faqs-frequently-asked-questions/can-adjuncts-collect -unemployment-compensation-between-terms; Coalition for the Academic Workforce. "One Faculty Serving All Students" (New Faculty Majority, 2010); Martin J. Finkelstein, Valerie Martin Conley, and Jack H. Schuster, *The Faculty Factor: Reassessing the American Academy in a Turbulent Era* (Baltimore: Johns Hopkins University Press, 2016).

18. Coalition for the Academic Workforce, "One Faculty"; Dan Edmonds, "More Than Half of College Faculty Are Adjuncts: Should You Care?," *Forbes*, May 28, 2015, www.forbes.com/sites/noodleeducation/2015/05/28/more-than -half-of-college-faculty-are-adjuncts-should-you-care/; Jack H. Schuster and Martin J. Finkelstein, *The American Faculty: The Restructuring of Academic Work and Careers* (Baltimore: Johns Hopkins University Press, 2006). We dislike the use of the term "adjunct," which means not essential. We believe these instructors are essential to higher education and chose to call them "contingent" instead. Kezar and Sam ("Understanding the New Majority") argued that all faculty should just be called faculty, as these different labels only serve to create hierarchies and divisions that serve neither individuals nor the campuses where they are employed.

19. Schuster and Finkelstein, *The American Faculty*; American Federation of Teachers, *American Academic: The State of the Higher Education Workforce* (Washington, DC: American Federation of Teachers, 2009); American Association of University Professors, "Visualizing Change."

20. John W. Curtis, "Inequities Persist for Women and Non-Tenure-Track Faculty: Economic Status of the Profession, 2004–05," *Academe* 91, no. 2 (2005): 19–98, https://doi.org/10.2307/40253410; Robert K. Toutkoushian and Marcia L. Bellas, "The Effects of Part-Time Employment and Gender on Faculty Earnings and Satisfaction," *The Journal of Higher Education* 74, no. 2 (March 1, 2003): 172–95, https://doi.org/10.1080/00221546.2003.11777195; Coalition for the Academic Workforce, "One Faculty"; Eugene L. Anderson, *The New Professoriate: Characteristics, Contributions, and Compensation* (Washington, DC: Center for Policy Analysis, American Council on Education. 2002), https://eric.ed.gov/?id =ED478300; CUPA-HR, "Representation and Pay of Women of Color in the Higher Education Workforce," 2018; C. Hollenshead, J. Waltman, L. August, L. Miller, G. Smith, and A. Bell, *Making the Best of Both Worlds: Findings from a*

National Institution-Level Survey on Non-Tenure-Track Faculty (Ann Arbor, MI: Center for the Education of Women, 2007).

21. Coalition for the Academic Workforce, "One Faculty"; Gappa and Leslie, *The Invisible Faculty*.

22. Gappa and Leslie, *The Invisible Faculty*; Hollenshead et al., *Making the Best*; Adrianna J. Kezar, "Examining Non-Tenure Track Faculty Perceptions of How Departmental Policies and Practices Shape Their Performance and Ability to Create Student Learning at Four-Year Institutions," *Research in Higher Education* 54, no. 5 (August 1, 2013): 571–98, https://doi.org/10/f4573b.

23. Valerie Martin Conley and David W. Leslie, "Part-Time Instructional Faculty and Staff: Who They Are, What They Do, and What They Think," *1993 National Study of Postsecondary Faculty*, https://eric.ed.gov/?id=ED464527; Gappa and Leslie, *The Invisible Faculty*; C. Outcalt, *A Profile of the Community College Professoriate, 1975–2000* (New York: Routledge, 2002); Baldwin and Chronister, *Teaching without Tenure*; Kezar and Sam, "Understanding the New Majority."

24. Colleeen Flaherty, "Colleges Assign Adjunct Hiring to a Third Party," *Inside Higher Ed*, July 21, 2014, www.insidehighered.com/news/2014/07/21/colleges-assign-adjunct-hiring-third-party; Rachel Ohm, "University of Tennessee Campuses Will Not Outsource Facilities Jobs," *Knoxville News Sentinel*, October 31, 2017, www.knoxnews.com/story/news/education/2017/10/31/university-tennessee-knoxville-not-outsource-facilities-jobs/816760001/.

25. Kevin Kiley, "Should Online Teaching Be Outsourced?," Online Learning Update, 2011, http://people.uis.edu/rschr1/onlinelearning/?p=2551; Alene Russell, "Outsourcing Instruction: Issues for Public Colleges and Universities," American Association of State Colleges and Universities, 2010, https://eric.ed.gov/?id=ED512015; Staff, "Purdue's Kaplan Deal Receives HLC Approval," *WLFI News*, 2018 www.wlfi.com/content/news/Purdue-University-receives-HLC-approval-for-Purdue-Global-475868393.html; Goldie Blumenstyk, "Purdue's Purchase of Kaplan Is a Big Bet—and a Sign of the Times," *The Chronicle of Higher Education*, April 28, 2017, www.chronicle.com/article/Purdue-s-Purchase-of-Kaplan/239931; Jillian Berman, "Why Mainstream Public University Purdue Is Buying For-Profit College Chain Kaplan," *MarketWatch*, April 27, 2017. www.marketwatch.com/story/a-prestigious-public-university-wants-to-acquire-this-for-profit-college-chain-2017-04-27.

26. Hollenshead et al., *Making the Best*; Baldwin and Chronister, *Teaching without Tenure*.

27. Rebecca Burns, "Adjunct Instructor: 'I Was Practically Giving My Work Away. It Was Charity,'" *Working In These Times*, October 15, 2014; Colleen Flaherty, "AAUP Report Says Adjunct Professor Was Likely Fired for Insisting on

Rigor in Courses," *Inside Higher Ed*, March 29, 2017, www.insidehighered.com /news/2017/03/29/aaup-report-says-adjunct-professor-was-likely-fired-insisting -rigor-courses; Peter N. Kirstein, "Seventh Circuit Protects Part-Time Faculty Union Leader, Robin Meade," *Academe Blog*, November 4, 2014, https:// academeblog.org/2014/11/04/seventh-circuit-protects-part-time-faculty-union -leader-robin-meade/; David M. Perry, "Why Can't 'Free Speech' Advocates Ever Defend Adjunct Professors and People of Color?," *Pacific Standard*, 2017, https:// psmag.com/education/when-will-you-defend-left-wing-free-speech; Baldwin and Chronister, *Teaching without Tenure*.

28. Kezar and Sam, "Understanding the New Majority."

29. Lydia Pleotis Howell, Chao-Yin Chen, Jesse P. Joad, Ralph Green, Edward J. Callahan, and Ann C. Bonham, "Issues and Challenges of Non-Tenure-Track Research Faculty: The UC Davis School of Medicine Experience," *Academic Medicine* 85, no. 6 (June 2010): 1041, https://doi.org/10.1097/ACM.0b013e3181dbfbf3; Inger Bergom, Jean Waltman, Louise August, and Carol Hollenshead, "Academic Researchers Speak," *Change: The Magazine of Higher Learning* 42, no. 2 (February 26, 2010): 45–49, https://doi.org/10.1080/00091380903562987.

30. Bergom et al. "Academic Researchers Speak."

31. "Salary: Research Faculty," Glassdoor, 2018, www.glassdoor.com/Salaries /research-faculty-salary-SRCH_KO0,16.htm.

32. Bergom et al., "Academic Researchers Speak."

33. Bergom et al., "Academic Researchers Speak."

34. Bergom et al., "Academic Researchers Speak."

35. Bergom et al., "Academic Researchers Speak"; Baldwin and Chronister, *Teaching without Tenure*.

36. National Academy of Sciences, *The Postdoctoral Experience Revisited* (Washington, DC: National Academies Press, 2014), https://doi.org/10.17226 /18982.

37. National Science Board, "Science and Engineering Indicators" (Arlington, VA: National Science Foundation, 2010), 566; Brendan Cantwell, "Are International Students Cash Cows? Examining the Relationship Between New International Undergraduate Enrollments and Institutional Revenue at Public Colleges and Universities in the US" *Journal of International Students* 5, no. 4 (2015): 14; National Academy of Sciences, *The Postdoctoral Experience Revisited*; Kendall Powell, "The Future of the Postdoc," *Nature News* 520, no. 7546 (April 9, 2015): 144, https://doi.org/10.1038/520144a; Paula Stephan, *How Economics Shapes Science* (Cambridge, MA: Harvard University Press, 2012); Jennifer M. Miller and Maryann P. Feldman, "The Sorcerer's Postdoc Apprentice: Uncertain Funding and Contingent Highly Skilled Labour," *Cambridge Journal of Regions, Economy and Society* 7, no. 2 (July 1, 2014): 289–305, https://doi.org/10.1093/cjres/rsu003.

38. Powell, "The Future of the Postdoc."

39. Powell, "The Future of the Postdoc"; Stephan, *How Economics Shapes Science*.

40. National Academy of Sciences, *The Postdoctoral Experience Revisited*; Stephan, *How Economics Shapes Science*; Paula Stephan, "How to Exploit Postdocs," *BioScience* 63, no. 4 (April 1, 2013): 245–46, https://doi.org/10.1525/bio.2013.63.4.2.

41. National Academy of Sciences, *The Postdoctoral Experience Revisited*; Brendan Cantwell and Barrett J. Taylor, "Internationalization of the Postdoctorate in the United States: Analyzing the Demand for International Postdoc Labor," *Higher Education* 66, no. 5 (November 1, 2013): 551–67, https://doi.org/10.1007/s10734-013-9621-0.

42. Audrey J. Jaeger and Alessandra J. Dinin, eds., *The Postdoc Landscape: The Invisible Scholars* (London: Academic Press, 2018); College and University Professionals Association for Human Resources, "The CUPA-HR Four-Year Faculty in Higher Education Salary Survey," 2018, www.cupahr.org/surveys/results/faculty-in-higher-education.

43. Jaeger and Dinin, *The Postdoc Landscape*.

44. Jenny J. Lee and Brendan Cantwell, "The Global Sorting Machine: An Examination of Neoracism among International Students and Postdoctoral Researchers," *Universities and the Public Sphere: Knowledge Creation and State Building in the Era of Globalization*, January 1, 2012, 47–63, https://doi.org/10.4324/9780203847848; Cantwell and Lee, "Unseen Workers in the Academic Factory: Perceptions of Neoracism among International Postdocs in the United States and the United Kingdom," *Harvard Educational Review* 80, no. 4 (December 1, 2010): 490–517, https://doi.org/10.17763/haer.80.4.w54750105q78p451.

45. Kryste Ferguson, Michael McTighe, Bhishma Amlani, and Tracy Costello, *Supporting the Needs of Postdocs* (Rockville, MD: National Postdoctoral Association, 2017), 18.

46. Mary Ann Mason, Marc Goulden, and Karie Frasch, "Why Graduate Students Reject the Fast Track," *Academe* 95 (2009): 1, www.aaup.org/article/why-graduate-students-reject-fast-track; Jessica Lee, Joan C. Williams, and Su Li, *Parents in the Pipeline: Retaining Postdoctoral Researchers and Families* (San Francisco: The Center for WorkLife Law, 2017).

47. Jaeger and Dinin, *The Postdoc Landscape*.

48. National Academy of Sciences, *The Postdoctoral Experience Revisited*.

49. Teresa Kroeger, Celine McNicholas, Marni von Wilpert, and Julia Wolfe, "The State of Graduate Student Employee Unions: Momentum to Organize among Graduate Student Workers Is Growing despite Opposition," *Economic Policy Institute*, January 11, 2018, www.epi.org/publication/graduate-student-employee

-unions; US Bureau of Labor Statistics. "Occupational Employment and Wages, May 2017," www.bls.gov/oes/current/oes251191.htm; American Association of University Professors, "Visualizing Change." GAs in public universities are covered by state laws, many of which have enabled unionization. GAs in private universities are covered by the NLRA.

50. US Bureau of Labor Statistics, "Occupational Employment and Wages"; Bousquet, *How the University Works*; Robert A. Rhoads and Gary Rhoades, "Graduate Employee Unionization as Symbol of and Challenge to the Corporatization of US Research Universities," *The Journal of Higher Education* 76, no. 3 (May 1, 2005): 243–75, https://doi.org/10.1080/00221546.2005.11772282; National Center for Education Statistics [NCES], "IPEDS 2018–2019 Glossary," National Center for Education Statistics, 2018.

51. Kroeger et al., "The State of Graduate Student Employee Unions"; Deeb-Paul Kitchen, "Can Graduate Students Re-Energize the Labor Movement?," *Thought & Action*, Fall 2014.

52. Marc Bousquet, "The Waste Product of Graduate Education: Toward a Dictatorship of the Flexible," *Social Text* 20, no. 1 (March 1, 2002): 81–104.

53. Bousquet, "The Waste Product of Graduate Education"; Bousquet, *How the University Works*; Bousquet, "A Ph.D. Should Result in a Tenure-Track Job, Not an Alt-Ac One," *Inside Higher Education*, 2015, www.insidehighered.com/views/2015/10/20/phd-should-result-tenure-track-job-not-alt-ac-one-essay.

54. Chris M. Golde, "The Role of the Department and Discipline in Doctoral Student Attrition: Lessons from Four Departments," *The Journal of Higher Education* 76, no. 6 (November 1, 2005): 669–700, https://doi.org/10.1080/00221546.2005.11772304; Rodney T. Hartnett and Joseph Katz, "The Education of Graduate Students," *The Journal of Higher Education* 48, no. 6 (November 1, 1977): 646–64, https://doi.org/10.1080/00221546.1977.11776583.

55. Evelynn M. Ellis, "The Impact of Race and Gender on Graduate School Socialization, Satisfaction with Doctoral Study, and Commitment to Degree Completion," *Western Journal of Black Studies* 25, no. 1 (Spring 2001): 30–45; Maria Ferreira, "Gender Issues Related to Graduate Student Attrition in Two Science Departments," *International Journal of Science Education* 25, no. 8 (August 1, 2003): 969–89, https://doi.org/10.1080/09500690305026; Chance W. Lewis, Rick Ginsberg, and Tim Davies, "The Experiences of African American PhD Students at a Predominantly White Carnegie I - Research Institution," in *Eighth Annual National Conference*, POCPWI (2003), 100–102, 4; R. Sowell, T. Zhang, K. Redd, and M. King, *PhD Completion and Attrition: Analysis of Baseline Program Data from the PhD Completion Project* (Washington, DC: Council of Graduate Schools, 2008); Scott Jaschik, "The Shrinking Phd Job Market," *Inside Higher Ed*, April 4,

2016, www.insidehighered.com/news/2016/04/04/new-data-show-tightening-phd -job-market-across-disciplines.

56. Joan C. Williams, Katherine W. Phillips, and Erika V. Hall. "Double Jeopardy? Gender Bias Against Women of Color in Science," UC Hastings College of Law, 2014.

57. American College Health Association, *American College Health Association-National College Health Assessment II: Reference Group Graduates Executive Summary Fall 2017* (Hanover, MD: American College Health Association, 2017); Stephen Stansfeld and Bridget Candy, "Psychosocial Work Environment and Mental Health—a Meta-analytic Review," *Scandinavian Journal of Work, Environment & Health* 32, no. 6 (2006): 443–62; Teresa M. Evans, Lindsay Bira, Jazmin Beltran Gastelum, L. Todd Weiss, and Nathan L. Vanderford, "Evidence for a Mental Health Crisis in Graduate Education," Comments and Opinion, *Nature Biotechnology*, March 6, 2018, https://doi.org/10.1038/nbt.4089; Peter Schmidt, "New Insights on What Psychologically Rattles Graduate Students," *The Chronicle of Higher Education*, November 12, 2016, www.chronicle.com/article/New -Insights-on-What/238399; Julie Posselt, "Normalizing Struggle: Dimensions of Faculty Support for Doctoral Students and Implications for Persistence and Well-Being," *The Journal of Higher Education* 89, no. 6 (2018): 1–26, https://doi.org /10.1080/00221546.2018.1449080; UC Berkeley Graduate Assembly, *Graduate Student Happiness & Well-Being Report* (Berkeley: UC Berkeley Graduate Assembly, 2014); Katia Levecque, Frederik Anseel, Alain De Beuckelaer, Johan Van der Heyden, and Lydia Gisle, "Work Organization and Mental Health Problems in PhD Students," *Research Policy* 46, no. 4 (May 1, 2017): 868–79, https://doi.org /10.1016/j.respol.2017.02.008.

58. Stansfeld and Candy, "Psychosocial Work Environment"; American College Health Association, "National College Health Assessment II"; Kay Devine and Karen H. Hunter, "PhD Student Emotional Exhaustion: The Role of Supportive Supervision and Self-Presentation Behaviours," *Innovations in Education and Teaching International* 54, no. 4 (July 4, 2017): 335–44, https://doi.org/10.1080 /14703297.2016.1174143; Gretchen M. Reevy and Grace Deason, "Predictors of Depression, Stress, and Anxiety among Non-Tenure Track Faculty," *Frontiers in Psychology* 5 (2014), https://doi.org/10.3389/fpsyg.2014.00701; Barry Chametzky, "Surviving Situational Suffering: A Classic Grounded Theory Study of Post-Secondary Part-Time Educators in the United States," *Grounded Theory Review* 14, no. 1 (2015): 15; Brooks Robert Harbison, "Stress in Tenure-Track and Non-Tenure-Track Faculty: What We Know and Where We Are Going" (master's thesis, The University of Texas at Austin, 2016), https://doi.org/10.15781 /T2MC8RK06; Miguel A. Padilla and Julia N. Thompson, "Burning Out Faculty at Doctoral Research Universities," *Stress and Health: Journal of the International*

Society for the Investigation of Stress 32, no. 5 (December 2016): 551–58, https://doi.org/10.1002/smi.2661.

59. Mark Huelsman, *The Debt Divide: The Racial and Class Bias Behind the "New Normal" of Student Borrowing* (New York: Demos, 2015); Fenaba R. Addo, Jason N. Houle, and Daniel Simon, "Young, Black, and (Still) in the Red: Parental Wealth, Race, and Student Loan Debt," *Race and Social Problems* 8, no. 1 (March 1, 2016): 64–76, https://doi.org/10.1007/s12552-016-9162-0; Judith Scott-Clayton and Jing Li, *Black-White Disparity in Student Loan Debt More Than Triples after Graduation* (Washington, DC: Brookings Institution, 2016); Kroeger et al., "The State of Graduate Student Employee Unions."

60. CUPA-HR, "The CUPA-HR Staff in Higher Education Salary Survey."

61. CUPA-HR, "The CUPA-HR Staff in Higher Education Salary Survey"; Tom Slee, *What's Yours Is Mine: Against the Sharing Economy* (London: Scribe UK, 2015).

62. Donna M. Desrochers and Rita Kirshstein, *Labor Intensive or Labor Expensive? Changing Staffing and Compensation Patterns in Higher Education*, Issue Brief (Washington, DC: Delta Cost Project at American Institutes for Research, 2014, https://eric.ed.gov/?id=ED558470.

63. David Graeber, "Are You in a BS Job? In Academe, You're Hardly Alone," *The Chronicle of Higher Education*, May 6, 2018, www.chronicle.com/article/Are-You-in-a-BS-Job-In/243318.

64. Benjamin Ginsberg, *The Fall of the Faculty* (New York: Oxford University Press, 2011); Graeber, "Are You in a BS Job?"

65. CUPA-HR, "The CUPA-HR Staff in Higher Education Salary Survey."

66. Graeber, "Are You in a BS Job?"; Steven Hurlburt and Michael McGarrah, *Cost Savings or Cost Shifting? The Relationship between Part-Time Contingent Faculty and Institutional Spending* (New York: TIAA Institute, 2016).

67. Hurlburt and McGarrah, *Cost Savings or Cost Shifting?*

68. Desrochers and Kirshstein, *Labor Intensive or Labor Expensive?*

69. Desrochers and Kirshstein, *Labor Intensive or Labor Expensive?*

70. Desrochers and Kirshstein, *Labor Intensive or Labor Expensive?*

71. CUPA-HR, "The CUPA-HR Staff in Higher Education Salary Survey"; D. Bauman, T. Davis, and Brian O'Leary, "Executive Compensation at Private and Public Colleges," *The Chronicle of Higher Education*, July 15, 2018, www.chronicle.com/interactives/executive-compensation.

72. Bauman et al., "Executive Compensation"; CUPA-HR, "The CUPA-HR Staff in Higher Education Salary Survey"; Rosser and Calkins, "ESPs."

73. Ginsberg, *The Fall of the Faculty*; Bryan J. Cook, "The American College President Study: Key Findings and Takeaways," American Council on Education, 2012, www.acenet.edu/the-presidency/columns-and-features/Pages/The-American

-College-President-Study.aspx; Jonathan S. Gagliardi, Lorelle L. Espinosa, Jonathan M. Turk, and Morgan Taylor, "American College President Study 2017," American Council on Education, 2017.

74. Jon Marcus, "University Bureaucracies Grew 15 Percent during the Recession, Even as Budgets Were Cut and Tuition Increased," *The Hechinger Report*, October 6, 2016, https://hechingerreport.org/university-bureaucracies-grew-15-percent-recession-even-budgets-cut-tuition-increased/.

75. E. E. Cummings and M. Grijalva, "Cummings, Grijalva Support Recommendations to Increase Transparency of Spending by For-Profit Colleges," press release, December 7, 2012, https://democrats-oversight.house.gov/news/press-releases/cummings-grijalva-support-recommendations-to-increase-transparency-of-spending.

76. Henry Lee Allen, "Faculty Workload and Productivity In For-Profit Institutions: The Good, the Bad, and the Ugly," *The 2013 NEA Almanac*, 11; Shelly K. Schwartz, "Pay for CEOs of For-Profit Colleges Top of the Class," CNBC, December 21, 2010, www.cnbc.com/id/40680879.

Three: Disintegrating Relationships and the Demise of Community

1. Sheila Slaughter and Larry L. Leslie, *Academic Capitalism: Politics, Policies, and the Entrepreneurial University* (Baltimore: Johns Hopkins University Press, 1999).

2. The past vision of a community of scholars was never inclusive and largely excluded woman and faculty of color. These foundations of exclusivity were built upon through the neoliberal logic.

3. Sheila Slaughter and Gary Rhoades, *Academic Capitalism and the New Economy: Markets, State, and Higher Education* (Baltimore: Johns Hopkins University Press, 2004).

4. Gary Rhoades, *Managed Professionals: Unionized Faculty and Restructuring Academic Labor* (Albany: State University of New York Press, 1998).

5. Clyde W. Barrow, "The Rationality Crisis in US Higher Education," *New Political Science* 32, no. 3 (September 1, 2010), 321.

6. Karen Thompson, "Contingent Faculty and Student Learning: Welcome to the Strativersity," *New Directions for Higher Education* 2003, no. 123 (2003): 41–47, https://doi.org/10.1002/he.119.

7. David Weil, *The Fissured Workplace* (Cambridge, MA: Harvard University Press, 2014).

8. Slaughter and Rhoades, *Academic Capitalism and the New Economy*.

9. James C. Hearn, Darrell R. Lewis, Lincoln Kallsen, Janet M. Holdsworth, and Lisa M. Jones, "'Incentives for Managed Growth': A Case Study of Incentives-

Based Planning and Budgeting in a Large Public Research University," *The Journal of Higher Education* 77, no. 2 (March 1, 2006): 286–316, https://doi.org/10.1080/00221546.2006.11778927. RCB involves each academic unit carrying its own costs and bringing in its own revenue. Academic unit leaders share a small portion of the revenue they generate to cover institutional overhead. Revenue that an academic unit generates from teaching, research, and extramural activities in excess of its expenses and the relatively small share distributed to the central administration remains with the unit to reinvest in its mission. Significant authority for managing the academic enterprise is shifted to deans and other academic unit leaders at RCB institutions.

10. Stephen Watt, "The Humanities, RCM, and Bullshit," *Western Humanities Review* 65, no. 3 (Fall 2011): 66–86.

11. Goldie Blumenstyk, "Apps Can Help Advise First-Generation Students. But It Takes a Human to Say, 'I Believe in You.'" *The Chronicle of Higher Education*, July 9, 2018, www.chronicle.com/article/Apps-Can-Help-Advise/243876; Beth Mcmurtrie, "How Artificial Intelligence Is Changing Teaching," *The Chronicle of Higher Education*, August 12, 2018, www.chronicle.com/article/How-Artificial-Intelligence-Is/244231.

12. Beth Mcmurtrie, "How Artificial Intelligence Is Changing Teaching," *The Chronicle of Higher Education*, August 12, 2018, www.chronicle.com/article/How-Artificial-Intelligence-Is/244231.

13. Slaughter and Rhoades, *Academic Capitalism and the New Economy*; Larry G. Gerber, *The Rise and Decline of Faculty Governance: Professionalization and the Modern American University* (Baltimore: John Hopkins University Press, 2014); Mary Burgan, *What Ever Happened to the Faculty? Drift and Decision in Higher Education* (Baltimore: Johns Hopkins University Press, 2006).

14. Gerber, *The Rise and Decline of Faculty Governance*; Burgan, *What Ever Happened to the Faculty?;* Adrianna Kezar, "Examining Non-Tenure Track Faculty Perceptions of How Departmental Policies and Practices Shape Their Performance and Ability to Create Student Learning at Four-Year Institutions," *Research in Higher Education* 54, no. 5 (August 1, 2013): 571–98, https://doi.org/10/f4573b; Adrianna Kezar and Sean Gehrke, "Grassroots Leadership: Responding to Declining Shared Governance in the Neoliberal World," in *Survival of the Fittest: The Shifting Contours of Higher Education in China and the United States*, edited by Qi Li and Cynthia Gerstl-Pepin, 101–17 (Berlin: Springer Berlin Heidelberg, 2014), https://doi.org/10.1007/978-3-642-39813-1_8.

15. Rhoades, *Managed Professionals*; Kezar and Gehrke, "Grassroots Leadership"; Teresa A. Sullivan, "Professional Control in the Complex University: Maintaining the Faculty Role," in *The American Academic Profession: Transformation in Contemporary Higher Education*, edited by Joseph C. Hermanowitz

(Baltimore: Johns Hopkins University Press, 2011); Robert Birnbaum, "The End of Shared Governance: Looking Ahead or Looking Back," *New Directions for Higher Education* 2004, no. 127 (2004): 5–22, https://doi.org/10.1002/he.152.

16. Gerber, *The Rise and Decline of Faculty Governance*; Jack H. Schuster and Martin J. Finkelstein, *The American Faculty: The Restructuring of Academic Work and Careers* (Baltimore: Johns Hopkins University Press, 2006).

17. Rhoades, *Managed Professionals*; Slaughter and Rhoades, *Academic Capitalism and the New Economy*; Gerber, *The Rise and Decline of Faculty Governance*; Burgan, *What Ever Happened to the Faculty?*; Association of Governing Boards, "AGB Board of Directors' Statement on Shared Governance," Association of Governing Boards, October 10, 2017, www.agb.org/statements/2017-1010/agb-board-of-directors-statement-on-shared-governance.

18. Barrow, "The Rationality Crisis in US Higher Education."

19. Wayne Carr Willis, "Empire State College and the Conflicted Legacy of Progressive Higher Education," in *Principles, Practices, and Creative Tensions in Progressive Higher Education: One Institution's Struggle to Sustain a Vision*, edited by Katherine Jelly and Alan Mandell, 29–42 (Rotterdam: SensePublishers, 2017), https://doi.org/10.1007/978-94-6300-884-6_2; Gordon Lafer, "Graduate Student Unions: Organizing in a Changed Academic Economy," *Labor Studies Journal* 28, no. 2 (June 1, 2003): 25–43, https://doi.org/10.1177/0160449X03028 00202.

20. Timothy K. Garfield, "Governance in a Union Environment," *New Directions for Community Colleges* 2008, no. 141 (2008): 25–33, https://doi.org/10.1002/cc.312.

21. Linda Evans, "Professionalism, Professionality and the Development of Education Professionals," *British Journal of Educational Studies* 56, no. 1 (March 1, 2008): 20–38, https://doi.org/10.1111/j.1467-8527.2007.00392.x; Christian Schneijderberg and Nadine Merkator, "The New Higher Education Professionals," in *The Academic Profession in Europe: New Tasks and New Challenges*, edited by Barbara M. Kehm and Ulrich Teichler, 53–92 (Dordrecht: Springer Netherlands, 2013), https://doi.org/10.1007/978-94-007-4614-5_5.

22. Celia Whitechurch, *Reconstructing Identities in Higher Education: The Rise of Third Space Professionals* (New York: Routledge, 2013).

23. Vicki J. Rosser, "Support Professionals: The Key Issues Survey," *NEA 2009 Almanac of Higher Education*, 6; Peter M. Magolda, *The Lives of Campus Custodians: Insights into Corporatization and Civic Disengagement in the Academy* (Sterling, VA: Stylus Publishing, 2016); Samantha Jane Armstrong Ash, "Student Affairs Support Staff: Empowered and Invisible" (PhD diss., Washington State University, 2013), http://search.proquest.com/docview/1502024967/abstract/A4E91723D0AF45EBPQ/1.

24. Judith M. Gappa, *The Invisible Faculty: Improving the Status of Part-Timers in Higher Education* (San Francisco: Jossey-Bass, 1993); Adrianna Kezar and Cecelia Sam, "Understanding the New Majority of Non-Tenure-Track Faculty in Higher Education—Demographics, Experiences, and Plans of Action," Association for the Study of Higher Education, 2010, http://doi.wiley.com/10.1002/aehe .3604; Daniel C. Feldman and William H. Turnley, "A Field Study of Adjunct Faculty: The Impact of Career Stage on Reactions to Non-Tenure-Track Jobs," *Journal of Career Development* 28, no. 1 (September 1, 2001): 1–16, https://doi.org /10.1177/0894845301028000101; Adrianna J. Kezar, "Departmental Cultures and Non-Tenure-Track Faculty: Willingness, Capacity, and Opportunity to Perform at Four-Year Institutions," *The Journal of Higher Education* 84, no. 2 (March 2013): 153–88, https://doi.org/10.1080/00221546.2013.11777284; Jean Waltman, Inger Bergom, Carol Hollenshead, Jeanne Miller, and Louise August, "Factors Contributing to Job Satisfaction and Dissatisfaction among Non-Tenure-Track Faculty," *The Journal of Higher Education* 83, no. 3 (May 1, 2012): 411–34, https://doi.org /10.1080/00221546.2012.11777250; Barbara K. Townsend, "Community College Organizational Climate for Minorities and Women," *Community College Journal of Research and Practice* 33, no. 9 (August 3, 2009): 731–44, https://doi.org/10 .1080/10668920903022458.

25. Inger Bergom, Jean Waltman, Louise August, and Carol Hollenshead, "Academic Researchers Speak," *Change: The Magazine of Higher Learning* 42, no. 2 (February 26, 2010): 45–49, https://doi.org/10.1080/00091380903562987.

26. Audrey J. Jaeger and Alessandra J. Dinin, *The Postdoc Landscape: The Invisible Scholars* (London: Academic Press, 2018); Patricia Hinchey and Isabel Kimmel, *The Graduate Grind* (New York: Falmer Press, 2000).

27. Gallup, "The Engaged University," Gallup.com, www.gallup.com/education /194321/higher-education-employee-engagement.aspx; Julie Ray and Stephanie Kafka, "Life in College Matters for Life after College," Gallup, 2014, https://news .gallup.com/poll/168848/life-college-matters-life-college.aspx. One could be suspicious of Gallup's motives to garner business opportunities rather than to help higher education. Yet their data do point out a key problem.

28. Michael Smilowitz, *Report of the Faculty Senate's 2013 Faculty Job Satisfaction Survey: Quantitative Analysis* (Harrisonburg, VA: James Madison University, 2013), www.jmu.edu/facultysenate/_files/notes/2013-09-18-faculty-satisfaction-survey.pdf; UIS Campus Planning and Budget Committee, *UIS Faculty Satisfaction Survey Report* (University of Illinois at Springfield, 2004), www.uis .edu/accreditation/wp-content/uploads/sites/23/2013/04/CPBCFacultySatisfactio nSurvey2004.pdf; COACHE, "UW Tacoma COACHE Report," COACHE, 2013, www.tacoma.uw.edu/sites/default/files/users/mcrosby/coache_provost_re port_universityofwashingtontacoma.pdf.

29. One national survey is the "Higher Education Insight Survey," which consists of approximately ninety items measuring faculty and staff satisfaction. Campuses can also obtain benchmarking data that allow institutions to see how employees' responses compare to those at other institutions. Another example is the "College Employee Satisfaction Survey" that features seventy items in five different areas: *Campus culture and policies*—employees rate their "importance and satisfaction" levels regarding various issues including employee training and recognition, pride in their work, departmental communication, and budgets and human resources, among other topics. *Institutional goals*—survey respondents rate the importance of different institutional goals such as staff morale, diversity efforts, and staff retention. The survey also asks respondents to rank the three goals, which should constitute the top three campus priorities. *Involvement in planning and decision-making*—survey respondents rate the level of involvement various campus constituents have in the decision-making process, from "not enough involvement to too much involvement." *Work environment*—respondents are asked to rate the importance of and their satisfaction with issues such as "employee empowerment," "supervisor relationships," "professional development," and "fulfillment and job satisfaction." These are all areas that for the last two decades, administrative leaders have routinely been eroding on campuses, with faculty and staff having less decision-making and input, more control and less empowerment, fewer opportunities for professional development and advancement, less resources and compensation, and poor relationships between employees and supervisors.

30. Leila Meyer, "Report: Higher Ed Neglecting Employee Engagement," *Campus Technology*, September 22, 2016, https://campustechnology.com/articles /2016/09/22/report-higher-ed-neglecting-employee-engagement.aspx; Cornerstone OnDemand and Ellucian, "Empowering Employees: The State of Employee Engagement and Retention in Higher Education," Ellucian, 2016; Ronald G. Ehrenberg and Liang Zhang, "Do Tenured and Tenure-Track Faculty Matter?," *The Journal of Human Resources* 40, no. 3 (2005): 647–59; Ronald Ehrenberg, Hirschel Kasper, and Daniel Rees, "Faculty Turnover at American Colleges and Universities: Analyses of AAUP Data," *Economics of Education Review* 10, no. 2 (January 1, 1991): 99–110, https://doi.org/10.1016/0272-7757(91)90002-7; CUPA-HR, "The CUPA-HR Four-Year Faculty in Higher Education Salary Survey," 2018, www.cupahr.org/surveys/results/faculty-in-higher-education; CUPA-HR, "The CUPA-HR Staff in Higher Education Salary Survey," 2018, www.cupahr.org /surveys/results/staff-in-higher-education.

31. Meyer, "Report"; Cornerstone OnDemand and Ellucian, "Empowering Employees."

Four: How Employment Practices Negatively Impact Student Learning and Outcomes

1. Adrianna J. Kezar, "Obtaining Integrity? Reviewing and Examining the Charter between Higher Education and Society," *The Review of Higher Education* 27, no. 4 (2004): 429–59, https://doi.org/10.1353/rhe.2004.0013; Philo A. Hutcheson, "McCarthyism and the Professoriate: A Historiographic Nightmare?," in *Higher Education: Handbook of Theory and Research*, edited by J. C. Smart, vol. 12 (New York: Springer Science & Business Media, 1997); Adrianna Kezar, Anthony C. Chambers, and John C. Burkhardt, *Higher Education for the Public Good: Emerging Voices from a National Movement* (New York: Wiley, 2005).

2. Adrianna J. Kezar, "Departmental Cultures and Non-Tenure-Track Faculty: Willingness, Capacity, and Opportunity to Perform at Four-Year Institutions," *The Journal of Higher Education* 84, no. 2 (March 2013): 153–88, https://doi.org/10.1080/00221546.2013.11777284; Valerie Martin Conley and David W. Leslie, "Part-Time Instructional Faculty and Staff: Who They Are, What They Do, and What They Think," in *1993 National Study of Postsecondary Faculty*, https://eric.ed.gov/?id=ED464527; C. Outcalt, *A Profile of the Community College Professoriate, 1975–2000* (New York: Routledge, 2002); Judith M. Gappa, *The Invisible Faculty: Improving the Status of Part-Timers in Higher Education* (San Francisco: Jossey-Bass, 1993); Adrianna Kezar and Cecelia Sam, "Understanding the New Majority of Non-Tenure-Track Faculty in Higher Education—Demographics, Experiences, and Plans of Action," Association for the Study of Higher Education, 2010, http://doi.wiley.com/10.1002/aehe.3604; Paul D. Umbach, "How Effective Are They? Exploring the Impact of Contingent Faculty on Undergraduate Education," *The Review of Higher Education* 30, no. 2 (2007): 91–123, https://doi.org/10.1353/rhe.2006.0080.

3. Kezar, "Departmental Cultures and Non-Tenure-Track Faculty."

4. Barry J. Zimmerman, "Investigating Self-Regulation and Motivation: Historical Background, Methodological Developments, and Future Prospects," *American Educational Research Journal* 45, no. 1 (March 1, 2008): 166–83, https://doi.org/10.3102/0002831207312909; Gloria Crisp, "The Impact of Mentoring on the Success of Community College Students," *The Review of Higher Education* 34, no. 1 (2010): 39–60, https://doi.org/10.1353/rhe.2010.0003.

5. M. Kevin Eagan and Audrey J. Jaeger, "Effects of Exposure to Part-Time Faculty on Community College Transfer," *Research in Higher Education* 50, no. 2 (March 2009): 168–88, https://doi.org/10.1007/s11162-008-9113-8; Umbach, "How Effective Are They?"; Paul D. Umbach and Matthew R. Wawrzynski, "Faculty Do Matter: The Role of College Faculty in Student Learning and Engagement," *Research in Higher Education* 46, no. 2 (March 1, 2005): 153–84, https://doi.org

/10/fp6fnq; Ernst Benjamin, *Exploring the Role of Contingent Instructional Staff in Undergraduate Learning*, New Directions for Higher Education 123 (San Francisco: Jossey-Bass, 2003); Center for Community College Student Engagement, *Contingent Commitments: Bringing Parttime Faculty into Focus* (Austin: The University of Texas at Austin, Program in Higher Education Leadership, 2014); Audrey J. Jaeger and M. Kevin Eagan, "Unintended Consequences: Examining the Effect of Part-Time Faculty Members on Associate's Degree Completion," *Community College Review* 36, no. 3 (January 1, 2009): 167–94, https://doi.org/10 .1177/0091552108327070; Daniel Jacoby, "Effects of Part-Time Faculty Employment on Community College Graduation Rates," *Journal of Higher Education* 77, no. 6 (2006): 1081–1103; Ernest T. Pascarella and Patrick T. Terenzini, *How College Affects Students: A Third Decade of Research* (New York: Wiley, 2005); Matthew J. Mayhew, Alyssa N. Rockenbach, Nicholas A. Bowman, Tricia A. D. Seifert, and Gregory C. Wolniak, *How College Affects Students: 21st Century Evidence That Higher Education Works* (New York: Wiley, 2016).

6. Peter M. Magolda, *The Lives of Campus Custodians: Insights into Corporatization and Civic Disengagement in the Academy* (Sterling, VA: Stylus, 2016).

7. Adrianna Kezar, Daniel Maxey, and Laura Badke, *The Imperative for Change: Fostering Understanding of the Necessity of Changing Non-Tenure-Track Faculty Policies and Practices*, The Delphi Project on the Changing Faculty and Student Success, 2014, https://pullias.usc.edu/wp-content/uploads/2014/01 /IMPERATIVE-FOR-CHANGE_WEB-2014.pdf; Kezar and Sam, "Understanding Non-Tenure Track Faculty"; Adrianna J. Kezar and Tom DePaola, "Understanding the Need for Unions: Contingent Faculty Working Conditions and the Relationship to Student Learning," in *Professors in the Gig Economy: Unionizing Adjunct Faculty in America*, edited by Kim Tolley (Baltimore: Johns Hopkins University Press, 2018).

8. Kezar, "Departmental Cultures and Non-Tenure-Track Faculty"; Kezar, "Examining Non-Tenure Track Faculty Perceptions of How Departmental Policies and Practices Shape Their Performance and Ability to Create Student Learning at Four-Year Institutions," *Research in Higher Education* 54, no. 5 (August 1, 2013): 571–98, https://doi.org/10/f4573b; Roger G. Baldwin and Matthew R. Wawrzynski, "Contingent Faculty as Teachers: What We Know; What We Need to Know," *American Behavioral Scientist* 55, no. 11 (November 1, 2011): 1485–1509, https:// doi.org/10.1177/0002764211409194; Eagan and Jaeger, "Effects of Exposure to Part-Time Faculty on Community College Transfer"; Ronald Ehrenberg and Liang Zhang, "Do Tenured and Tenure-Track Faculty Matter?," *The Journal of Human Resources* 40, no. 3 (2005): 647–59.

9. Ronald G. Ehrenberg, *What's Happening to Public Higher Education? The Shifting Financial Burden* (Baltimore: Johns Hopkins University Press, 2007); Jae-

ger and Eagan, "Unintended Consequences"; Jacoby, "Effects of Part-Time Faculty Employment"; Eric Bettinger and Bridget Terry Long, "Help or Hinder? Adjunct Professors and Student Outcomes," 2005, 20.

10. Charles Harrington and Timothy Schibik, "Caveat Emptor: Is There a Relationship between Part-Time Faculty Utilization and Student Learning Outcomes and Retention?," AIR 2001 Annual Forum Paper, June 2001, https://eric.ed.gov/?id=ED456785; Florence Xiaotao Ran and Di Xu, "How and Why Do Adjunct Instructors Affect Students' Academic Outcomes? Evidence from Two-Year and Four-Year Colleges," CAPSEE Working Paper (Center for Analysis of Postsecondary Education and Employment, New York, NY, January 2017), https://eric.ed.gov/?id=ED574812; Eric P. Bettinger and Bridget Terry Long, "Does Cheaper Mean Better? The Impact of Using Adjunct Instructors on Student Outcomes," *Review of Economics and Statistics* 92, no. 3 (August 2010): 598–613, https://doi.org/10.1162/REST_a_00014.

11. Betheny Gross and Dan Goldhaber, *Community College Transfer and Articulation Policies: Looking Beneath the Surface*, CRPE Working Paper 2009-1, Center on Reinventing Public Education, 2009, https://eric.ed.gov/?id=ED504665; Eagan and Jaeger, "Effects of Exposure to Part-Time Faculty on Community College Transfer."

12. Jerome Seymour Bruner, *The Culture of Education* (Cambridge, MA: Harvard University Press, 1996); Umbach, "How Effective Are They?"

13. Baldwin and Wawrzynski, "Contingent Faculty as Teachers"; Benjamin, *Exploring the Role of Contingent Instructional Staff in Undergraduate Learning*; Umbach, "How Effective Are They?"; Umbach and Wawrzynski, "Faculty Do Matter."

14. Jean Lave and Etienne Wenger, *Situated Learning: Legitimate Peripheral Participation* (New York: Cambridge University Press, 1991); Albert Bandura, *Social Learning Theory* (Englewood Cliffs, NJ: Prentice-Hall, 1977); Bandura, "Social Cognitive Theory: An Agentic Perspective," *Annual Review of Psychology* 2001, no. 52 (2001): 1–26; L. S. Vygotsky and Michael Cole, *Mind in Society: The Development of Higher Psychological Processes* (Cambridge, MA: Harvard University Press, 1978); Immordino-Yang, "Implications of Affective and Social Neuroscience for Educational Theory." Bandura first coined the term Social Learning Theory, then coined the term Social Cognitive Theory as the theory developed. We will use the term Social Cognitive Theory for the remainder of the chapter.

15. Bandura, "Social Cognitive Theory: An Agentic Perspective"; Bandura, "The Self System in Reciprocal Determinism," *American Psychologist* 33, no. 4 (1978): 197; Bandura, *Social Foundations of Thought and Action: A Social Cognitive Theory* (Englewood Cliffs, NJ: Prentice-Hall, 1986); Alberta M. Gloria and Ester R. Rodriguez, "Counseling Latino University Students: Psychosociocultural

Issues for Consideration," *Journal of Counseling & Development* 78, no. 2 (April 2000): 145–54, https://doi.org/10.1002/j.1556-6676.2000.tb02572.x.

16. Bandura, *Social Foundations of Thought and Action*; Gloria and Rodriguez, "Counseling Latino University Students."

17. Bandura, *Social Learning Theory* (Englewood Cliffs, NJ: Prentice-Hall, 1977); Bandura, *Social Foundations of Thought and Action*; Pascarella and Terenzini, *How College Affects Students*; Carol A. Lundberg and Laurie A. Schreiner, "Quality and Frequency of Faculty-Student Interaction as Predictors of Learning: An Analysis by Student Race/Ethnicity," *Journal of College Student Development* 45, no. 5 (2004): 549–65, https://doi.org/10.1353/csd.2004.0061; Mayhew et al., *How College Affects Students*; Jaeger and Eagan, "Unintended Consequences"; Veronica Bordes and Patricia Arredondo, "Mentoring and 1st-Year Latina/o College Students," *Journal of Hispanic Higher Education* 4, no. 2 (April 1, 2005): 114–33, https://doi.org/10.1177/1538192704273855; Mark A. Lamport, "Student-Faculty Informal Interaction and the Effect on College Student Outcomes: A Review of the Literature," *Adolescence* 28, no. 112 (Winter 1993): 971–90; Bradley E. Cox and Elizabeth Orehovec, "Faculty-Student Interaction Outside the Classroom: A Typology from a Residential College," *The Review of Higher Education* 30, no. 4 (June 21, 2007): 343–62, https://doi.org/10.1353/rhe.2007.0033; Bradley E. Cox, Kadian L. McIntosh, Patrick T. Terenzini, Robert D. Reason, and Brenda R. Lutovsky Quaye, "Pedagogical Signals of Faculty Approachability: Factors Shaping Faculty–Student Interaction Outside the Classroom," *Research in Higher Education* 51, no. 8 (December 1, 2010): 767–88, https://doi.org/10.1007/s11162-010-9178-z.

18. Bandura, *Social Foundations of Thought and Action*; Bandura, "Social Cognitive Theory of Moral Thought and Action," in *Handbook of Moral Behavior and Development*, edited by W. M. Kurtines and J. L. Gewirtz, 1:45–103 (Hillsdale, NJ: Erlbaum, 1991).

19. Bandura, *Social Foundations of Thought and Action*.

20. Alberta M. Gloria, Jeanett Castellanos, and Veronica Orozco, "Perceived Educational Barriers, Cultural Fit, Coping Responses, and Psychological Well-Being of Latina Undergraduates," *Hispanic Journal of Behavioral Sciences* 27, no. 2 (May 1, 2005): 161–83, https://doi.org/10.1177/0739986305275097.

21. Kevin Cokley, "Perceived Faculty Encouragement and Its Influence on College Students," *Journal of College Student Development* 41, no. 3 (2000): 348–52; Meera Komarraju, Sergey Musulkin, and Gargi Bhattacharya, "Role of Student-Faculty Interactions in Developing College Students' Academic Self-Concept, Motivation, and Achievement," *Journal of College Student Development* 51, no. 3 (May 23, 2010): 332–42, https://doi.org/10.1353/csd.0.0137; Linda J. Sax, Alyssa N. Bryant, and Casandra E. Harper, "The Differential Effects

of Student-Faculty Interaction on College Outcomes for Women and Men," *Journal of College Student Development* 46, no. 6 (November 1, 2005): 642–57, https://doi.org/10.1353/csd.2005.0067.

22. Cokley, "Perceived Faculty Encouragement"; Komarraju et al., "Role of Student-Faculty Interactions"; Sax et al., "The Differential Effects"; Kelly A. Rocca, "Student Participation in the College Classroom: An Extended Multidisciplinary Literature Review," *Communication Education* 59, no. 2 (April 1, 2010): 185–213, https://doi.org/10.1080/03634520903505936; Polly A. Fassinger, "Understanding Classroom Interaction," *The Journal of Higher Education* 66, no. 1 (January 1, 1995): 82–96, https://doi.org/10.1080/00221546.1995.11774758; Robert R. Weaver and Jiang Qi, "Classroom Organization and Participation: College Students' Perceptions," *The Journal of Higher Education* 76, no. 5 (September 1, 2005): 570–601, https://doi.org/10.1080/00221546.2005.11772299.

23. Laura I. Rendon, "Beyond Involvement: Creating Validating Academic and Social Communities in the Community College," 1994, https://eric.ed.gov/?id=ED374728; Rendon, "Community College Puente: A Validating Model of Education," *Educational Policy* 16, no. 4 (September 1, 2002): 642–67, https://doi.org/10.1177/0895904802016004010; Laura Rendon Linares and Susan Munoz, "Revisiting Validation Theory: Theoretical Foundations, Applications, and Extensions," *Enrollment Management Journal* 5, no. 2 (2011): 24; S. Hurtado, A. Ruiz Alvarado, and C. Guillermo-Wann, "Creating Inclusive Environments: The Mediating Effect of Faculty and Staff Validation on the Relationship of Discrimination/Bias to Students' Sense of Belonging," *Journal Committed to Social Change on Race and Ethnicity* 1, no. 1 (October 13, 2015): 60–80, https://escholarship.org/uc/item/5z728go; Rendon, "Validating Culturally Diverse Students: Toward a New Model of Learning and Student Development," *Innovative Higher Education* 19, no. 1 (September 1, 1994): 33–51, https://doi.org/10.1007/BF01191156; Mandy Martin Lohfink and Michael B. Paulsen, "Comparing the Determinants of Persistence for First-Generation and Continuing-Generation Students," *Journal of College Student Development* 46, no. 4 (2005): 409–28, https://doi.org/10.1353/csd.2005.0040; Jeff Davis, *First-Generation Student Experience* (Sterling, VA: Stylus, 2010); Rendon, "Facilitating Retention and Transfer for First Generation Students in Community Colleges," March 1, 1995, https://eric.ed.gov/?id=ED383369; Carol A. Lundberg, Laurie A. Schreiner, Kristin Hovaguimian, and Sharyn Slavin Miller, "First-Generation Status and Student Race/Ethnicity as Distinct Predictors of Student Involvement and Learning," *Journal of Student Affairs Research and Practice* 44, no. 1 (January 20, 2007), https://doi.org/10.2202/1949-6605.1755; Jennifer Engle, "Postsecondary Access and Success for First-Generation College Students," *American Academic* 3 (2007): 25–48; Penny J. McConnell, "ERIC Review: What Community Colleges Should Do to Assist First-Generation Students,"

Community College Review 28, no. 3 (December 1, 2000): 75–87, https://doi.org /10.1177/009155210002800305; Karen Kurotsuchi Inkelas, Zaneeta E. Daver, Kristen E. Vogt, and Jeannie Brown Leonard, "Living–Learning Programs and First-Generation College Students' Academic and Social Transition to College," *Research in Higher Education* 48, no. 4 (June 1, 2007): 403–34, https://doi.org /10.1007/s11162-006-9031-6; Daniel Solorzano, Miguel Ceja, and Tara Yosso, "Critical Race Theory, Racial Microaggressions, and Campus Racial Climate: The Experiences of African American College Students," *The Journal of Negro Education* 69, no. 1/2 (2000), www.jstor.org/stable/2696265; Samuel D. Museus, "The Role of Ethnic Student Organizations in Fostering African American and Asian American Students' Cultural Adjustment and Membership at Predominantly White Institutions," *Journal of College Student Development* 49, no. 6 (2008): 568–86, https://doi.org/10.1353/csd.0.0039; Elisabeth A. Barnett, "Validation Experiences and Persistence among Community College Students," *The Review of Higher Education* 34, no. 2 (December 16, 2010): 193–230, https://doi.org/10.1353/rhe.2010 .0019; Barnett, "Faculty Validation and Persistence Among Nontraditional Community College Students," *Enrollment Management Journal* 5, no. 2 (2011): 161; Rendon, "Facilitating Retention and Transfer"; Mitchell J. Chang, "Preservation or Transformation: Where's the Real Educational Discourse on Diversity?," *The Review of Higher Education* 25, no. 2 (Winter 2002): 125–40; Sharon L. Holmes, Larry H. Ebbers, Daniel C. Robinson, and Abel G. Mugenda, "Validating African American Students at Predominantly White Institutions," *Journal of College Student Retention: Research, Theory & Practice* 2, no. 1 (May 1, 2000): 41–58, https:// doi.org/10.2190/XP0F-KRQW-F547-Y2XM.

24. Nancy K. Schlossberg, "Marginality and Mattering: Key Issues in Building Community," *New Directions for Student Services* 1989, no. 48 (August 2, 2006): 5–15, https://doi.org/10.1002/ss.37119894803; Morris Rosenberg and B. McCullough, "Mattering: Inferred Significance and Mental Health among Adolescents," *Research in Community and Mental Health* 2 (January 1, 1981): 163–82; Sarah K. Dixon, and Sharon E. Robinson Kurpius, "Depression and College Stress Among University Undergraduates: Do Mattering and Self-Esteem Make a Difference?," *Journal of College Student Development* 49, no. 5 (2008): 412–24, https://doi.org/10.1353/csd.0.0024; Adrian Huerta and Seth Fishman, "Marginality and Mattering: Urban Latino Male Undergraduates in Higher Education," *Journal of the First-Year Experience and Students in Transition* 26, no. 1 (January 1, 2014): 85–100.

25. Gail Crombie, Sandra W. Pyke, Naida Silverthorn, Alison Jones, and Sergio Piccinin, "Students' Perceptions of Their Classroom Participation and Instructor as a Function of Gender and Context," *The Journal of Higher Education* 74, no. 1 (2003): 51–76; Elise J. Dallimore, Julie H. Hertenstein, and Marjorie B.

Platt, "Classroom Participation and Discussion Effectiveness: Student-Generated Strategies," *Communication Education* 53, no. 1 (January 1, 2004), https://doi.org /10.1080/0363452032000135805; Richard West and Judy C. Pearson. "Anteced-ent and Consequent Conditions of Student Questioning: An Analysis of Classroom Discourse across the University," *Communication Education* 43, no. 4 (October 1, 1994): 299–311, https://doi.org/10.1080/03634529409378988.

26. Terrell L. Strayhorn, "Fittin' In: Do Diverse Interactions with Peers Affect Sense of Belonging for Black Men at Predominantly White Institutions?," *NASPA Journal* 45, no. 4 (October 1, 2008): 501–27, https://doi.org/10/cmz97z; Nomsa E. Geleta, Adrienne Dixon, and Susan Curtin, "Collaboration Rebuilds a Sense of Belonging for Students of Color Using the Sanctuary Model as a Framework," *Making Connections* 16, no. 1 (July 2015): 27–34; Sylvia Hurtado and Deborah Faye Carter, "Effects of College Transition and Perceptions of the Campus Racial Climate on Latino College Students' Sense of Belonging," *Sociology of Education* 70, no. 4 (1997): 324–45, https://doi.org/10/g8w; Amy K. Ribera, Angie L. Miller, and Amber D. Dumford, "Sense of Peer Belonging and Institutional Acceptance in the First Year: The Role of High-Impact Practices," *Journal of College Student Development* 58, no. 4 (2017): 545–63, https://doi.org/10/gc6xs2; V. Thandi Sulé, "Hip-Hop Is the Healer: Sense of Belonging and Diversity Among Hip-Hop Col-legians," *Journal of College Student Development* 57, no. 2 (2016): 181–96, https://doi.org/10/f8gdvb; Sungjun Won, Christopher A. Wolters, and Stefanie A. Mueller, "Sense of Belonging and Self-Regulated Learning: Testing Achievement Goals as Mediators," *The Journal of Experimental Education* (February 22, 2017): 1–17, https://doi.org/10/gc6xst; J. Luke Wood and Frank Harris III, "The Effect of Academic Engagement on Sense of Belonging: A Hierarchical, Multilevel Analy-sis of Black Men in Community Colleges," *Spectrum: A Journal on Black Men* 4, no. 1 (2015): 21, https://doi.org/10/gc6xss; A. H. Maslow, *Toward a Psychology of Being*, vol. 50 (Princeton, NJ: Van Nostrand, 1962); R. F. Baumeister and M. R. Leary, "The Need to Belong: Desire for Interpersonal Attachments as a Funda-mental Human Motivation," *Psychological Bulletin* 117, no. 3 (1995): 497–529; Terrell L. Strayhorn, *College Students' Sense of Belonging: A Key to Educational Success for All Students* (New York: Routledge, 2012).

27. Sulé, "Hip-Hop Is the Healer"; Strayhorn, *College Students' Sense of Be-longing*; Rosenberg and McCullough, "Mattering."

28. Arthur W. Chickering and Zelda F. Gamson, "Seven Principles for Good Practice in Undergraduate Education," *AAHE Bulletin*, March 1987, https://eric .ed.gov/?id=ED282491; George D. Kuh, "The Other Curriculum: Out-of-Class Ex-periences Associated with Student Learning and Personal Development," *The Journal of Higher Education* 66, no. 2 (1995): 123–55, https://doi.org/10.2307 /2943909; Richard J. Light, *Making the Most of College: Students Speak Their*

Minds (Cambridge, MA: Harvard University Press, 2001); George D. Kuh, Jillian Kinzie, Jennifer A. Buckley, Brian K. Bridges, and John C. Hayek, *What Matters to Student Success: A Review of the Literature*, Commissioned Report for the National Symposium on Postsecondary Student Success (Washington, DC: National Postsecondary Education Cooperative, 2006). Much of this section draws on the following article: A. Kezar and D. Maxey, "Faculty Matter: So Why Doesn't Everyone Think So?," *Thought & Action 30* (2014): 29–44.

29. Cox et al., "Pedagogical Signals of Faculty Approachability," 768.

30. George D. Kuh and Shouping Hu, "The Effects of Student-Faculty Interaction in the 1990s," *The Review of Higher Education 24*, no. 3 (March 1, 2001): 309–32, https://doi.org/10.1353/rhe.2001.0005; Philip E. Jacob, *Changing Values in College: An Exploratory Study of the Impact of College Teaching* (New York: Harper, 1957), 8; Kuh, "The Other Curriculum"; Shouping Hu and George D. Kuh, "Diversity Experiences and College Student Learning and Personal Development," *Journal of College Student Development 44*, no. 3 (May 23, 2003): 320–34, https://doi.org/10.1353/csd.2003.0026.

31. Alexander W. Astin, *What Matters in College? Four Critical Years Revisited* (San Francisco: Jossey-Bass, 1993); Hu and Kuh, "Diversity Experiences"; Kuh and Hu, "The Effects of Student-Faculty Interaction In the 1990s"; Pascarella and Terenzini, *How College Affects Students*; Bordes and Arredondo, "Mentoring and 1st-Year Latina/o College Students"; Gloria, Castellanos, and Orozco, "Perceived Educational Barriers"; Lamport, "Student-Faculty Informal Interaction"; Cox and Orehovec, "Faculty-Student Interaction Outside the Classroom"; Cox et al., "Pedagogical Signals of Faculty Approachability"; W. Brad Johnson, Gail Rose, and Lewis Z. Schlosser, "Student-Faculty Mentoring: Theoretical and Methodological Issues," in *The Blackwell Handbook of Mentoring: A Multiple Perspectives Approach*, edited by Tammy D. Allen and Lillian T. Eby (New York: John Wiley & Sons, 2011); Kuh et al., *What Matters to Student Success*, 41.

32. John Braxton, Nathaniel Bray, and Joseph Berger, "Faculty Teaching Skills and Their Influence on the College Student Departure Process," *Journal of College Student Development 41*, no. 2 (January 1, 2000): 215–27; Cara Lundquist, Rebecca J. Spalding, and R. Eric Landrum, "College Students' Thoughts about Leaving the University: The Impact of Faculty Attitudes and Behaviors," *Journal of College Student Retention: Research, Theory & Practice 4*, no. 2 (August 1, 2002): 123–33, https://doi.org/10.2190/FLAL-7AM5-Q6K3-L40P; Huiming Wang and Judith Wilson Grimes, "A Systematic Approach to Assessing Retention Programs: Identifying Critical Points for Meaningful Interventions and Validating Outcomes Assessment," *Journal of College Student Retention: Research, Theory & Practice 2*, no. 1 (May 1, 2000): 59–68, https://doi.org/10.2190/HYY4-XTBH -RJFD-LU5Y; David W. Johnson, *Academic Controversy: Enriching College In-*

struction through Intellectual Conflict, ASHE-ERIC Higher Education Report, vol. 25, no. 3 (Washington, DC: ERIC Clearinghouse on Higher Education, 1997), http://eric.ed.gov/?id=ED409829; Robert M. Carini, George D. Kuh, and Stephen P. Klein, "Student Engagement and Student Learning: Testing the Linkages," Research in Higher Education 47, no. 1 (February 1, 2006): 1–32, https://doi.org /10.1007/s11162-005-8150-9; Guadalupe Anaya, "College Experiences and Student Learning: The Influence of Active Learning, College Environments, and Co-curricular Activities," Journal of College Student Development 37, no. 6 (1996): 611–22; Guadalupe Anaya and Darnell G. Cole, "Latina/o Student Achievement: Exploring the Influence of Student-Faculty Interactions on College Grades," Journal of College Student Development 42, no. 1 (February 2001): 3. Studies control for incoming characteristics and other college experiences. However, there is no way to control for students who perform well or who are inclined to persist tending to seek out more faculty interactions. Finally, the effects of student-faculty interaction are conditional. For example, students who were better prepared academically and who devoted more effort to their studies interacted more frequently with faculty members. It is not clear whether this is because such students were more assertive in seeking out faculty members or whether faculty members invited students who performed well academically to make contact (e.g., writing laudatory comments in the margins of a student's paper suggesting they talk further about the topic).

33. M. Arredondo, "Faculty-Student Interaction: Uncovering the Types of Interactions That Raise Undergraduate Degree Aspirations," Review of Higher Education 20, no. 2 (1997): 234; Braxton et al., "Faculty Teaching Skills"; James C. Hearn, "Impacts of Undergraduate Experiences on Aspirations and Plans for Graduate and Professional Education," Research in Higher Education 27, no. 2 (1987): 119–41; Johnson, Academic Controversy; Lundquist et al., "College Students' Thoughts"; Wang and Grimes, "A Systematic Approach"; Sylvia Hurtado, Marcela Cuellar, and Chelsea Guillermo-Wann, "Quantitative Measures of Students' Sense of Validation: Advancing the Study of Diverse Learning Environments," Enrollment Management Journal 5, no. 2 (2011): 161; Wynetta Y. Lee, "Striving toward Effective Retention: The Effect of Race on Mentoring African American Students," Peabody Journal of Education 74, no. 2 (April 1999): 27–43, https://doi.org/10.1207/s15327930pje7402_4.

34. Arredondo, "Faculty-Student Interaction"; Braxton et al., "Faculty Teaching Skills"; Johnson, Academic Controversy; Lundquist et al., "College Students' Thoughts"; Wang and Grimes, "A Systematic Approach"; Light, Making the Most of College; Kuh and Hu, "The Effects of Student-Faculty Interaction In the 1990s"; Ernest T. Pascarella, Patrick T. Terenzini, and James Hibel, "Student-Faculty Interactional Settings and Their Relationship to Predicted Academic

Performance," *The Journal of Higher Education* 49, no. 5 (September 1, 1978): 450–63, https://doi.org/10.1080/00221546.1978.11780395; Cokley, "Perceived Faculty Encouragement."

35. Lundberg and Schreiner, "Quality and Frequency"; Anaya and Cole, "Latina/o Student Achievement"; Valerie C. McKay and Jeremy Estrella, "First-Generation Student Success: The Role of Faculty Interaction in Service Learning Courses," *Communication Education* 57, no. 3 (July 1, 2008): 356–372, https://doi.org/10.1080/03634520801966123.

36. Robert Dean Reason, Patrick T. Terenzi, and Robert J. Domingo, "Developing Social and Personal Competence in the First Year of College," *The Review of Higher Education* 30, no. 3 (2007): 271–99, https://doi.org/10.1353/rhe.2007.0012.

37. Pascarella et al., "Student-Faculty Interactional Settings"; Cox et al., "Pedagogical Signals of Faculty Approachability"; Arredondo, "Faculty-Student Interaction"; Sylvia Hurtado, M. Kevin Eagan, Minh C. Tran, Christopher B. Newman, Mitchell J. Chang, and Paolo Velasco, "'We Do Science Here': Underrepresented Students' Interactions with Faculty in Different College Contexts," *Journal of Social Issues* 67, no. 3 (September 1, 2011): 553–79, https://doi.org/10.1111/j.1540-4560.2011.01714.x; McKay and Estrella, "First-Generation Student Success"; Philip Smallwood, "'More Creative than Creation': On the Idea of Criticism and the Student Critic," *Arts and Humanities in Higher Education* 1, no. 1 (June 1, 2002): 59–71, https://doi.org/10.1177/1474022202001001005.

38. See, for example, Kuh and Hu, "The Effects of Student-Faculty Interaction in the 1990s."

39. R. V. Alderman, "Faculty and Student Out-of-Classroom Interaction: Student Perceptions of Quality of Interaction" (PhD diss., Texas A&M University, 2008).

40. Daniel F. Chambliss and Christopher G. Takacs, *How College Works* (Cambridge, MA: Harvard University Press, 2014), 3.

41. Gallup, "Great Jobs Great Lives: The 2014 Gallup-Purdue Index Report," Gallup, 2014.

42. George D. Kuh, Jillian Kinzie, John H. Schuh, and Elizabeth J. Whitt, *Student Success in College: Creating Conditions That Matter* (San Francisco: Jossey-Bass, 2010).

43. Samantha Jane Armstrong Ash, "Student Affairs Support Staff: Empowered and Invisible" (PhD diss., Washington State University, 2013), Proquest (1502024967).

Five: The Growth of Unions and New Broad-Based Organizing Strategies

1. Barry Hirsch and David MacPherson, "Union Membership and Coverage Database from the CPS [Data from Unionstat]," 2017, http://unionstats.gsu.edu

/CPS; US Bureau of Labor Statistics, "Occupational Employment and Wages, May 2017," www.bls.gov/oes/current/oes251191.htm.

2. William A. Herbert and Jacob Apkarian, "Everything Passes, Everything Changes: Unionization and Collective Bargaining in Higher Education," SSRN Scholarly Paper (Rochester, NY: Social Science Research Network, December 9, 2017), http://papers.ssrn.com/abstract=3085214; Timothy Reese Cain, "Campus Unions: Organized Faculty and Graduate Students in US Higher Education," *ASHE Higher Education Report* 43, no. 3 (2017): 7–163, https://doi.org/10.1002 /aehe.20119; Philo A. Hutcheson, *A Professional Professoriate: Unionization, Bureaucratization, and the AAUP*, 1st ed. (Nashville, TN: Vanderbilt University Press, 2000); Gary Rhoades, *Managed Professionals: Unionized Faculty and Restructuring Academic Labor* (Albany: State University of New York Press, 1998); Adrianna Kezar and Cecelia Sam, "Understanding the New Majority of Non-Tenure-Track Faculty in Higher Education—Demographics, Experiences, and Plans of Action," Association for the Study of Higher Education, 2010, http://doi .wiley.com/10.1002/aehe.3604.

3. Herbert and Apkarian, "Everything Passes, Everything Changes."

4. Cain, "Campus Unions."

5. Joe Berry and Michelle Savarese, "Directory of US Faculty Contracts and Bargaining Agents in Institutions of Higher Education," National Center for the Study of Collective Bargaining in Higher Education and the Professions, Hunter College, CUNY, New York, 2012.

6. Hirsch and MacPherson, "Union Membership and Coverage Database."

7. Herbert and Apkarian, "Everything Passes, Everything Changes."

8. Herbert and Apkarian, "Everything Passes, Everything Changes."

9. Josh Verges, "Appeals Court Rejects Attempt to Unionize All UMN Twin Cities Faculty," *Twin Cities*, September 5, 2017, www.twincities.com/2017/09/05 /appeals-court-rejects-attempt-to-unionize-all-umn-twin-cities-faculty.

10. Herbert and Apkarian, "Everything Passes, Everything Changes."

11. David Weil, *The Fissured Workplace* (Cambridge, MA: Harvard University Press, 2014).

12. Berry and Savarese, "Directory of US Faculty Contracts."

13. Richard W. Hurd and Gregory Woodhead, "The Unionization of Clerical Workers at Large US Universities and Colleges," *Newsletter of the National Center for the Study of Collective Bargaining in Higher Education and the Professions* 15, no. 3 (1987): 1–8; Hurd, "Non-Faculty Unionization at Institutions of Higher Education," in *Directory of Non-Faculty Bargaining Agents in Institutions of Higher Education*, edited by J. M. Douglas, ix–xii (New York: National Center for the Study of Collective Bargaining in Higher Education and the Professions, 1991).

14. Richard W. Hurd, "The Unionization of Clerical, Technical, and Professional Employees in Higher Education: Threat or Opportunity," in *Managing the Industrial Labor Relations Process in Higher Education*, edited by D. J. Julius, 315–27 (Washington, DC: College and University Professional Association for Human Resources, 1993), 16.

15. Ronald Ehrenberg and Liang Zhang, "The Changing Nature of Faculty Employment," *Working Papers*, April 1, 2004, https://digitalcommons.ilr.cornell.edu/workingpapers/43.

16. Rachel Applegate, "Who Benefits? Unionization and Academic Libraries and Librarians," *The Library Quarterly* 79, no. 4 (October 1, 2009): 443–63, https://doi.org/10.1086/605383.

17. Richard H. Bee, Terry Ann Beronja, and Genevra Mann, "Analysis of the Unionization of Academic Advisors," *NACADA Journal* 10, no. 1 (1990): 35–40.

18. Daniel J. Julius and Patricia J. Gumport, "Graduate Student Unionization: Catalysts and Consequences," *The Review of Higher Education* 26, no. 2 (2002): 187–216, https://doi.org/10.1353/rhe.2002.0033; Tom Schenk, Jr., "The Effects of Graduate-Student Unionization" (PhD diss., Iowa State University, 2007).

19. Congress enacted the NLRA in 1935 to protect the rights of employees and employers, to encourage collective bargaining, and to curtail certain private-sector labor and management practices, which can harm the general welfare of workers, businesses, and the US economy.

20. The National Labor Relations Board is an independent US government agency with responsibilities for enforcing US labor law in relation to collective bargaining and unfair labor practices.

21. Berry and Savarese, "Directory of US Faculty Contracts."

22. NLRB, The Trustees of Columbia University in the City of New York, No. 02-RC-143012 (NLRB 2017).

23. Eleanor J. Bader, "Graduate Student Unions Are Growing—and Fighting for Social Justice," *Truthout*, January 26, 2018, https://truthout.org/articles/graduate-student-unions-are-growing-and-fighting-for-social-justice.

24. National Postdoctoral Association [NPA], "National Postdoctoral Association Position Statement on Unions," 2006, https://cdn.ymaws.com/www.nationalpostdoc.org/resource/resmgr/Docs/npa-position-statement-on-un.pdf.

25. University of Washington Postdoc Organizing Committee, "University of Washington Postdocs," May 14, 2018, https://uaw.org/university-washington-postdocs-official-union/; UAW Local 5810, "Contract," 2017, http://uaw5810.org/know-your-rights/contract/; Sayil Camacho and Robert A. Rhoads, "Breaking the Silence: The Unionization of Postdoctoral Workers at the University of California," *The Journal of Higher Education* 86, no. 2 (2015): 295–325, https://doi.org/10.1353/jhe.2015.0010.

26. University of Washington Postdoc Organizing Committee, "University of Washington Postdocs"; Flaherty, Colleen, "Could Postdoc Unions Be the Next Big Thing in Collective Bargaining among Academics?," *Inside Higher Ed*, 2017, www .insidehighered.com/news/2017/10/31/could-postdoc-unions-be-next-big-thing -collective-bargaining-among-academics.

27. Camacho and Rhoads, "Breaking the Silence"; A. Bankston and G. S. McDowell, "Monitoring the Compliance of the Academic Enterprise with the Fair Labor Standards Act," F1000Research, 2016; Flaherty, "Could Postdoc Unions?"

28. Since the US Supreme Court's infamous NLRB v. Yeshiva University decision in 1980, faculty members at private colleges and universities have confronted major roadblocks to unionization. *Yeshiva* labels most tenure-track faculty as "managerial," excluding them from the right to unionize under the NLRA.

29. Gordon Lafer, "Graduate Student Unions: Organizing in a Changed Academic Economy," *Labor Studies Journal* 28, no. 2 (June 1, 2003): 25–43, https:// doi.org/10.1177/0160449X0302800202.

30. New York University and International Union, United Automobile, Aerospace and Agricultural Implement Workers of America, AFL-CIO, Case No. 2-RC-22082, April 3, 2000; National Labor Relations Board, New York University v. NLRB, 364 F. Supp. 160 (SDNY 1973).

31. Brown University and International Union, United Automobile, Aerospace and Agricultural Implement Workers of America, UAW AFL-CIO, Petitioner. Case 1-RC-21368, July 13, 2004.

32. CGEU, "Coalition of Graduate Employee Unions," Coalition of Graduate Employee Unions, 2018, www.thecgeu.org.

33. https://web.archive.org/web/20181002121258/http://www.thecgeu.org /wiki/United_States.

34. NLRB v. Yeshiva Univ; NLRB v. Catholic Bishop of Chicago. The NLRB (defendant) exercised jurisdiction over lay faculty members at two groups of religious high schools owned by the Catholic Bishop of Chicago and the Diocese of Fort Wayne–South Bend, Inc. (plaintiffs). The NLRB certified certain unions as the bargaining agents for these teachers and ordered the schools to bargain with those unions. Additionally, charges of unfair labor practices were filed against the schools under the National Labor Relations Act, 29 USC §§ 151–69. At a hearing before the NLRB, the schools argued that the challenged practices were mandated by the schools' religious creeds and that the NLRB could not exercise jurisdiction over church-operated schools. The NLRB disagreed and ordered the schools to cease the challenged practices and enter into collective bargaining agreements with the unions. The schools challenged the NLRB's order in the United States Court of Appeals for the Seventh Circuit. The court of appeals held in favor of the schools

and declined to enforce the order. The NLRB petitioned the United States Supreme Court for review.

35. NLRB v. Yeshiva University was the controversial ruling that stated tenure-stream faculty were not afforded rights to a union because they were determined to have managerial authority. The Pacific Lutheran University decision (2901) built on that by establishing that employees of religious organizations may be excluded from unionization.

36. Herbert and Apkarian, "Everything Passes, Everything Changes"; Berry and Savarese, "Directory of US Faculty Contracts."

37. Laura Pulido, "Faculty Governance at the University of Southern California," in *The Imperial University: Academic Repression and Scholarly Dissent*, edited by Piya Chatterjee and Sunaina Maira, 99–121 (Minneapolis: University of Minnesota Press, 2014).

38. Gary Rhoades, "Bread and Roses, and Quality Too? A New Faculty Majority Negotiating the New Academy," *The Journal of Higher Education* 88, no. 5 (September 3, 2017): 645–71, https://doi.org/10.1080/00221546.2016.1257310; SEIU, "The High Cost of Adjunct Living," SEIU, 2015, http://seiufacultyforward .org/wp-content/uploads/2016/10/29035-White-paper-Florida-Final.pdf.

39. Daniel J. Julius, "The Slippery Slope of 'Unique,'" *Journal of Collective Bargaining in the Academy* 9 (2017): 5; Sara Horowitz, "Freelancers Union Looks to Bring Portable Benefits to On-Demand Workers Nationwide," *Freelancers Union*, May 10, 2016, https://blog.freelancersunion.org/2016/05/10/freelancers -union-looks-to-bring-portable-benefits-to-on-demand-workers-nationwide-2/.

40. Paul Johnston, *Success While Others Fail: Social Movement Unionism and the Public Workplace* (Ithaca, NY: ILR Press, 1994); Gary Rhoades and Robert A. Rhoads, "The Public Discourse of US Graduate Employee Unions: Social Movement Identities, Ideologies, and Strategies," *The Review of Higher Education* 26, no. 2 (2002): 163–86, https://doi.org/10.1353/rhe.2002.0035; Lowell Turner, Harry C. Katz, and Richard W. Hurd, eds., *Rekindling the Movement: Labor's Quest for Relevance in the 21st Century* (Ithaca, NY: Cornell University Press, 2001); Gordon Lafer, "The Corporate Assault on Higher Education and Union Responses," *Thought & Action* 33, no. 2 (2017): 11–36; NYSUT Communications, "Adjunct Pay an Urgent Issue for Unions," accessed March 29, 2018, www .nysut.org/news/2017/april/ra/adjunct-pay-an-urgent-issue-for-unions; California Faculty Association, "California Faculty Association Collective Bargaining Agreement," Los Angeles, 2014.

41. California Faculty Association, "Equity Interrupted," Los Angeles, 2017; Gary Rhoades, "What Are We Negotiating For? Public Interest Bargaining," *Journal of Collective Bargaining in the Academy* 7 (2015): 15; Joe Berry, *Reclaiming the Ivory Tower: Organizing Adjuncts to Change Higher Education* (New York:

Monthly Review Press, 2005); Marc Bousquet, "A Ph.D. Should Result in a Tenure-Track Job, Not an Alt-Ac One," *Inside Higher Education*, October 20, 2015, www.insidehighered.com/views/2015/10/20/phd-should-result-tenure-track-job-not-alt-ac-one-essay; Adrianna Kezar and Cecilia Sam, "Governance as a Catalyst for Policy Change: Creating a Contingent Faculty Friendly Academy," *Educational Policy* 28, no. 3 (May 1, 2014): 425–62, https://doi.org/10.1177/0895904812465112; AFT, "Grad Employee Union Wins Full Pay for Diversity Work," *American Federation of Teachers*, September 6, 2017, www.aft.org/news/grad-employee-union-wins-full-pay-diversity-work.

42. Adom Getachew, "Bringing Unions to the Fight," *Jacobin*, 2017, http://jacobinmag.com/2017/02/graduate-workers-unions-racial-justice-diversity-yale-geso/.

43. Molly McCafferty, "Grad Union Establishes Sexual Harassment Committee" *The Harvard Crimson*, May 11, 2018, www.thecrimson.com/article/2018/5/11/hgsu-times-up-established/; UAW Local 4121, "UAW Local 4121," 2015, www.uaw4121.org.

44. CGEU, "Resolution on Taking an Active Anti-racist Stand in Our Unions and Support the Movement for Black Lives," 2016; CGEU, "Resolution to Address the Inequitable Treatment of International Graduate Student Workers," 2016.

45. Shannon Ikebe and Alexandra Holstrom-Smith, "Union Democracy, Student Labor, and the Fight for Public Education," *Berkeley Journal of Sociology* 58 (2014): 42–50.

46. Mary Ellen Benedict, "The Effect of Unionization on Faculty Salaries 1978–1996: A Test of Empirical Methods," *Journal of Collective Negotiations* 31, no. 3 (January 1, 2007): 251–74, https://doi.org/10.2190/CN.31.3.e; Christine M. Wickens, "The Organizational Impact of University Labor Unions," *Higher Education* 56, no. 5 (November 1, 2008): 545–64, https://doi.org/10.1007/s10734-008-9110-z; Coalition for the Academic Workforce, "One Faculty Serving All Students," *New Faculty Majority*, 2010.

47. Vicki J. Rosser, "'How Did You Hear That You Might Lose Your Job?'"

48. Kristen Edwards and Kim Tolley, "Do Unions Help Adjuncts?," *The Chronicle of Higher Education*, June 3, 2018, www.chronicle.com/article/Do-Unions-Help-Adjuncts-/243566.

49. Coalition for the Academic Workforce, "One Faculty Serving All Students."

50. Rhoades, "Bread and Roses, and Quality Too?"

51. Vicki J. Rosser, "Support Professionals: The Key Issues Survey," *NEA 2009 Almanac of Higher Education*, 6.

52. Rosser, "'How Did You Hear That You Might Lose Your Job?'"; Kezar and Sam, "Understanding the New Majority."

53. Rosser, "Support Professionals"; Rosser, "'How Did You Hear That You Might Lose Your Job?'"

54. Rosser, "Support Professionals"; Rosser, "Education Support Professionals."

55. Caroline Sabina Wekullo, "Outsourcing in Higher Education: The Known and Unknown about the Practice," *Journal of Higher Education Policy and Management* 39, no. 4 (July 4, 2017): 453–68, https://doi.org/10.1080/1360080X.2017.1330805; Rosser, "Support Professionals."

56. Doug Lederman, "Arbitrator Sides with Eastern Michigan in Dispute with Union over Online Learning," *Inside Higher Ed*, January 15, 2018, www.insidehighered.com/digital-learning/article/2018/01/15/arbitrator-sides-eastern-michigan-dispute-union-over-online.

57. Thomas Walker, Jessica Buttermore, and Jeffrey Lichtenstein, "Tennessee Campus Workers Foil Billionaire Governor's Outsourcing Scheme," *Labor Notes*, November 22, 2017, www.labornotes.org/2017/11/tennessee-campus-workers-foil-billionaire-governors-outsourcing-scheme.

58. C. Maitland, Gary Rhoades, and M. F. Smith, "Unions and Senates: Governance and Distance Education," *The NEA 2009 Almanac of Higher Education*.

59. David F. Noble, *Digital Diploma Mills: The Automation of Higher Education* (New York: Monthly Review Press, 2001).

60. Ronald G. Ehrenberg, *Governing Academia: Who Is in Charge at the Modern University?* (Ithaca, NY: Cornell University Press, 2004); Rhoades, "Bread and Roses, and Quality Too?"; Cain, "Campus Unions"; Daniel B. Klaff and Ronald G. Ehrenberg, "Collective Bargaining and Staff Salaries in American Colleges and Universities," *ILR Review* 57, no. 1 (October 1, 2003): 92–104, https://doi.org/10.1177/001979390305700105; Stephen G. Katsinas, J. A. Ogun, and N. J. Bray, "Monetary Compensation of Full-Time Faculty at American Public Regional Universities: The Impact of Geography and the Existence of Collective Bargaining," *Journal of Collective Bargaining in the Academy* 8 (2016): 29.

61. Ehrenberg, *Governing Academia*; GEU-UAW, "GEU-UAW Collective Bargaining Agreement," 2015.

62. Charles Wassell, David Hedrick, Steven Henson, and John Krieg, "Wage Distribution Impacts of Higher Education Faculty Unionization," *Journal of Collective Bargaining in the Academy* 7, no. 1 (February 28, 2016), http://thekeep.eiu.edu/jcba/vol7/iss1/4; Katsinas et al., "Monetary Compensation of Full-Time Faculty"; Coalition on the Academic Workforce, "A Portrait of Part-Time Faculty Members," 2012.

63. Karen Halverson Cross, "Unionization and the Development of Policies for Non-Tenure Track Faculty: A Comparative Study of Research Universities,"

Journal of Collective Bargaining in the Academy 9 (2017): 39; Timothy Reese Cain, "Campus Unions: Organized Faculty and Graduate Students in US Higher Education," *ASHE Higher Education Report* 43, no. 3 (2017): 7–163, https://doi .org/10.1002/aehe.20119.

64. Mark Cassell and Odeh Halaseh, "The Impact of Unionization on University Performance," *Journal of Collective Bargaining in the Academy* 6, no. 1 (2014), http://thekeep.eiu.edu/jcba/vol6/iss1/3; Deeb-Paul Kitchen, "The Union Makes Us Strong: A Case Study in the Graduate Labor Movement" (PhD diss., University of Florida, 2011), Proquest (3467578).

65. Schenk, "The Effects of Graduate-Student Unionization"; Sean E. Rogers, Adrienne E. Eaton, and Paula B. Voos, "Effects of Unionization on Graduate Student Employees: Faculty-Student Relations, Academic Freedom, and Pay," *ILR Review* 66, no. 2 (April 2013): 487–510, https://doi.org/10.1177/001979391306600208; Gordon J. Hewitt, "Graduate Student Employee Collective Bargaining and the Educational Relationship between Faculty and Graduate Students," *Journal of Collective Negotiations* 29, no. 2 (June 1, 2000): 153–66, https://doi.org /10.2190/P07G-C8RF-5GG0-4VH8.

Six: Whither the Struggle

1. Barry Eidlin and Micah Uetricht, "The Problem of Workplace Democracy," *New Labor Forum* 27, no. 1 (January 1, 2018): 70–79, https://doi.org/10.1177 /1095796017745037.

2. Eidlin and Uetricht, "The Problem of Workplace Democracy."

3. Eidlin and Uetricht, "The Problem of Workplace Democracy."

4. Markus Pausch, "From a Democratic Ideal to a Managerial Tool and Back," *The Innovation Journal: The Public Sector Innovation Journal* 19, no. 1 (2013): 1.

5. David Michael Smith, "Workplace Democracy at College of the Mainland," *Peace Review* 12, no. 2 (June 1, 2000): 257–62, https://doi.org/10.1080 /10402650050057924.

6. Jake Rosenfeld, *What Unions No Longer Do* (Cambridge, MA: Harvard University Press, 2014).

7. While we advocate for more collectivist collective bargaining, we do acknowledge that in the history of organizing, tenure-track faculty, for example, did not always adequately support the bargaining interests of non-tenure-track faculty. There is evidence that the approach we are advocating for may not work and that inequalities in power may play out in detrimental ways.

8. A. C. Brown, "The Impact of Interest-Based Bargaining on Community College Faculty and Administrative Relationships" (PhD diss., Northern Arizona

University, 2015); Gary Rhoades, "What Are We Negotiating For? Public Interest Bargaining," *Journal of Collective Bargaining in the Academy* 7 (2015): 15.

9. Consult the Delphi Project's thorough list of resources for a good starting point.

10. American Federation of Teachers (AFT), "Grad Employee Union Wins Full Pay for Diversity Work," *American Federation of Teachers*, September 6, 2017, www.aft.org/news/grad-employee-union-wins-full-pay-diversity-work; Molly Mc-Cafferty, "Grad Union Establishes Sexual Harassment Committee," *The Harvard Crimson*, May 11, 2018, www.thecrimson.com/article/2018/5/11/hgsu-times-up -established/; UAW Local 4121, "UAW Local 4121," 2015, www.uaw4121.org/.

11. Association of Governing Boards, "AGB Board of Directors' Statement on Shared Governance," Association of Governing Boards, October 10, 2017, www .agb.org/statements/2017-1010/agb-board-of-directors-statement-on-shared -governance.

12. Adrianna Kezar and Cecilia Sam, *Non-Tenure-Track Faculty in Higher Education: Theories and Tensions*, ASHE Higher Education Report (San Francisco: Jossey-Bass, January 11, 2011).

13. Karen M. Cardozo, "Academic Labor: Who Cares?," *Critical Sociology* 43, no. 3 (May 1, 2017): 405–28, https://doi.org/10.1177/0896920516641733.

14. Timothy M. Renick, "How to Best Harness Student-Success Technology," *The Chronicle of Higher Education*, July 1, 2018, www.chronicle.com/article/How -to-Best-Harness/243798.

15. David Weil, *The Fissured Workplace* (Cambridge, MA: Harvard University Press, 2014); Maria Maisto, "Adjuncts, Blogs and the DOL," *Majority Rule*, July 25, 2015, https://extraordinaryfacultynfm.wordpress.com/2015/07/25/adjuncts -blogs-and-the-dol/.

16. Erin Dunlop Velez, "Newly Released Student Loan Data Bust Several Myths about Student Loan Repayment," *Evolllution*, May 9, 2018, https:// evolllution.com/attracting-students/todays_learner/newly-released-student-loan -data-bust-several-myths-about-student-loan-repayment/.

17. Judith Scott-Clayton and Jing Li, *Black-White Disparity in Student Loan Debt More Than Triples after Graduation* (Washington, DC: Brookings Institute, 2016).

18. Scott Fullwiler, Stephanie Kelton, Catherine Ruetschlin, and Marshall Steinbaum, *The Macroeconomic Effects of Student Debt Cancellation* (Annandale-on-Hudson, NY: Levy Economics Institute, 2018).

19. Christopher Newfield, *The Great Mistake: How We Wrecked Public Universities and How We Can Fix Them* (Baltimore: Johns Hopkins University Press, 2016); Michael Mitchell, Michael Leachman, and Kathleen Masterson, "A Lost Decade in Higher Education Funding," Center on Budget and Policy Priorities,

August 22, 2017, www.cbpp.org/research/state-budget-and-tax/a-lost-decade-in -higher-education-funding; Robert Samuels, *Why Public Higher Education Should Be Free: How to Decrease Cost and Increase Quality at American Universities* (Newark, NJ: Rutgers University Press, 2013); Sara Goldrick-Rab, *Paying the Price: College Costs, Financial Aid, and the Betrayal of the American Dream* (Chicago: University of Chicago Press, 2016).

20. Richard Cano, "Name-Calling Begins in Battle over #InvestInEd Ballot Measure," *Azcentral*, July 12, 2018, www.azcentral.com/story/news/politics /arizona-education/2018/07/12/invested-ballot-measure-attacks-get-personal -arizona-chamber-commerce-noah-karvelis-redfored/776074002.

21. Danielle Lerner, "Proposed Arizona Bill, HB 2017, Looks to Limit School Walkouts like Red for Ed Movement," *ABC Arizona*, January 17. 2019, www .abc15.com/news/state/proposed-arizona-bill-h-b-2017-looks-to-limit-school -walkouts-like-the-red-for-ed-movement; Noah Karvelis, "You Need Rank and File to Win: How Arizona Teachers Built a Movement," *Rethinking Schools* 33, no. 2 (Winter 2018–19), www.rethinkingschools.org/articles/you-need-rank-and-file-to -win-how-arizona-teachers-built-a-movement; Ali Vetnar, "Invest in Ed Demands New Money during 2019 Legislative Session," *KTAR News*, January 11, 2019, http://ktar.com/story/2391495/invest-in-ed-demands-new-money-during-2019 -legislative-session/.

22. Five Colleges Consortium, "The Consortium," accessed August 31, 2018, www.fivecolleges.edu/consortium; Judith M. Gappa, *The Invisible Faculty: Improving the Status of Part-Timers in Higher Education* (San Francisco: Jossey-Bass, 1993).

23. David Rolf, Shelby Clark, and Corrie Watterson Bryant, *Portable Benefits in the 21st Century* (Washington, DC: Aspen Institute, 2016).

24. Adrianna Kezar and Daniel Maxey, *Envisioning the Faculty for the Twenty-First Century: Moving to a Mission-Oriented and Learner-Centered Model* (New Brunswick, NJ: Rutgers University Press, 2016).

25. Kezar and Maxey, *Adapting by Design*, 2nd ed. (Los Angeles: The Delphi Project on the Changing Faculty and Student Success, 2015), https://pullias.usc .edu/wp-content/uploads/2015/06/DELPHI-PROJECT_ADAPTING-BY -DESIGN_2ED.pdf.

26. Sarah A. Bunton and William T. Mallon, "The Impact of Centers and Institutes on Faculty Life: Findings from a Study of Basic Science and Internal Medicine Faculty at Research-Intensive Medical Schools," *Academic Medicine* 81, no. 8 (August 2006): 734–43. https://doi.org/10.1097/00001888-200608000-00012.

27. Kezar, *Enhancing Campus Capacity for Leadership an Examination of Grassroots Leaders in Higher Education* (Stanford, CA: Stanford University Press, 2011).

References

....

Addo, Fenaba R., Jason N. Houle, and Daniel Simon. "Young, Black, and (Still) in the Red: Parental Wealth, Race, and Student Loan Debt." *Race and Social Problems* 8, no. 1 (March 1, 2016): 64–76. https://doi.org/10.1007/s12552-016-9162-0.

Ad-Hoc Committee on Grade Inflation. *Final Report of the Ad-Hoc Committee on Grade Inflation.* Washington, DC: American University, 2016.

"Administrative Jobs." HigherEdJobs. Accessed July 30, 2018. www.higheredjobs.com/admin/.

Alderman, R. V. "Faculty and Student Out-of-Classroom Interaction: Student Perceptions of Quality of Interaction." PhD diss., Texas A&M University, 2008.

Allen, Henry Lee. "Faculty Workload and Productivity in For-Profit Institutions: The Good, the Bad, and the Ugly." *The 2013 NEA Almanac,* 77–87.

American Association of University Professors. "Visualizing Change: Report on the Economic Status of the Profession." *Academe,* 2017.

American College Health Association. *American College Health Association-National College Health Assessment II: Reference Group Graduates Executive Summary Fall 2017.* Hanover, MD: American College Health Association, 2017.

American Federation of Teachers. *American Academic: The State of the Higher Education Workforce.* Washington, DC: American Federation of Teachers, 2009.

———. "Grad Employee Union Wins Full Pay for Diversity Work." American Federation of Teachers, September 6, 2017. www.aft.org/news/grad-employee-union-wins-full-pay-diversity-work.

Anaya, Guadalupe. "College Experiences and Student Learning: The Influence of Active Learning, College Environments and Cocurricular Activities." *Journal of College Student Development* 37, no. 6 (1996): 611–22.

Anaya, Guadalupe, and Darnell G. Cole. "Latina/o Student Achievement: Exploring the Influence of Student-Faculty Interactions on College Grades." *Journal of College Student Development* 42, no. 1 (February 2001): 3–14.

Anderson, Eugene L. *The New Professoriate: Characteristics, Contributions, and Compensation*. Washington, DC: Center for Policy Analysis, American Council on Education, 2002. https://eric.ed.gov/?id=ED478300.

Applegate, Rachel. "Who Benefits? Unionization and Academic Libraries and Librarians." *The Library Quarterly* 79, no. 4 (October 1, 2009): 443–63. https:// doi.org/10.1086/605383.

Armstrong Ash, and Samantha Jane. "Student Affairs Support Staff: Empowered and Invisible." PhD diss., Washington State University, 2013. Proquest (1502024967).

Arredondo, M. "Faculty-Student Interaction: Uncovering the Types of Interactions That Raise Undergraduate Degree Aspirations." *Review of Higher Education* 20, no. 2 (1997): 2–24.

Association of Governing Boards. "AGB Board of Directors' Statement on Shared Governance." Association of Governing Boards, October 10, 2017. www.agb .org/statements/2017-1010/agb-board-of-directors-statement-on-shared -governance.

Astin, Alexander W. *What Matters in College? Four Critical Years Revisited*. San Francisco: Jossey-Bass, 1993.

Bader, Eleanor J. "Graduate Student Unions Are Growing—and Fighting for Social Justice." *Truthout*, January 26, 2018. https://truthout.org/articles/graduate -student-unions-are-growing-and-fighting-for-social-justice/.

Baldwin, Davarian L. "When Universities Swallow Cities." *The Chronicle of Higher Education*, July 30, 2017. www.chronicle.com/article/When-Univer sities-Swallow/240739.

Baldwin, Roger G., and Jay L. Chronister. *Teaching without Tenure: Policies and Practices for a New Era*. Baltimore: Johns Hopkins University Press, 2001. http://ebookcentral.proquest.com/lib/socal/detail.action?docID=3318123.

Baldwin, Roger G., and Matthew R. Wawrzynski. "Contingent Faculty as Teachers: What We Know; What We Need to Know." *American Behavioral Scientist* 55, no. 11 (November 1, 2011): 1485–1509. https://doi.org/10.1177 /0002764211409194.

Bandura, Albert. "The Self System in Reciprocal Determinism." *American Psychologist* 33, no. 4 (1978): 344–58.

———. "Social Cognitive Theory: An Agentic Perspective." *Annual Review of Psychology* 2001, no. 52 (2001): 1–26.

———. "Social Cognitive Theory of Moral Thought and Action." In *Handbook of Moral Behavior and Development*, vol. 1, edited by W. M. Kurtines and J. L. Gewirtz, 45–103. Hillsdale, NJ: Erlbaum, 1991.

———. *Social Foundations of Thought and Action: A Social Cognitive Theory*. Englewood Cliffs, NJ: Prentice-Hall, 1986.

———. *Social Learning Theory*. Englewood Cliffs, NJ: Prentice-Hall, 1977.

Bandura, Albert, Nancy E. Adams, Arthur B. Hardy, and Gary N. Howells. "Tests of the Generality of Self-Efficacy Theory." *Cognitive Therapy and Research* 4, no. 1 (March 1, 1980): 39–66. https://doi.org/10.1007/BF01173354.

Bankston, A., and G. S. McDowell. "Monitoring the Compliance of the Academic Enterprise with the Fair Labor Standards Act." F1000Research, 2016.

Barnett, Elisabeth A. "Faculty Validation and Persistence among Nontraditional Community College Students." *Enrollment Management Journal* 5, no. 2 (2011): 161.

———. "Validation Experiences and Persistence among Community College Students." *The Review of Higher Education* 34, no. 2 (December 16, 2010): 193–230. https://doi.org/10.1353/rhe.2010.0019.

Barrow, Clyde W. "The Rationality Crisis in US Higher Education." *New Political Science* 32, no. 3 (September 1, 2010): 317–44. https://doi.org/10.1080/07393148.2010.498197.

Bauman, D., T. Davis, and Brian O'Leary. "Executive Compensation at Private and Public Colleges." *The Chronicle of Higher Education*, July 15, 2018. www.chronicle.com/interactives/executive-compensation.

Baumeister, R. F., and M. R. Leary. "The Need to Belong: Desire for Interpersonal Attachments as a Fundamental Human Motivation." *Psychological Bulletin* 117, no. 3 (1995): 497–529.

Bee, Richard H., Terry Ann Beronja, and Genevra Mann. "Analysis of the Unionization of Academic Advisors." *NACADA Journal* 10, no. 1 (1990): 35–40.

Benedict, Mary Ellen. "The Effect of Unionization on Faculty Salaries 1978–1996: A Test of Empirical Methods." *Journal of Collective Negotiations* 31, no. 3 (January 1, 2007): 251–74. https://doi.org/10.2190/CN.31.3.e.

Benjamin, Ernst. *Exploring the Role of Contingent Instructional Staff in Undergraduate Learning*. New Directions for Higher Education 123. San Francisco: Jossey-Bass, 2003.

Bergom, Inger, Jean Waltman, Louise August, and Carol Hollenshead. "Academic Researchers Speak." *Change: The Magazine of Higher Learning* 42, no. 2 (February 26, 2010): 45–49. https://doi.org/10.1080/00091380903562987.

Berman, Jillian. "Why Mainstream Public University Purdue Is Buying For-Profit College Chain Kaplan." *MarketWatch*, April 27, 2017. www.marketwatch.com/story/a-prestigious-public-university-wants-to-acquire-this-for-profit-college-chain-2017-04-27.

Berry, Joe. *Reclaiming the Ivory Tower: Organizing Adjuncts to Change Higher Education*. New York: Monthly Review Press, 2005.

Berry, Joe, and Michelle Savarese. "Directory of US Faculty Contracts and Bargaining Agents in Institutions of Higher Education." National Center for the Study of Collective Bargaining in Higher Education and the Professions, Hunter College, CUNY, New York, 2012.

Bettinger, Eric P., and Bridget Terry Long. "Does Cheaper Mean Better? The Impact of Using Adjunct Instructors on Student Outcomes." *Review of Economics and Statistics* 92, no. 3 (August 2010): 598–613. https://doi.org/10.1162/REST_a_00014.

———. "Help or Hinder? Adjunct Professors and Student Outcomes," 2005.

Birnbaum, Robert. "The End of Shared Governance: Looking Ahead or Looking Back." *New Directions for Higher Education* 2004, no. 127 (2004): 5–22. https://doi.org/10.1002/he.152.

Blumenstyk, Goldie. "Apps Can Help Advise First-Generation Students. But It Takes a Human to Say, 'I Believe in You.'" *The Chronicle of Higher Education*, July 9, 2018. www.chronicle.com/article/Apps-Can-Help-Advise/243876.

———. "Purdue's Purchase of Kaplan Is a Big Bet—and a Sign of the Times." *The Chronicle of Higher Education*, April 28, 2017. www.chronicle.com/article/Purdue-s-Purchase-of-Kaplan/239931.

Bordes, Veronica, and Patricia Arredondo. "Mentoring and 1st-Year Latina/o College Students." *Journal of Hispanic Higher Education* 4, no. 2 (April 1, 2005): 114–33. https://doi.org/10.1177/1538192704273855.

Boring, Anne, Kellie Ottoboni, and Philip Stark. "Student Evaluations of Teaching (Mostly) Do Not Measure Teaching Effectiveness." *ScienceOpen Research*, January 7, 2016. https://doi.org/10.14293/S2199-1006.1.SOR-EDU.AETBZC.v1.

Bousquet, Marc. "Good MOOCs, Bad MOOCs." Brainstorm, *The Chronicle of Higher Education*, July 25, 2012. www.chronicle.com/blogs/brainstorm/good-moocs-bad-moocs/50361.

———. *How the University Works: Higher Education and the Low-Wage Nation.* Cultural Front. New York: New York University Press, 2008.

———. "A PhD Should Result in a Tenure-Track Job, Not an Alt-Ac One." *Inside Higher Education*, October 20, 2015. www.insidehighered.com/views/2015/10/20/phd-should-result-tenure-track-job-not-alt-ac-one-essay.

———. "The Waste Product of Graduate Education: Toward a Dictatorship of the Flexible." *Social Text* 20, no. 1 (March 1, 2002): 81–104.

Braxton, John, Nathaniel Bray, and Joseph Berger. "Faculty Teaching Skills and Their Influence on the College Student Departure Process." *Journal of College Student Development* 41, no. 2 (January 1, 2000): 215–27.

Brown, A. C. "The Impact of Interest-Based Bargaining on Community College Faculty and Administrative Relationships." PhD diss., Northern Arizona University, 2015.

Brown, Wendy. *Undoing the Demos: Neoliberalism's Stealth Revolution*. Cambridge, MA: MIT Press, 2015.

Brown University and International Union, United Automobile, Aerospace and Agricultural Implement Workers of America, UAW AFL–CIO, Petitioner, No. Case 1-RC-21368 (2004).

Bruner, Jerome Seymour. *The Culture of Education*. Cambridge, MA: Harvard University Press, 1996.

Bunton, Sarah A., and William T. Mallon. "The Impact of Centers and Institutes on Faculty Life: Findings from a Study of Basic Science and Internal Medicine Faculty at Research-Intensive Medical Schools." *Academic Medicine* 81, no. 8 (August 2006): 734–43. https://doi.org/10.1097/00001888-200608000-00012.

Burgan, Mary. *What Ever Happened to the Faculty? Drift and Decision in Higher Education*. Baltimore: Johns Hopkins University Press, 2006.

Burns, Rebecca. "Adjunct Instructor: 'I Was Practically Giving My Work Away. It Was Charity.'" *Working in These Times*, October 15, 2014. http://inthesetimes.com/working/entry/17253/adjunct_instructor_i_was_practically_giving_my_work_away_it_was_charity.

Bushman, Mary F., and John E. Dean. "Outsourcing of Non-Mission-Critical Functions: A Solution to the Rising Cost of College Attendance." Collegecosts.info, 2005.

Cain, Timothy Reese. "Campus Unions: Organized Faculty and Graduate Students in US Higher Education." *ASHE Higher Education Report* 43, no. 3 (2017): 7–163. https://doi.org/10.1002/aehe.20119.

California Faculty Association. "California Faculty Association Collective Bargaining Agreement." Los Angeles, 2014.

———. "Equity Interrupted." Los Angeles, 2017.

Camacho, Sayil, and Robert A. Rhoads. "Breaking the Silence: The Unionization of Postdoctoral Workers at the University of California." *The Journal of Higher Education* 86, no. 2 (2015): 295–325. https://doi.org/10.1353/jhe.2015.0010.

Cano, Richard. "Name-Calling Begins in Battle over #InvestInEd Ballot Measure." *Azcentral*, July 12, 2018. www.azcentral.com/story/news/politics/arizona-education/2018/07/12/invested-ballot-measure-attacks-get-personal-arizona-chamber-commerce-noah-karvelis-redfored/776074002/.

Cantwell, Brendan. "Are International Students Cash Cows? Examining the Relationship Between New International Undergraduate Enrollments and

Institutional Revenue at Public Colleges and Universities in the US." *Journal of International Students* 5, no. 4 (2015): 512–25.

Cantwell, Brendan, and Jenny Lee. "Unseen Workers in the Academic Factory: Perceptions of Neoracism among International Postdocs in the United States and the United Kingdom." *Harvard Educational Review* 80, no. 4 (December 1, 2010): 490–517. https://doi.org/10.17763/haer.80.4.w54750105q7 8p451.

Cantwell, Brendan, and Barrett J. Taylor. "Internationalization of the Postdoctorate in the United States: Analyzing the Demand for International Postdoc Labor." *Higher Education* 66, no. 5 (November 1, 2013): 551–67. https://doi.org/10.1007/s10734-013-9621-0.

Cardozo, Karen M. "Academic Labor: Who Cares?" *Critical Sociology* 43, no. 3 (May 1, 2017): 405–28. https://doi.org/10.1177/0896920516641733.

Carini, Robert M., George D. Kuh, and Stephen P. Klein. "Student Engagement and Student Learning: Testing the Linkages." *Research in Higher Education* 47, no. 1 (February 1, 2006): 1–32. https://doi.org/10.1007/s11162-005-8150-9.

Carre, Francois. "(In)Dependent Contractor Misclassification." Economic Policy Institute, 2015. www.epi.org/publication/independent-contractor-misclassification/.

Cassell, Mark, and Odeh Halaseh. "The Impact of Unionization on University Performance." *Journal of Collective Bargaining in the Academy* 6, no. 1 (2014). http://thekeep.eiu.edu/jcba/vol6/iss1/3.

Center for Community College Student Engagement. *Contingent Commitments: Bringing Parttime Faculty into Focus.* Austin: The University of Texas at Austin, Program in Higher Education Leadership, 2014.

CGEU. "Coalition of Graduate Employee Unions." Coalition of Graduate Employee Unions, 2018. www.thecgeu.org/.

———. "Resolution to Address the Inequitable Treatment of International Graduate Student Workers." 2016. www.thecgeu.org/2016-conference-resolutions /resolution-to-address-the-inequitable-treatment-of-international-graduate -student-workers/.

———. "Resolution on Taking an Active Anti-racist Stand in Our Unions and Support the Movement for Black Lives." 2016. www.thecgeu.org/2016 -conference-resolutions/resolution-on-taking-an-active-anti-racist-stand-in -our-unions-and-support-the-movement-for-black-lives/.

Chambliss, Daniel F., and Christopher G. Takacs. *How College Works.* Cambridge, MA: Harvard University Press, 2014.

Chametzky, Barry. "Surviving Situational Suffering: A Classic Grounded Theory Study of Post-Secondary Part-Time Educators in the United States." *Grounded Theory Review* 14, no. 1 (2015): 25–39.

Chang, Mitchell J. "Preservation or Transformation: Where's the Real Educational Discourse on Diversity?" *The Review of Higher Education* 25, no. 2 (Winter 2002): 125–40.

Chickering, Arthur W., and Zelda F. Gamson. "Seven Principles for Good Practice in Undergraduate Education." *AAHE Bulletin*, March 1987. https://eric.ed.gov/?id=ED282491.

COACHE. "UW Tacoma COACHE Report." COACHE, 2013. www.tacoma.uw.edu/sites/default/files/users/mcrosby/coache_provost_report_universityofwashingtontacoma.pdf.

Coalition on the Academic Workforce. "One Faculty Serving All Students." New Faculty Majority, 2010.

———. "A Portrait of Part-Time Faculty Members," 2012.

Cokley, Kevin. "Perceived Faculty Encouragement and Its Influence on College Students." *Journal of College Student Development* 41, no. 3 (2000): 348–52.

College and University Professionals Association for Human Resources [CUPA-HR]. "The CUPA-HR Four-Year Faculty in Higher Education Salary Survey." 2018. www.cupahr.org/surveys/results/faculty-in-higher-education/.

———. "The CUPA-HR Staff in Higher Education Salary Survey." 2018. www.cupahr.org/surveys/results/staff-in-higher-education/.

———. "Representation and Pay of Women of Color in the Higher Education Workforce." 2018.

Conley, Valerie Martin. "Retirement and Benefits: One Size Does Not Fit All." *NEA 2016 Almanac of Higher Education*, 69–79.

Conley, Valerie Martin, and David W. Leslie. "Part-Time Instructional Faculty and Staff: Who They Are, What They Do, and What They Think." *1993 National Study of Postsecondary Faculty.* https://eric.ed.gov/?id=ED464527.

Cook, Bryan J. "The American College President Study: Key Findings and Takeaways." American Council on Education, 2012. www.acenet.edu/the-presidency/columns-and-features/Pages/The-American-College-President-Study.aspx.

Cornerstone OnDemand and Ellucian. "Empowering Employees: The State of Employee Engagement and Retention in Higher Education." Ellucian, 2016.

Cox, Bradley E., Kadian L. McIntosh, Patrick T. Terenzini, Robert D. Reason, and Brenda R. Lutovsky Quaye. "Pedagogical Signals of Faculty Approachability: Factors Shaping Faculty–Student Interaction Outside the Classroom." *Research in Higher Education* 51, no. 8 (December 1, 2010): 767–88. https://doi.org/10.1007/s11162-010-9178-z.

Cox, Bradley E., and Elizabeth Orehovec. "Faculty-Student Interaction Outside the Classroom: A Typology from a Residential College." *The Review of Higher*

Education 30, no. 4 (June 21, 2007): 343–62. https://doi.org/10.1353/rhe
.2007.0033.

Crisp, Gloria. "The Impact of Mentoring on the Success of Community College
Students." *The Review of Higher Education* 34, no. 1 (2010): 39–60. https://
doi.org/10.1353/rhe.2010.0003.

Crombie, Gail, Sandra W. Pyke, Naida Silverthorn, Alison Jones, and Sergio Piccinin. "Students' Perceptions of Their Classroom Participation and Instructor as a Function of Gender and Context." *The Journal of Higher Education*
74, no. 1 (2003): 51–76.

Cross, John G., and Edie N. Goldenberg. *Off-Track Profs: Nontenured Teachers
in Higher Education.* Cambridge, MA: MIT Press, 2009.

Cross, Karen Halverson. "Unionization and the Development of Policies for Non-
Tenure Track Faculty: A Comparative Study of Research Universities." *Journal of Collective Bargaining in the Academy* 9 (2017): 1–38.

Cummings, E. E., and M. Grijalva. "Cummings, Grijalva Support Recommendations to Increase Transparency of Spending by For-Profit Colleges." Press release, December 7, 2012. https://democrats-oversight.house.gov/news/press
-releases/cummings-grijalva-support-recommendations-to-increase
-transparency-of-spending.

Curtis, John W. "Inequities Persist for Women and Non-Tenure-Track Faculty:
Economic Status of the Profession, 2004–05." *Academe* 91, no. 2 (2005): 19–
98. https://doi.org/10.2307/40253410.

Dallimore, Elise J., Julie H. Hertenstein, and Marjorie B. Platt. "Classroom Participation and Discussion Effectiveness: Student-Generated Strategies." *Communication Education* 53, no. 1 (January 1, 2004). https://doi.org/10.1080
/0363452032000135805.

Davies, William. "The Sharing Economy Comes to Campus." *The Chronicle of
Higher Education,* January 29, 2017. www.chronicle.com/article/The-Sharing
-Economy-Comes-to/238992.

Davis, Jeff. *First-Generation Student Experience.* Sterling, VA: Stylus, 2010.

Deloitte. *Deloitte's 2016 Global Outsourcing Survey.* London: Deloitte Consulting, 2016.

———. "Outsourcing Trends in 2016—from Our Global Outsourcing Survey."
Deloitte United States. Accessed July 15, 2018. www2.deloitte.com/us/en
/pages/operations/articles/key-insights-from-deloitte-2016-outsourcing
-survey.html.

The Delphi Project on the Changing Faculty and Student Success. "The Delphi
Project on the Changing Faculty and Student Success." Pullias Center. Accessed August 31, 2018. https://pullias.usc.edu/delphi/.

DePaola, Tom, and Adrianna Kezar. "The Changing Face of Employment at Research Universities." *New Directions for Institutional Research* 2018, no. 176 (2017): 83–96. https://doi.org/10.1002/ir.20246.

Desrochers, Donna M., and Rita Kirshstein. *Labor Intensive or Labor Expensive? Changing Staffing and Compensation Patterns in Higher Education*. Issue Brief. Washington, DC: Delta Cost Project at American Institutes for Research, 2014. https://eric.ed.gov/?id=ED558470.

Devine, Kay, and Karen H. Hunter. "PhD Student Emotional Exhaustion: The Role of Supportive Supervision and Self-Presentation Behaviours." *Innovations in Education and Teaching International* 54, no. 4 (July 4, 2017): 335–44. https://doi.org/10.1080/14703297.2016.1174143.

Dixon, Sarah K., and Sharon E. Robinson Kurpius. "Depression and College Stress among University Undergraduates: Do Mattering and Self-Esteem Make a Difference?" *Journal of College Student Development* 49, no. 5 (2008): 412–24. https://doi.org/10.1353/csd.0.0024.

DPE Research Department. "The Misclassification of Employees as Independent Contractors." AFL-CIO, 2016.

Dunlop Velez, Erin. "Newly Released Student Loan Data Bust Several Myths about Student Loan Repayment." *Evolllution*, May 9, 2018. https://evolllution.com/attracting-students/todays_learner/newly-released-student-loan-data-bust-several-myths-about-student-loan-repayment.

Eagan, M. Kevin, and Audrey J. Jaeger. "Effects of Exposure to Part-Time Faculty on Community College Transfer." *Research in Higher Education* 50, no. 2 (March 2009): 168–88. https://doi.org/10.1007/s11162-008-9113-8.

Edmonds, Dan. "More Than Half of College Faculty Are Adjuncts: Should You Care?" *Forbes*, May 28, 2015. www.forbes.com/sites/noodleeducation/2015/05/28/more-than-half-of-college-faculty-are-adjuncts-should-you-care/.

Edwards, Kristen, and Kim Tolley. "Do Unions Help Adjuncts?" *The Chronicle of Higher Education*, June 3, 2018. www.chronicle.com/article/Do-Unions-Help-Adjuncts-/243566.

Ehrenberg, Ronald G. *Governing Academia: Who Is in Charge at the Modern University?* Ithaca, NY: Cornell University Press, 2004.

Ehrenberg, Ronald, and Liang Zhang. "The Changing Nature of Faculty Employment." *Working Papers*, April 1, 2004. https://digitalcommons.ilr.cornell.edu/workingpapers/43.

———. "Do Tenured and Tenure-Track Faculty Matter?" *The Journal of Human Resources* 40, no. 3 (2005): 647–59.

———. *What's Happening to Public Higher Education? The Shifting Financial Burden*. Baltimore: Johns Hopkins University Press, 2007.

Ehrenberg, Ronald, Hirschel Kasper, and Daniel Rees. "Faculty Turnover at American Colleges and Universities: Analyses of AAUP Data." *Economics of Education Review* 10, no. 2 (January 1, 1991): 99–110. https://doi.org/10.1016/0272-7757(91)90002-7.

Eidlin, Barry, and Micah Uetricht. "The Problem of Workplace Democracy." *New Labor Forum* 27, no. 1 (January 1, 2018): 70–79. https://doi.org/10.1177/1095796017745037.

Ellis, Evelynn M. "The Impact of Race and Gender on Graduate School Socialization, Satisfaction with Doctoral Study, and Commitment to Degree Completion." *Western Journal of Black Studies* 25, no. 1 (Spring 2001): 30–45.

Engle, Jennifer. "Postsecondary Access and Success for First-Generation College Students." *American Academic* 3 (2007): 25–48.

Evans, Linda. "Professionalism, Professionality and the Development of Education Professionals." *British Journal of Educational Studies* 56, no. 1 (March 1, 2008): 20–38. https://doi.org/10.1111/j.1467-8527.2007.00392.x.

Evans, Teresa M., Lindsay Bira, Jazmin Beltran Gastelum, L. Todd Weiss, and Nathan L. Vanderford. "Evidence for a Mental Health Crisis in Graduate Education." Comments and Opinion, *Nature Biotechnology*, March 6, 2018. https://doi.org/10.1038/nbt.4089.

Fassinger, Polly A. "Understanding Classroom Interaction." *The Journal of Higher Education* 66, no. 1 (January 1, 1995): 82–96. https://doi.org/10.1080/00221546.1995.11774758.

Feldman, Daniel C., and William H. Turnley. "A Field Study of Adjunct Faculty: The Impact of Career Stage on Reactions to Non-Tenure-Track Jobs." *Journal of Career Development* 28, no. 1 (September 1, 2001): 1–16. https://doi.org/10.1177/089484530102800101.

Ferguson, Kryste, Michael McTighe, Bhishma Amlani, and Tracy Costello. *Supporting the Needs of Postdocs*. Rockville, MD: National Postdoctoral Association, 2017.

Ferreira, Maria. "Gender Issues Related to Graduate Student Attrition in Two Science Departments." *International Journal of Science Education* 25, no. 8 (August 1, 2003): 969–89. https://doi.org/10.1080/09500690305026.

Finkelstein, Martin J., Valerie Martin Conley, and Jack H. Schuster. *The Faculty Factor: Reassessing the American Academy in a Turbulent Era*. Baltimore: Johns Hopkins University Press, 2016.

Five Colleges Consortium. "The Consortium." Accessed August 31, 2018. www.fivecolleges.edu/consortium.

Flaherty, Colleen. "AAUP Report Says Adjunct Professor Was Likely Fired for Insisting on Rigor in Courses." *Inside Higher Ed*, March 29, 2017. www

.insidehighered.com/news/2017/03/29/aaup-report-says-adjunct-professor
-was-likely-fired-insisting-rigor-courses.

———. "Colleges Assign Adjunct Hiring to a Third Party." *Inside Higher Ed*,
July 21, 2014. www.insidehighered.com/news/2014/07/21/colleges-assign
-adjunct-hiring-third-party.

———. "Could Postdoc Unions Be the Next Big Thing in Collective Bargaining
among Academics?" *Inside Higher Ed*, October 31, 2017. www.insidehighered
.com/news/2017/10/31/could-postdoc-unions-be-next-big-thing-collective
-bargaining-among-academics.

Flannery, Mary Ellen. "The Homeless Professor Who Lives in Her Car." *NEA
Today*, November 1, 2017. http://neatoday.org/2017/11/01/homeless
-professor/.

Florida, Richard, Gary Gates, Brian Knudsen, and Kevin Stolarick. *The University
and the Creative Economy*. Pittsburgh, PA: H. J. Heinz III School of Public
Policy, Carnegie Mellon University, 2006.

Foucault, Michel. *The Birth of Biopolitics: Lectures at the Collège de France,
1978–79*. Edited by Michel Senellart. New York: Palgrave Macmillan,
2008.

———. *Discipline and Punish: The Birth of the Prison*. Translated by Alan Sheridan. 2nd ed. New York: Vintage Books, 1995.

Fredrickson, Caroline. "There Is No Excuse for How Universities Treat Adjuncts."
The Atlantic, September 15, 2015. www.theatlantic.com/business/archive
/2015/09/higher-education-college-adjunct-professor-salary/404461/.

Fullwiler, Scott, Stephanie Kelton, Catherine Ruetschlin, and Marshall Steinbaum.
The Macroeconomic Effects of Student Debt Cancellation. Annandale-on-
Hudson, NY: Levy Economics Institute, 2018.

Gagliardi, Jonathan S., Lorelle L. Espinosa, Jonathan M. Turk, and Morgan Taylor. "American College President Study 2017." American Council on Education, 2017.

Gallup. "The Engaged University." Gallup.com. Accessed July 2, 2018. www.gallup
.com/education/194321/higher-education-employee-engagement.aspx.

———. "Great Jobs Great Lives: The 2014 Gallup-Purdue Index Report." Gallup, 2014.

Gappa, Judith M. *The Invisible Faculty: Improving the Status of Part-Timers in
Higher Education*. San Francisco: Jossey-Bass, 1993.

Garfield, Timothy K. "Governance in a Union Environment." *New Directions for
Community Colleges* 2008, no. 141 (2008): 25–33. https://doi.org/10.1002
/cc.312.

Gee, Alastair. "Facing Poverty, Academics Turn to Sex Work and Sleeping in Cars."
US News, *The Guardian*, September 28, 2017. www.theguardian.com/us

-news/2017/sep/28/adjunct-professors-homeless-sex-work-academia -poverty.

Gehrke, Sean, and Adrianna Kezar. "Unbundling the Faculty Role in Higher Education: Utilizing Historical, Theoretical, and Empirical Frameworks to Inform Future Research." In *Higher Education: Handbook of Theory and Research*, edited by Michael B. Paulsen, vol. 30, 93–150. Cham, Switzerland: Springer International Publishing, 2015. https://doi.org/10.1007/978-3-319-12835-1_3.

Geleta, Nomsa E., Adrienne Dixon, and Susan Curtin. "Collaboration Rebuilds a Sense of Belonging for Students of Color Using the Sanctuary Model as a Framework." *Making Connections* 16, no. 1 (July 2015): 27–34.

Gerber, Larry G. *The Rise and Decline of Faculty Governance: Professionalization and the Modern American University*. Baltimore: John Hopkins University Press, 2014.

Getachew, Adom. "Bringing Unions to the Fight." *Jacobin*, 2017. http://jacobinmag .com/2017/02/graduate-workers-unions-racial-justice-diversity-yale-geso/.

GEU-UAW. "GEU-UAW Collective Bargaining Agreement," 2015. http:// uconngradunion.org/home/resources/current-members/full-contract.

Gillespie, Patrick. "Intuit: Gig Economy Is 34% of US Workforce." CNNMoney, May 24, 2017. https://money.cnn.com/2017/05/24/news/economy/gig-eco nomy-intuit/index.html.

Ginsberg, Benjamin. *The Fall of the Faculty*. Oxford, UK: Oxford University Press, 2011.

Gloria, Alberta M., Jeanett Castellanos, and Veronica Orozco. "Perceived Educational Barriers, Cultural Fit, Coping Responses, and Psychological Well-Being of Latina Undergraduates." *Hispanic Journal of Behavioral Sciences* 27, no. 2 (May 1, 2005): 161–83. https://doi.org/10.1177/0739986305275097.

Gloria, Alberta M., and Ester R. Rodriguez. "Counseling Latino University Students: Psychosociocultural Issues for Consideration." *Journal of Counseling & Development* 78, no. 2 (April 2000): 145–54. https://doi.org/10.1002/j .1556-6676.2000.tb02572.x.

Gold, Robert S. *A Jazz Lexicon*. 1st ed. A. A. Knopf, 1964.

Goldberg, David. "The Dangers of the Uberization of Higher Education." *Inside Higher Ed*, August 12, 2016. www.insidehighered.com/views/2016/08/12 /dangers-uberization-higher-education-essay.

Golde, Chris M. "The Role of the Department and Discipline in Doctoral Student Attrition: Lessons from Four Departments." *The Journal of Higher Education* 76, no. 6 (November 1, 2005): 669–700. https://doi.org/10.1080/00221546 .2005.11772304.

Goldrick-Rab, Sara. *Paying the Price: College Costs, Financial Aid, and the Betrayal of the American Dream*. Chicago: University of Chicago Press, 2016.

Gordon J. Hewitt. "Graduate Student Employee Collective Bargaining and the Educational Relationship between Faculty and Graduate Students." *Journal of Collective Negotiations* 29, no. 2 (June 1, 2000): 153–66. https://doi.org /10.2190/P07G-C8RF-5GG0-4VH8.

Graeber, David. "Are You in a BS Job? In Academe, You're Hardly Alone." *The Chronicle of Higher Education*, May 6, 2018. www.chronicle.com/article/Are -You-in-a-BS-Job-In/243318.

Graunke, Steven S., and Sherry A. Woosley. "An Exploration of the Factors That Affect the Academic Success of College Sophomores." *College Student Journal* 39, no. 2 (June 2005): 367–76.

Gross, Betheny, and Dan Goldhaber. *Community College Transfer and Articulation Policies: Looking Beneath the Surface.* CRPE Working Paper 2009-1. Center on Reinventing Public Education, 2009. https://eric.ed.gov/?id =ED504665.

Hall, Gary. *The Uberification of the University.* Minneapolis: University of Minnesota Press, 2016.

Hannák, Anikó, Claudia Wagner, David Garcia, Alan Mislove, Markus Strohmaier, and Christo Wilson. "Bias in Online Freelance Marketplaces: Evidence from TaskRabbit and Fiverr." *Proceedings of the 2017 ACM Conference on Computer Supported Cooperative Work and Social Computing,* 1914-33. New York: ACM Press, 2017. https://doi.org/10.1145/2998181 .2998327.

Harbison, Brooks Robert. "Stress in Tenure-Track and Non-Tenure-Track Faculty: What We Know and Where We Are Going." Master's thesis, The University of Texas at Austin, 2016. https://doi.org/10.15781/T2MC8RK06.

Harrington, Charles, and Timothy Schibik. "Caveat Emptor: Is There a Relationship between Part-Time Faculty Utilization and Student Learning Outcomes and Retention?" AIR 2001 Annual Forum Paper, June 2001. https://eric.ed .gov/?id=ED456785.

Hartnett, Rodney T., and Joseph Katz. "The Education of Graduate Students." *The Journal of Higher Education* 48, no. 6 (November 1, 1977): 646–64. https:// doi.org/10.1080/00221546.1977.11776583.

Harvey, David. *Spaces of Neoliberalization: Towards a Theory of Uneven Geographical Development.* Stuttgart: Franz Steiner Verlag, 2005.

Head, Sarah King. "MOOCs—The Revolution Has Begun, Says Moody's." *University World News*, September 23, 2012. www.universityworldnews.com /article.php?story=20120920124146236.

Hearn, James C. "Impacts of Undergraduate Experiences on Aspirations and Plans for Graduate and Professional Education." *Research in Higher Education* 27, no. 2 (1987): 119–41.

Hearn, James C., Darrell R. Lewis, Lincoln Kallsen, Janet M. Holdsworth, and Lisa M. Jones. "'Incentives for Managed Growth': A Case Study of Incentives-Based Planning and Budgeting in a Large Public Research University." *The Journal of Higher Education* 77, no. 2 (March 1, 2006): 286–316. https://doi .org/10.1080/00221546.2006.11778927.

Herbert, William A., and Jacob Apkarian. "Everything Passes, Everything Changes: Unionization and Collective Bargaining in Higher Education." SSRN Scholarly Paper. Rochester, NY: Social Science Research Network, December 9, 2017. http://papers.ssrn.com/abstract=3085214.

Hinchey, Patricia, and Isabel Kimmel. *The Graduate Grind*. New York: Falmer Press, 2000.

Hirsch, Barry, and David MacPherson. "Union Membership and Coverage Database from the CPS [Data from Unionstat]," 2017. http://unionstats.gsu.edu /CPS.

Hoerr, John. *We Can't Eat Prestige: The Women Who Organized Harvard*. Philadelphia: Temple University Press, 2001.

Hollenshead, Carol, Jean Waltman, Louise August, Jeanne Miller, Gilia Smith, and Allison Bell. *Making the Best of Both Worlds: Findings from a National Institution-Level Survey on Non-Tenure-Track Faculty*. Ann Arbor, MI: Center for the Education of Women, 2007.

Holmes, Sharon L., Larry H. Ebbers, Daniel C. Robinson, and Abel G. Mugenda. "Validating African American Students at Predominantly White Institutions." *Journal of College Student Retention: Research, Theory & Practice* 2, no. 1 (May 1, 2000): 41–58. https://doi.org/10.2190/XP0F-KRQW-F547-Y2XM.

Horowitz, Sara. "Freelancers Union Looks to Bring Portable Benefits to On-Demand Workers Nationwide." *Freelancers Union,* May 10, 2016. https:// blog.freelancersunion.org/2016/05/10/freelancers-union-looks-to-bring -portable-benefits-to-on-demand-workers-nationwide-2/.

Howell, Lydia Pleotis, Chao-Yin Chen, Jesse P. Joad, Ralph Green, Edward J. Callahan, and Ann C. Bonham. "Issues and Challenges of Non-Tenure-Track Research Faculty: The UC Davis School of Medicine Experience." *Academic Medicine* 85, no. 6 (June 2010): 1041. https://doi.org/10.1097/ACM.0b013e3 181dbfbf3.

Hu, Shouping, and George D. Kuh. "Diversity Experiences and College Student Learning and Personal Development." *Journal of College Student Development* 44, no. 3 (May 23, 2003): 320–34. https://doi.org/10.1353/csd.2003 .0026.

Huelsman, Mark. *The Debt Divide: The Racial and Class Bias behind the "New Normal" of Student Borrowing*. New York: Demos, 2015.

Huerta, Adrian, and Seth Fishman. "Marginality and Mattering: Urban Latino Male Undergraduates in Higher Education." *Journal of the First-Year Experience and Students in Transition* 26, no. 1 (January 1, 2014): 85–100.

Hurd, Richard W. "Non-Faculty Unionization at Institutions of Higher Education." In *Directory of Non-Faculty Bargaining Agents in Institutions of Higher Education*, edited by J. M. Douglas, ix–xii. New York: National Center for the Study of Collective Bargaining in Higher Education and the Professions, 1991.

———. "The Unionization of Clerical, Technical, and Professional Employees in Higher Education: Threat or Opportunity." In *Managing the Industrial Labor Relations Process in Higher Education*, edited by D. J. Julius, 315–27. Washington, DC: College and University Professional Association for Human Resources, 1993.

Hurd, Richard W., and Gregory Woodhead. "The Unionization of Clerical Workers at Large US Universities and Colleges." *Newsletter of the National Center for the Study of Collective Bargaining in Higher Education and the Professions* 15, no. 3 (1987): 1–8.

Hurlburt, Steven, and Michael McGarrah. *Cost Savings or Cost Shifting? The Relationship between Part-Time Contingent Faculty and Institutional Spending*." New York: TIAA Institute, 2016.

Hurtado, S., A. Ruiz Alvarado, and C. Guillermo-Wann. "Creating Inclusive Environments: The Mediating Effect of Faculty and Staff Validation on the Relationship of Discrimination/Bias to Students' Sense of Belonging." *Journal Committed to Social Change on Race and Ethnicity* 1, no. 1 (October 13, 2015): 60–80. https://escholarship.org/uc/item/5z7283g0.

Hurtado, Sylvia, and Deborah Faye Carter. "Effects of College Transition and Perceptions of the Campus Racial Climate on Latino College Students' Sense of Belonging." *Sociology of Education* 70, no. 4 (1997): 324–45. https://doi.org/10/g8w.

Hurtado, Sylvia, Marcela Cuellar, and Chelsea Guillermo-Wann. "Quantitative Measures of Students' Sense of Validation: Advancing the Study of Diverse Learning Environments." *Enrollment Management Journal* 5, no. 2 (2011): 161.

Hurtado, Sylvia, M. Kevin Eagan, Minh C. Tran, Christopher B. Newman, Mitchell J. Chang, and Paolo Velasco. "'We Do Science Here': Underrepresented Students' Interactions with Faculty in Different College Contexts." *Journal of Social Issues* 67, no. 3 (September 1, 2011): 553–79. https://doi.org/10.1111/j.1540-4560.2011.01714.x.

Hutcheson, Philo A. "McCarthyism and the Professoriate: A Historiographic Nightmare?" In *Higher Education: Handbook of Theory and Research*, edited by J. C. Smart, vol. 12. New York. Springer Science & Business Media, 1997.

———. *A Professional Professoriate: Unionization, Bureaucratization, and the AAUP.* 1st ed. Vanderbilt Issues in Higher Education. Nashville, TN: Vanderbilt University Press, 2000.

Huws, Ursula. *Labor in the Global Digital Economy: The Cybertariat Comes of Age.* New York: Monthly Review Press, 2014.

Hyman, Louis. "Where Are All the Uber Drivers? Not in These Government Statistics." *Los Angeles Times,* July 27, 2018. www.latimes.com/opinion/op-ed/la -oe-hyman-contingent-temp-workers-20180729-story.html.

Ikebe, Shannon, and Alexandra Holstrom-Smith. "Union Democracy, Student Labor, and the Fight for Public Education." *Berkeley Journal of Sociology* 58 (2014): 42–50.

Immordino-Yang, Mary Helen. "Implications of Affective and Social Neuroscience for Educational Theory." *Educational Philosophy and Theory* 43, no. 1 (January 1, 2011): 98–103. https://doi.org/10.1111/j.1469-5812.2010 .00713.x.

Inkelas, Karen Kurotsuchi, Zaneeta E. Daver, Kristen E. Vogt, and Jeannie Brown Leonard. "Living-Learning Programs and First-Generation College Students' Academic and Social Transition to College." *Research in Higher Education* 48, no. 4 (June 1, 2007): 403–34. https://doi.org/10.1007/s11162 -006-9031-6.

Jacob, Philip E. *Changing Values in College: An Exploratory Study of the Impact of College Teaching.* New York: Harper, 1957.

Jacobs, Ken, Ian Perry, and Jenifer MacGillvary. "The High Public Cost of Low Wages." *Center for Labor Research and Education*, April 13, 2015. http:// laborcenter.berkeley.edu/the-high-public-cost-of-low-wages/.

Jacoby, Daniel. "Effects of Part-Time Faculty Employment on Community College Graduation Rates." *Journal of Higher Education* 77, no. 6 (2006): 1081–1103.

Jaeger, Audrey J., and Alessandra J. Dinin, eds. *The Postdoc Landscape: The Invisible Scholars.* London: Academic Press, 2018.

Jaeger, Audrey J., and M. Kevin Eagan. "Unintended Consequences: Examining the Effect of Part-Time Faculty Members on Associate's Degree Completion." *Community College Review* 36, no. 3 (January 1, 2009): 167–94. https://doi .org/10.1177/0091552108327070.

Jaschik, Scott. "The Shrinking Phd Job Market." *Inside Higher Ed*, April 4, 2016. www.insidehighered.com/news/2016/04/04/new-data-show-tightening-phd -job-market-across-disciplines.

Johnson, David W. *Academic Controversy. Enriching College Instruction through Intellectual Conflict.* ASHE-ERIC Higher Education Report, vol. 25, no. 3. Washington, DC: ERIC Clearinghouse on Higher Education, 1997. http://eric.ed.gov/?id=ED409829.

Johnson, W. Brad, Gail Rose, and Lewis Z. Schlosser. "Student-Faculty Mentoring: Theoretical and Methodological Issues." In *The Blackwell Handbook of Mentoring: A Multiple Perspectives Approach*, edited by Tammy D. Allen and Lillian T. Eby. New York: Wiley, 2011.

Johnsrud, Linda K. "Higher Education Staff: Bearing the Brunt of Cost Containment." *NEA 2000 Almanac of Higher Education*, 101–118.

———. "Higher Education Support Professionals: Demographics and Worklife Issues." *NEA 2004 Almanac of Higher Education*, 105–126.

———. "Higher Education Support Professionals: The Fear of Speaking Out." *NEA 2003 Almanac of Higher Education*, 109–118.

———. "The Worklife Issues of Higher Education Support Personnel." *NEA 1999 Almanac of Higher Education*, 111–124.

Johnsrud, Linda K., and Vicki J. Rosser. "Faculty Members' Morale and Their Intention to Leave." *The Journal of Higher Education* 73, no. 4 (July 1, 2002): 518–42. https://doi.org/10.1080/00221546.2002.11777162.

Johnston, Paul. *Success While Others Fail: Social Movement Unionism and the Public Workplace.* Ithaca, NY: ILR Press, 1994.

Juillerat, Stephanie. "Assessing the Expectations and Satisfactions of Sophomores." In *Visible Solutions for Invisible Students: Helping Sophomores Succeed*, edited by Laurie A. Schreiner and Jerry Pattengale, 19–29. Columbia, SC: National Resource Center for the First Year Experience and Students in Transition, University of South Carolina, 2000.

Julius, Daniel J. "The Slippery Slope of 'Unique.'" *Journal of Collective Bargaining in the Academy* 9 (2017): 1–4.

Julius, Daniel J., and Patricia J. Gumport. "Graduate Student Unionization: Catalysts and Consequences." *The Review of Higher Education* 26, no. 2 (2002): 187–216. https://doi.org/10.1353/rhe.2002.0033.

Kalleberg, Arne L., and Michael Dunn. "Good Jobs, Bad Jobs in the Gig Economy." *Perspectives on Work* 20 (2016): 10–14.

Karvelis, Noah. "You Need Rank and File to Win: How Arizona Teachers Built a Movement." *Rethinking Schools* 33, no. 2 (Winter 2018–19). www.rethinkingschools.org/articles/you-need-rank-and-file-to-win-how-arizona-teachers-built-a-movement.

Katsinas, Stephen G., J. A. Ogun, and N. J. Bray. "Monetary Compensation of Full-Time Faculty at American Public Regional Universities: The Impact of

Geography and the Existence of Collective Bargaining." *Journal of Collective Bargaining in the Academy* 8 (2016): 1–28.

Katz, Lawrence F., and Alan B. Krueger. "The Rise and Nature of Alternative Work Arrangements in the United States, 1995–2015." Working Paper. National Bureau of Economic Research, September 2016. https://doi.org/10.3386 /w22667.

Kelly-Woessner, April, and Matthew C. Woessner. "My Professor Is a Partisan Hack: How Perceptions of a Professor's Political Views Affect Student Course Evaluations." *PS: Political Science & Politics* 39, no. 3 (July 2006): 495–501. https://doi.org/10.1017/S104909650606080X.

Kezar, Adrianna J. "Departmental Cultures and Non-Tenure-Track Faculty: Willingness, Capacity, and Opportunity to Perform at Four-Year Institutions." *The Journal of Higher Education* 84, no. 2 (March 2013): 153–88. https://doi .org/10.1080/00221546.2013.11777284.

———. *Enhancing Campus Capacity for Leadership an Examination of Grassroots Leaders in Higher Education.* Stanford, CA: Stanford University Press, 2011.

———. "Examining Non-Tenure Track Faculty Perceptions of How Departmental Policies and Practices Shape Their Performance and Ability to Create Student Learning at Four-Year Institutions." *Research in Higher Education* 54, no. 5 (August 1, 2013): 571–98. https://doi.org/10/f4573b.

———. "Obtaining Integrity? Reviewing and Examining the Charter between Higher Education and Society." *The Review of Higher Education* 27, no. 4 (2004): 429–59. https://doi.org/10.1353/rhe.2004.0013.

Kezar, Adrianna, Anthony C. Chambers, and John C. Burkhardt. *Higher Education for the Public Good: Emerging Voices from a National Movement.* New York: Wiley, 2005.

Kezar, Adrianna J., and Tom DePaola. "Understanding the Need for Unions: Contingent Faculty Working Conditions and the Relationship to Student Learning." In *Professors in the Gig Economy: Unionizing Adjunct Faculty in America*, by Kim Tolley. Baltimore: Johns Hopkins University Press, 2018.

Kezar, Adrianna, and Sean Gehrke. "Grassroots Leadership: Responding to Declining Shared Governance in the Neoliberal World." In *Survival of the Fittest: The Shifting Contours of Higher Education in China and the United States*, edited by Qi Li and Cynthia Gerstl-Pepin, 101–17. Berlin: Springer Berlin Heidelberg, 2014. https://doi.org/10.1007/978-3-642-39813-1_8.

Kezar, Adrianna, and Daniel Maxey. *Adapting by Design.* 2nd ed. Los Angeles: The Delphi Project, 2015. https://pullias.usc.edu/wp-content/uploads/2015/06 /DELPHI-PROJECT_ADAPTING-BY-DESIGN_2ED.pdf.

————, eds. *Envisioning the Faculty for the Twenty-First Century: Moving to a Mission-Oriented and Learner-Centered Model*. New Brunswick, NJ: Rutgers University Press, 2016.

Kezar, Adrianna, Daniel Maxey, and Laura Badke. *The Imperative for Change: Fostering Understanding of the Necessity of Changing Non-Tenure-Track Faculty Policies and Practices*. The Delphi Project on the Changing Faculty and Student Success. Los Angeles: USC Pullias Center for Higher Education, 2014. https://pullias.usc.edu/wp-content/uploads/2014/01/IMPERATIVE -FOR-CHANGE_WEB-2014.pdf.

Kezar, Adrianna, and Cecelia Sam. "Governance as a Catalyst for Policy Change: Creating a Contingent Faculty Friendly Academy." *Educational Policy* 28, no. 3 (May 1, 2014): 425–62. https://doi.org/10.1177/0895904812465112.

————. *Non-Tenure-Track Faculty in Higher Education: Theories and Tensions*. ASHE Higher Education Report. San Francisco: Jossey-Bass, 2011.

————. "Understanding the New Majority of Non-Tenure-Track Faculty in Higher Education—Demographics, Experiences, and Plans of Action." Association for the Study of Higher Education, 2010. http://doi.wiley.com/10.1002/aehe .3604.

————. "Understanding Non-Tenure Track Faculty: New Assumptions and Theories for Conceptualizing Behavior." *American Behavioral Scientist* 55, no. 11 (November 1, 2011): 1419–42. https://doi.org/10.1177/0002764211 408879.

Kiley, Kevin. "Should Online Teaching Be Outsourced?" Online Learning Update, 2011. http://people.uis.edu/rschr1/onlinelearning/?p=2551.

Kirstein, Peter N. "Seventh Circuit Protects Part-Time Faculty Union Leader, Robin Meade." *Academe Blog*, November 4, 2014. https://academeblog.org/2014/11 /04/seventh-circuit-protects-part-time-faculty-union-leader-robin-meade/.

Kitchen, Deeb-Paul. "Can Graduate Students Re-energize the Labor Movement?" *Thought & Action* (Fall 2014): 47–62.

————. "The Union Makes Us Strong: A Case Study in the Graduate Labor Movement." PhD diss., University of Florida, 2011. Proquest (3467578).

Klaff, Daniel B., and Ronald G. Ehrenberg. "Collective Bargaining and Staff Salaries in American Colleges and Universities." *ILR Review* 57, no. 1 (October 1, 2003): 92–104. https://doi.org/10.1177/001979390305700105.

Komarraju, Meera, Sergey Musulkin, and Gargi Bhattacharya. "Role of Student-Faculty Interactions in Developing College Students' Academic Self-Concept, Motivation, and Achievement." *Journal of College Student Development* 51, no. 3 (May 23, 2010): 332–42. https://doi.org/10.1353/csd.0.0137.

Kreider, Benjamin. "Risk Shift and the Gig Economy." Economic Policy Institute, 2015. www.epi.org/blog/risk-shift-and-the-gig-economy/.

Kroeger, Teresa, Celine McNicholas, Marni von Wilpert, and Julia Wolfe. "The State of Graduate Student Employee Unions: Momentum to Organize among Graduate Student Workers Is Growing Despite Opposition." Economic Policy Institute, January 11, 2018. www.epi.org/publication/graduate-student-employee-unions/.

Kuh, George D. "The Other Curriculum: Out-of-Class Experiences Associated with Student Learning and Personal Development." *The Journal of Higher Education* 66, no. 2 (1995): 123–55. https://doi.org/10.2307/2943909.

Kuh, George D., and Shouping Hu. "The Effects of Student-Faculty Interaction in the 1990s." *The Review of Higher Education* 24, no. 3 (March 1, 2001): 309–32. https://doi.org/10.1353/rhe.2001.0005.

Kuh, George D., Jillian Kinzie, Jennifer A. Buckley, Brian K. Bridges, and John C. Hayek. What *Matters to Student Success: A Review of the Literature*. Commissioned Report for the National Symposium on Postsecondary Student Success. Washington, DC: National Postsecondary Education Cooperative, 2006.

Kuh, George D., Jillian Kinzie, John H. Schuh, and Elizabeth J. Whitt. *Student Success in College: Creating Conditions That Matter*. San Francisco: Jossey-Bass, 2010.

Lafer, Gordon. "The Corporate Assault on Higher Education and Union Responses." *Thought & Action* 33, no. 2 (2017): 11–36.

———. "Graduate Student Unions: Organizing in a Changed Academic Economy." *Labor Studies Journal* 28, no. 2 (June 1, 2003): 25–43. https://doi.org/10.1177/0160449X0302800202.

Lamport, Mark A. "Student-Faculty Informal Interaction and the Effect on College Student Outcomes: A Review of the Literature." *Adolescence* 28, no. 112 (Winter 1993): 971–90.

Lauer, Mike. "Update on the Postdoctoral Benefit Survey." NIH Extramural Nexus, November 30, 2015. https://nexus.od.nih.gov/all/2015/11/30/update-postdoctoral-benefit-survey/.

Lave, Jean, and Etienne Wenger. *Situated Learning: Legitimate Peripheral Participation*. New York: Cambridge University Press, 1991.

Lederman, Doug. "Arbitrator Sides with Eastern Michigan in Dispute with Union over Online Learning." *Inside Higher Ed*, January 15, 2018. www.insidehighered.com/digital-learning/article/2018/01/15/arbitrator-sides-eastern-michigan-dispute-union-over-online.

Lee, Jenny J., and Brendan Cantwell. "The Global Sorting Machine: An Examination of Neoracism among International Students and Postdoctoral Researchers." *Universities and the Public Sphere: Knowledge Creation and*

State Building in the Era of Globalization, January 1, 2012, 47–63. https://doi.org/10.4324/9780203847848.

Lee, Jenny J., and Charles Rice. "Welcome to America? International Student Perceptions of Discrimination." *Higher Education* 53, no. 3 (March 1, 2007): 381–409. https://doi.org/10.1007/s10734-005-4508-3.

Lee, Jessica, Joan C. Williams, and Su Li. *Parents in the Pipeline: Retaining Postdoctoral Researchers and Families.* San Francisco: The Center for WorkLife Law, 2017.

Lee, Wynetta Y. "Striving toward Effective Retention: The Effect of Race on Mentoring African American Students." *Peabody Journal of Education* 74, no. 2 (April 1999): 27–43. https://doi.org/10.1207/s15327930pje7402_4.

Lerner, Danielle. "Proposed Arizona Bill, HB 2017, Looks to Limit School Walkouts like Red for Ed Movement." *ABC Arizona*, January 17. 2019. www.abc15.com/news/state/proposed-arizona-bill-h-b-2017-looks-to-limit-school-walkouts-like-the-red-for-ed-movement.

Levecque, Katia, Frederik Anseel, Alain De Beuckelaer, Johan Van der Heyden, and Lydia Gisle. "Work Organization and Mental Health Problems in PhD Students." *Research Policy* 46, no. 4 (May 1, 2017): 868–79. https://doi.org/10.1016/j.respol.2017.02.008.

Lewis, Chance W., Rick Ginsberg, and Tim Davies. "The Experiences of African American PhD Students at a Predominantly White Carnegie I Research Institution." In *Eighth Annual National Conference, POCPWI*, 100–102, 2003.

Light, Richard J. *Making the Most of College: Students Speak Their Minds.* Cambridge, MA: Harvard University Press, 2001.

Lundberg, Carol A., and Laurie A. Schreiner. "Quality and Frequency of Faculty-Student Interaction as Predictors of Learning: An Analysis by Student Race/Ethnicity." *Journal of College Student Development* 45, no. 5 (2004): 549–65. https://doi.org/10.1353/csd.2004.0061.

Lundberg, Carol A., Laurie A. Schreiner, Kristin Hovaguimian, and Sharyn Slavin Miller. "First-Generation Status and Student Race/Ethnicity as Distinct Predictors of Student Involvement and Learning." *Journal of Student Affairs Research and Practice* 44, no. 1 (January 20, 2007). https://doi.org/10.2202/1949-6605.1755.

Lundquist, Cara, Rebecca J. Spalding, and R. Eric Landrum. "College Students' Thoughts about Leaving the University: The Impact of Faculty Attitudes and Behaviors." *Journal of College Student Retention: Research, Theory & Practice* 4, no. 2 (August 1, 2002): 123–33. https://doi.org/10.2190/FLAL-7AM5-Q6K3-L40P.

Mac, Ryan. "Amazon Releases Diversity Numbers for the First Time and Surprise, It's Mostly Male and White." *Forbes*, October 31, 2014. www.forbes.com /sites/ryanmac/2014/10/31/amazon-releases-diversity-numbers-for-first-time -and-surprise-its-mostly-male-and-white/#3958de8124cf.

MacNell, Lillian, Adam Driscoll, and Andrea N. Hunt. "What's in a Name: Exposing Gender Bias in Student Ratings of Teaching." *Innovative Higher Education* 40, no. 4 (August 1, 2015): 291–303. https://doi.org/10.1007/s10755-014 -9313-4.

Magolda, Peter M. *The Lives of Campus Custodians: Insights into Corporatization and Civic Disengagement in the Academy*. Sterling, VA: Stylus Publishing, 2016.

Maisto, Maria. "Adjuncts, Blogs and the DOL." *Majority Rule*, July 25, 2015. https://extraordinaryfacultynfm.wordpress.com/2015/07/25/adjuncts-blogs -and-the-dol/.

Maitland, C., Gary Rhoades, and M. F. Smith. "Unions and Senates: Governance and Distance Education." *The NEA 2009 Almanac of Higher Education*, 75–84.

Marcus, Jon. "University Bureaucracies Grew 15 Percent during the Recession, Even as Budgets Were Cut and Tuition Increased." *The Hechinger Report*, October 6, 2016. https://hechingerreport.org/university-bureaucracies-grew -15-percent-recession-even-budgets-cut-tuition-increased/.

Martin Lohfink, Mandy, and Michael B. Paulsen. "Comparing the Determinants of Persistence for First-Generation and Continuing-Generation Students." *Journal of College Student Development* 46, no. 4 (2005): 409–28. https://doi .org/10.1353/csd.2005.0040.

Maslow, A. H. *Toward a Psychology of Being*. Vol. 50. Princeton, NJ: Van Nostrand, 1962.

Mason, Mary Ann, Marc Goulden, and Karie Frasch. "Why Graduate Students Reject the Fast Track." *Academe* 95 (2009): 1. www.aaup.org/article/why -graduate-students-reject-fast-track#.XGURluLYrcI.

Mayhew, Matthew J., Alyssa N. Rockenbach, Nicholas A. Bowman, Tricia A. D. Seifert, and Gregory C. Wolniak. *How College Affects Students: 21st Century Evidence That Higher Education Works*. New York: Wiley, 2016.

McCafferty, Molly. "Grad Union Establishes Sexual Harassment Committee." *The Harvard Crimson*, May 11, 2018. www.thecrimson.com/article/2018/5/11 /hgsu-times-up-established/.

McConnell, Penny J. "ERIC Review: What Community Colleges Should Do to Assist First-Generation Students." *Community College Review* 28, no. 3 (December 1, 2000): 75–87. https://doi.org/10.1177/009155210002800305.

McKay, Valerie C., and Jeremy Estrella. "First-Generation Student Success: The Role of Faculty Interaction in Service Learning Courses." *Communication Education* 57, no. 3 (July 1, 2008): 356–72. https://doi.org/10.1080/03634520801966123.

Mcmurtrie, Beth. "How Artificial Intelligence Is Changing Teaching." *The Chronicle of Higher Education*, August 12, 2018. www.chronicle.com/article/How-Artificial-Intelligence-Is/244231.

Mello, James A. "In Support of Others: An Examination of Psychological Capital and Job Satisfaction in Academic Staff." *Journal of Academic Administration in Higher Education* 9, no. 2 (2013): 1–9.

Merritt, Deborah J. "Bias, the Brain, and Student Evaluations of Teaching." *St. John's Law Review* 82 (2008): 235–88.

Meyer, Leila. "Report: Higher Ed Neglecting Employee Engagement." *Campus Technology*, September 22, 2016. https://campustechnology.com/articles/2016/09/22/report-higher-ed-neglecting-employee-engagement.aspx.

Miller, Jennifer M., and Maryann P. Feldman. "The Sorcerer's Postdoc Apprentice: Uncertain Funding and Contingent Highly Skilled Labour." *Cambridge Journal of Regions, Economy and Society* 7, no. 2 (July 1, 2014): 289–305. https://doi.org/10.1093/cjres/rsu003.

Miller, Michelle, and Eric Harris Bernstein. *New Frontiers of Worker Power: Challenges and Opportunities in the Modern Economy.* New York: Roosevelt Institute, 2017. http://rooseveltinstitute.org/new-frontiers-worker-power/.

Mitchell, Kristina M. W., and Jonathan Martin. "Gender Bias in Student Evaluations." *PS: Political Science & Politics* 51, no. 3 (July 2018): 648–52. https://doi.org/10.1017/S104909651800001X.

Mitchell, Michael, Michael Leachman, and Kathleen Masterson. "A Lost Decade in Higher Education Funding." Center on Budget and Policy Priorities, August 22, 2017. www.cbpp.org/research/state-budget-and-tax/a-lost-decade-in-higher-education-funding.

Muryn Kaminski, Jennifer A., and Anne H. Reilly. "Career Development of Women in Information Technology." *SAM Advanced Management Journal* 69, no. 4 (Autumn 2004): 20–30.

Museus, Samuel D. "The Role of Ethnic Student Organizations in Fostering African American and Asian American Students' Cultural Adjustment and Membership at Predominantly White Institutions." *Journal of College Student Development* 49, no. 6 (2008): 568–86. https://doi.org/10.1353/csd.0.0039.

National Academy of Sciences. *The Postdoctoral Experience Revisited.* Washington, DC: National Academies Press, 2014. https://doi.org/10.17226/18982.

National Center for Education Statistics. "Digest of Education Statistics." 2016. https://nces.ed.gov/programs/digest/d16/tables/dt16_315.10.asp.

National Center for Education Statistics [NCES]. "IPEDS 2018–2019 Glossary." National Center for Education Statistics, 2018.

National Labor Relations Board [NLRB]. New York University v. NLRB, 364 F. Supp. 160 (SDNY 1973).

———. NLRB v. Catholic Bishop of Chicago, No. 440 US 490 (NLRB 1979).

———. NLRB v. Yeshiva Univ., No. 444 US 672 (NLRB 1980).

———. The Trustees of Columbia University in the City of New York, No. 02–RC–143012 (NLRB 2017).

National Postdoctoral Association [NPA]. "National Postdoctoral Association Position Statement on Unions," 2006. https://cdn.ymaws.com/www.nationalpostdoc.org/resource/resmgr/Docs/npa-position-statement-on-un.pdf.

National Science Board. *Science and Engineering Indicators*. Arlington, VA: National Science Foundation. 2010, 566.

New Faculty Majority. "Can Adjuncts Collect Unemployment Compensation between Terms?," 2017. www.newfacultymajority.info/faqs-frequently-asked-questions/can-adjuncts-collect-unemployment-compensation-between-terms.

Newfield, Christopher. *The Great Mistake: How We Wrecked Public Universities and How We Can Fix Them*. Baltimore: Johns Hopkins University Press, 2016.

Nikolakakos, Elaine, Jennifer L. Reeves, and Sheldon Shuch. "An Examination of the Causes of Grade Inflation in a Teacher Education Program and Implications for Practice." *College and University* 87, no. 3 (Winter 2012): 2–13.

Noble, David F. *Digital Diploma Mills: The Automation of Higher Education*. New York: Monthly Review Press, 2001.

NYSUT Communications. "Adjunct Pay an Urgent Issue for Unions." Accessed March 29, 2018. www.nysut.org/news/2017/april/ra/adjunct-pay-an-urgent-issue-for-unions.

Ohm, Rachel. "University of Tennessee Campuses Will Not Outsource Facilities Jobs." *Knoxville News Sentinel*, October 31, 2017. www.knoxnews.com/story/news/education/2017/10/31/university-tennessee-knoxville-not-outsource-facilities-jobs/816760001/.

Outcalt, C. *A Profile of the Community College Professoriate, 1975–2000*. New York: Routledge, 2002.

Padilla, Miguel A., and Julia N. Thompson. "Burning Out Faculty at Doctoral Research Universities." *Stress and Health: Journal of the International Society for the Investigation of Stress* 32, no. 5 (December 2016): 551–58. https://doi.org/10.1002/smi.2661.

Pascarella, Ernest T. "Student-Faculty Informal Contact and College Outcomes." *Review of Educational Research* 50, no. 4 (December 1, 1980): 545–95. https://doi.org/10.3102/00346543050004545.

Pascarella, Ernest T., and Patrick T. Terenzini. *How College Affects Students: A Third Decade of Research*. New York: Wiley, 2005.

Pascarella, Ernest T., Patrick T. Terenzini, and James Hibel. "Student-Faculty Interactional Settings and Their Relationship to Predicted Academic Performance." *The Journal of Higher Education* 49, no. 5 (September 1, 1978): 450–63. https://doi.org/10.1080/00221546.1978.11780395.

Pausch, Markus. "From a Democratic Ideal to a Managerial Tool and Back." *The Innovation Journal: The Public Sector Innovation Journal* 19, no. 1 (2013): 1.

Peck, Jamie. *Constructions of Neoliberal Reason*. Oxford: Oxford University Press, 2010.

Perry, David M. "Why Can't 'Free Speech' Advocates Ever Defend Adjunct Professors and People of Color?" *Pacific Standard*, 2017. https://psmag.com/education/when-will-you-defend-left-wing-free-speech.

Petriglieri, Gianpiero, Susan J. Ashford, and Amy Wrzesniewski. "Agony and Ecstasy in the Gig Economy: Cultivating Holding Environments for Precarious and Personalized Work Identities." *Administrative Science Quarterly*, February 6, 2018. https://doi.org/10.1177/0001839218759646.

Platzer, David, and Anne Allison. "Academic Precarity in American Anthropology." *Cultural Anthropology*, February 12, 2018. https://culanth.org/fieldsights/1310-academic-precarity-in-american-anthropology.

Posselt, Julie. "Normalizing Struggle: Dimensions of Faculty Support for Doctoral Students and Implications for Persistence and Well-Being." *The Journal of Higher Education* 89, no. 6 (2018): 1–26. https://doi.org/10.1080/00221546.2018.1449080.

Powell, Kendall. "The Future of the Postdoc." *Nature News* 520, no. 7546 (April 9, 2015): 144. https://doi.org/10.1038/520144a.

Pulido, Laura. "Faculty Governance at the University of Southern California." In *The Imperial University: Academic Repression and Scholarly Dissent*, edited by Piya Chatterjee and Sunaina Maira, 99–121. Minneapolis: University of Minnesota Press, 2014.

Ran, Florence Xiaotao, and Di Xu. "How and Why Do Adjunct Instructors Affect Students' Academic Outcomes? Evidence from Two-Year and Four-Year Colleges." A CAPSEE Working Paper, Center for Analysis of Postsecondary Education and Employment, New York, NY, January 2017. https://eric.ed.gov/?id=ED574812.

Ray, Julie, and Stephanie Kafka. "Life in College Matters for Life after College." Gallup, 2014. https://news.gallup.com/poll/168848/life-college-matters-life -college.aspx.

Reason, Robert Dean., Patrick T. Terenzi, and Robert J. Domingo. "Developing Social and Personal Competence in the First Year of College." *The Review of Higher Education* 30, no. 3 (2007): 271–99. https://doi.org/10.1353/rhe.2007 .0012.

Reevy, Gretchen M., and Grace Deason. "Predictors of Depression, Stress, and Anxiety among Non-Tenure Track Faculty." *Frontiers in Psychology* 5 (2014). https://doi.org/10.3389/fpsyg.2014.00701.

Rendon, Laura I. "Beyond Involvement: Creating Validating Academic and Social Communities in the Community College." 1994. https://eric.ed.gov/?id =ED374728.

———. "Community College Puente: A Validating Model of Education." *Educational Policy* 16, no. 4 (September 1, 2002): 642–67. https://doi.org/10.1177 /0895904802016004010.

———. "Facilitating Retention and Transfer for First Generation Students in Community Colleges." Paper presented at the New Mexico Institute, Rural Community College Initiative, Espanola, NM, March 1, 1995. https://eric.ed.gov /?id=ED383369.

———. "Validating Culturally Diverse Students: Toward a New Model of Learning and Student Development." *Innovative Higher Education* 19, no. 1 (September 1, 1994): 33–51. https://doi.org/10.1007/BF01191156.

Rendon Linares, Laura, and Susan Munoz. "Revisiting Validation Theory: Theoretical Foundations, Applications, and Extensions." *Enrollment Management Journal* 5, no. 2 (2011): 24.

Renick, Timothy M. "How to Best Harness Student-Success Technology." *The Chronicle of Higher Education*, July 1, 2018. www.chronicle.com/article /How-to-Best-Harness/243798.

Rhoades, Gary. "Bread and Roses, and Quality Too? A New Faculty Majority Negotiating the New Academy." *The Journal of Higher Education* 88, no. 5 (September 3, 2017): 645–71. https://doi.org/10.1080/00221546.2016.1257310.

———. *Managed Professionals: Unionized Faculty and Restructuring Academic Labor*. Albany: State University of New York Press, 1998.

———. "What Are We Negotiating For? Public Interest Bargaining." *Journal of Collective Bargaining in the Academy* 7 (2015): 15.

Rhoades, Gary, and Christine Maitland. "Bargaining for Full-Time, Non-Tenure Track Faculty: Best Practices." *NEA 2008 Almanac of Higher Education*, 67–73.

Rhoades, Gary, and Robert A. Rhoads. "The Public Discourse of US Graduate Employee Unions: Social Movement Identities, Ideologies, and Strategies." *The Review of Higher Education* 26, no. 2 (2002): 163–86. https://doi.org/10.1353/rhe.2002.0035.

Rhoads, Robert A., and Gary Rhoades. "Graduate Employee Unionization as Symbol of and Challenge to the Corporatization of US Research Universities." *The Journal of Higher Education* 76, no. 3 (May 1, 2005): 243–75. https://doi.org/10.1080/00221546.2005.11772282.

Ribera, Amy K., Angie L. Miller, and Amber D. Dumford. "Sense of Peer Belonging and Institutional Acceptance in the First Year: The Role of High-Impact Practices." *Journal of College Student Development* 58, no. 4 (2017): 545–63. https://doi.org/10/gc6xs2.

Rocca, Kelly A. "Student Participation in the College Classroom: An Extended Multidisciplinary Literature Review." *Communication Education* 59, no. 2 (April 1, 2010): 185–213. https://doi.org/10.1080/03634520903505936.

Rogers, Sean E., Adrienne E. Eaton, and Paula B. Voos. "Effects of Unionization on Graduate Student Employees: Faculty-Student Relations, Academic Freedom, and Pay." *ILR Review* 66, no. 2 (April 2013): 487–510. https://doi.org/10.1177/001979391306600208.

Rolf, David, Shelby Clark, and Corrie Watterson Bryant. *Portable Benefits in the 21st Century*. Washington, DC: The Aspen Institute, 2016.

Rosenberg, Morris, and B. Mccullough. "Mattering: Inferred Significance and Mental Health among Adolescents." *Research in Community and Mental Health* 2 (January 1, 1981): 163–82.

Rosenfeld, Jake. *What Unions No Longer Do*. Cambridge, MA: Harvard University Press, 2014. https://doi.org/10.4159/harvard.9780674726215.

Rosser, Sue V., and Eliesh O'Neil Lane. "Key Barriers for Academic Institutions Seeking to Retain Female Scientists and Engineers: Family-Unfriendly Policies, Low Numbers, Stereotypes, and Harassment." *Journal of Women and Minorities in Science and Engineering* 8, no. 2 (2002). https://doi.org/10.1615/JWomenMinorScienEng.v8.i2.40.

Rosser, Vicki J. "Education Support Professionals: Employment Status and Financial Exigency." *NEA 2011 Almanac of Higher Education*, 67–73.

———. "'How Did You Hear That You Might Lose Your Job?'" *NEA 2012 Almanac of Higher Education*, 113–116.

———. "Support Professionals: The Key Issues Survey." *NEA 2009 Almanac of Higher Education*, 93–97.

Rosser, Vicki J., and Celeste M. Calkins. "ESPs: Employment and Living Wage Update." In *NEA 2017 Almanac of Higher Education*, 87–96.

Russell, Alene. "Outsourcing Instruction: Issues for Public Colleges and Universities." American Association of State Colleges and Universities, 2010. https://eric.ed.gov/?id=ED512015.

"Salary: Research Faculty." Glassdoor, 2018. www.glassdoor.com/Salaries/research-faculty-salary-SRCH_KO0,16.htm.

Samuels, Robert. *Why Public Higher Education Should Be Free: How to Decrease Cost and Increase Quality at American Universities*. Newark, NJ: Rutgers University Press, 2013.

Sax, Linda J., Alyssa N. Bryant, and Casandra E. Harper. "The Differential Effects of Student-Faculty Interaction on College Outcomes for Women and Men." *Journal of College Student Development* 46, no. 6 (November 1, 2005): 642–57. https://doi.org/10.1353/csd.2005.0067.

Schenk, Tom, Jr. "The Effects of Graduate-Student Unionization." PhD diss., Iowa State University, 2007. http://lib.dr.iastate.edu/cgi/viewcontent.cgi?article=15881&context=rtd.

Schlossberg, Nancy K. "Marginality and Mattering: Key Issues in Building Community." *New Directions for Student Services* 1989, no. 48 (August 2, 2006): 5–15. https://doi.org/10.1002/ss.37119894803.

Schmidt, Peter. "New Insights on What Psychologically Rattles Graduate Students." *The Chronicle of Higher Education*, November 12, 2016. www.chronicle.com/article/New-Insights-on-What/238399.

Schneijderberg, Christian, and Nadine Merkator. "The New Higher Education Professionals." In *The Academic Profession in Europe: New Tasks and New Challenges*, edited by Barbara M. Kehm and Ulrich Teichler, 53–92. Dordrecht: Springer Netherlands, 2013. https://doi.org/10.1007/978-94-007-4614-5_5.

Schuster, Jack H., and Martin J. Finkelstein. *The American Faculty: The Restructuring of Academic Work and Careers*. Baltimore: Johns Hopkins University Press, 2006.

Schwartz, Shelly K. "Pay for CEOs of For-Profit Colleges Top of the Class." CNBC, December 21, 2010. www.cnbc.com/id/40680879.

Scott-Clayton, Judith, and Jing Li. *Black-White Disparity in Student Loan Debt More Than Triples after Graduation*. Washington, DC: Brookings Institution, 2016.

SEIU. "The High Cost of Adjunct Living." SEIU, 2015. http://seiufacultyforward.org/wp-content/uploads/2016/10/29035-White-paper-Florida-Final.pdf.

Slaughter, Sheila, and Larry L. Leslie. *Academic Capitalism: Politics, Policies, and the Entrepreneurial University*. Baltimore: Johns Hopkins University Press, 1999.

Slaughter, Sheila, and Gary Rhoades. *Academic Capitalism and the New Economy: Markets, State, and Higher Education*. Baltimore: Johns Hopkins University Press, 2004.

Slee, Tom. *What's Yours Is Mine: Against the Sharing Economy*. London: Scribe UK, 2015.

Smallwood, Philip. "'More Creative Than Creation': On the Idea of Criticism and the Student Critic." *Arts and Humanities in Higher Education* 1, no. 1 (June 1, 2002): 59–71. https://doi.org/10.1177/1474022202001001005.

Smilowitz, Michael. *Report of the Faculty Senate's 2013 Faculty Job Satisfaction Survey: Quantitative Analysis*. Harrisonburg, VA: James Madison University, 2013. www.jmu.edu/facultysenate/_files/notes/2013-09-18-faculty-satisfaction-survey.pdf.

Smith, David Michael. "Workplace Democracy at College of the Mainland." *Peace Review* 12, no. 2 (June 1, 2000): 257–62. https://doi.org/10.1080/10402650050057924.

Solorzano, Daniel, Miguel Ceja, and Tara Yosso. "Critical Race Theory, Racial Microaggressions, and Campus Racial Climate: The Experiences of African American College Students." *The Journal of Negro Education* 69, no. 1/2 (2000). http://www.jstor.org/stable/2696265.

Sowell, R., T. Zhang, K. Redd, and M. King. *Ph.D. Completion and Attrition: Analysis of Baseline Program Data from the PhD Completion Project*. Washington, DC: Council of Graduate Schools, 2008.

Staff. "Purdue's Kaplan Deal Receives HLC Approval." *WLFI News*, 2018. www.wlfi.com/content/news/Purdue-University-receives-HLC-approval-for-Purdue-Global-475868393.html.

Stansfeld, Stephen, and Bridget Candy. "Psychosocial Work Environment and Mental Health: A Meta-analytic Review." *Scandinavian Journal of Work, Environment & Health* 32, no. 6 (2006): 443–62.

Stark, Philip, and Richard Freishtat. "An Evaluation of Course Evaluations." *ScienceOpen Research*, September 29, 2014. https://doi.org/10.14293/S2199-1006.1.SOR-EDU.AOFRQA.v1.

Stephan, Paula. *How Economics Shapes Science*. Cambridge, MA: Harvard University Press, 2012.

———. "How to Exploit Postdocs." *BioScience* 63, no. 4 (April 1, 2013): 245–46. https://doi.org/10.1525/bio.2013.63.4.2.

Strayhorn, Terrell L. *College Students' Sense of Belonging: A Key to Educational Success for All Students*. New York: Routledge, 2012.

———. "Fittin' In: Do Diverse Interactions with Peers Affect Sense of Belonging for Black Men at Predominantly White Institutions?" *NASPA Journal* 45, no. 4 (October 1, 2008): 501–27. https://doi.org/10/cmz97z.

Street, Steve, Maria Maisto, Esther Merves, and Gary Rhoades. Who Is Professor "Staff," and How Can This Person Teach So Many Classes? Center for the Future of Higher Education Policy, 2012.

Sulé, V. Thandi. "Hip-Hop Is the Healer: Sense of Belonging and Diversity among Hip-Hop Collegians." *Journal of College Student Development* 57, no. 2 (2016): 181–96. https://doi.org/10/f8gdvb.

Sullivan, Teresa A. "Professional Control in the Complex University: Maintaining the Faculty Role." In *The American Academic Profession: Transformation in Contemporary Higher Education*, edited by Joseph C. Hermanowitz. Baltimore: The Johns Hopkins University Press, 2011.

"The 2017 Almanac." National Education Association. www.nea.org//home/70231.htm.

Thomas Walker, Jessica Buttermore, and Jeffrey Lichtenstein. "Tennessee Campus Workers Foil Billionaire Governor's Outsourcing Scheme." *Labor Notes,* November 22, 2017. www.labornotes.org/2017/11/tennessee-campus-workers -foil-billionaire-governors-outsourcing-scheme.

Thompson, Karen. "Contingent Faculty and Student Learning: Welcome to the Strativersity." *New Directions for Higher Education* 2003, no. 123 (2003): 41–47. https://doi.org/10.1002/he.119.

Toutkoushian, Robert K., and Marcia L. Bellas. "The Effects of Part-Time Employment and Gender on Faculty Earnings and Satisfaction." *The Journal of Higher Education* 74, no. 2 (March 1, 2003): 172–95. https://doi.org/10.1080 /00221546.2003.11777195.

Townsend, Barbara K. "Community College Organizational Climate for Minorities and Women." *Community College Journal of Research and Practice* 33, no. 9 (August 3, 2009): 731–44. https://doi.org/10.1080/106689209 03022458.

Turner, Lowell, Harry C. Katz, and Richard W. Hurd, eds. *Rekindling the Movement: Labor's Quest for Relevance in the 21st Century.* Frank W. Pierce Memorial Lectureship and Conference Series. Ithaca, NY: Cornell University Press, 2001.

UAW Local 4121. "UAW Local 4121." UAW Local 4121, 2015. www.uaw4121.org/.

UAW Local 5810. "Contract." 2017. http://uaw5810.org/know-your-rights /contract/.

UC Berkeley Graduate Assembly. *Graduate Student Happiness & Well-Being Report.* Berkeley: UC Berkeley Graduate Assembly, 2014.

UIS Campus Planning and Budget Committee. *UIS Faculty Satisfaction Survey Report.* Springfield: University of Illinois at Springfield, 2004. www.uis.edu /accreditation/wp-content/uploads/sites/23/2013/04/CPBCFacultySatisfactio nSurvey2004.pdf.

Umbach, Paul D. "How Effective Are They? Exploring the Impact of Contingent Faculty on Undergraduate Education." *The Review of Higher Education* 30, no. 2 (2007): 91–123. https://doi.org/10.1353/rhe.2006.0080.

Umbach, Paul D., and Matthew R. Wawrzynski. "Faculty Do Matter: The Role of College Faculty in Student Learning and Engagement." *Research in Higher Education* 46, no. 2 (March 1, 2005): 153–84. https://doi.org/10/fp6fnq.

University of Washington Postdoc Organizing Committee. "University of Washington Postdocs: We Are a Union!," May 14, 2018. https://uaw.org/university-washington-postdocs-official-union/.

Upwork. "Freelancing in America: 2017 Survey," 2017. www.upwork.com/i/freelancing-in-america/2017/.

US Bureau of Labor Statistics. "Occupational Employment and Wages, May 2017." Bureau of Labor Statistics, 2017. www.bls.gov/oes/current/oes251191.htm.

US Government Accountability Office. "Contingent Workforce: Size, Characteristics, Compensation, and Work Experiences of Adjunct and Other Non-Tenure-Track Faculty." November 20, 2017. www.gao.gov/products/GAO-18-49.

Verges, Josh. "Appeals Court Rejects Attempt to Unionize All UMN Twin Cities Faculty." *Twin Cities*, September 5, 2017. www.twincities.com/2017/09/05/appeals-court-rejects-attempt-to-unionize-all-umn-twin-cities-faculty/.

Vetnar, Ali. "Invest in Ed Demands New Money during 2019 Legislative Session." *KTAR News*, January 11, 2019. http://ktar.com/story/2391495/invest-in-ed-demands-new-money-during-2019-legislative-session/.

Vygotsky, L. S., and Michael Cole. *Mind in Society: The Development of Higher Psychological Processes*. Cambridge, MA: Harvard University Press, 1978.

Waltman, Jean, Inger Bergom, Carol Hollenshead, Jeanne Miller, and Louise August. "Factors Contributing to Job Satisfaction and Dissatisfaction among Non-Tenure-Track Faculty." *The Journal of Higher Education* 83, no. 3 (May 1, 2012): 411–34. https://doi.org/10.1080/00221546.2012.11777250.

Wang, Huiming, and Judith Wilson Grimes. "A Systematic Approach to Assessing Retention Programs: Identifying Critical Points for Meaningful Interventions and Validating Outcomes Assessment." *Journal of College Student Retention: Research, Theory & Practice* 2, no. 1 (May 1, 2000): 59–68. https://doi.org/10.2190/HYY4-XTBH-RJFD-LU5Y.

Wassell, Charles, David Hedrick, Steven Henson, and John Krieg. "Wage Distribution Impacts of Higher Education Faculty Unionization." *Journal of Collective Bargaining in the Academy* 7, no. 1 (February 28, 2016). http://thekeep.eiu.edu/jcba/vol7/iss1/4.

Watt, Stephen. "The Humanities, RCM, and Bullshit." *Western Humanities Review* 65, no. 3 (Fall 2011): 66–86.

Weaver, Robert R., and Jiang Qi. "Classroom Organization and Participation: College Students' Perceptions." *The Journal of Higher Education* 76, no. 5 (September 1, 2005): 570–601. https://doi.org/10.1080/00221546.2005 .11772299.

Weil, David. "Lots of Employees Get Misclassified as Contractors. Here's Why It Matters." *Harvard Business Review*, July 5, 2017. https://hbr.org/2017 /07/lots-of-employees-get-misclassified-as-contractors-heres-why-it -matters.

———. *The Fissured Workplace*. Cambridge, MA: Harvard University Press, 2014.

Wekullo, Caroline Sabina. "Outsourcing in Higher Education: The Known and Unknown about the Practice." *Journal of Higher Education Policy and Management* 39, no. 4 (July 4, 2017): 453–68. https://doi.org/10.1080/1360080X .2017.1330805.

West, Richard, and Judy C. Pearson. "Antecedent and Consequent Conditions of Student Questioning: An Analysis of Classroom Discourse across the University." *Communication Education* 43, no. 4 (October 1, 1994): 299–311. https://doi.org/10.1080/03634529409378988.

Whitechurch, Celia. *Reconstructing Identities in Higher Education: The Rise of Third Space Professionals*. New York: Routledge, 2013.

Wickens, Christine M. "The Organizational Impact of University Labor Unions." *Higher Education* 56, no. 5 (November 1, 2008): 545–64. https://doi.org/10 .1007/s10734-008-9110-z.

Williams, Joan C., Katherine W. Phillips, and Erika V. Hall. *Double Jeopardy? Gender Bias Against Women of Color in Science*. San Francisco: UC Hastings College of Law, 2014.

Willis, Wayne Carr. "Empire State College and the Conflicted Legacy of Progressive Higher Education." In *Principles, Practices, and Creative Tensions in Progressive Higher Education: One Institution's Struggle to Sustain a Vision*, edited by Katherine Jelly and Alan Mandell, 29–42. Rotterdam: SensePublishers, 2017. https://doi.org/10.1007/978-94-6300-884-6_2.

Won, Sungjun, Christopher A. Wolters, and Stefanie A. Mueller. "Sense of Belonging and Self-Regulated Learning: Testing Achievement Goals as Mediators." *The Journal of Experimental Education*, February 22, 2017, 1–17. https://doi .org/10/gc6xst.

Wood, J. Luke, and Frank Harris III. "The Effect of Academic Engagement on Sense of Belonging: A Hierarchical, Multilevel Analysis of Black Men in Community Colleges." *Spectrum: A Journal on Black Men* 4, no. 1 (2015): 21. https://doi.org/10/gc6xss.

Workday. "Higher Education Financial Mgmt, HR, and Student Software." Accessed August 31, 2018. www.workday.com/en-us/industries/higher-education.html.

Young, Jeffrey R. "Here Comes Professor Everybody." *The Chronicle of Higher Education*, February 2, 2015. www.chronicle.com/article/Here-Comes-Professor-Everybody/151445.

Zimmerman, Barry J. "Investigating Self-Regulation and Motivation: Historical Background, Methodological Developments, and Future Prospects." *American Educational Research Journal* 45, no. 1 (March 1, 2008): 166–83. https://doi.org/10.3102/0002831207312909.

Index

academic capitalism, 2, 13–35, 76–98.
  See also corporatization;
  neoliberalism
academic self-confidence, 107–8
academic self-efficacy, 107–8
accountability, 14, 42, 57, 69, 71, 79,
  83, 89–90. *See also* surveillance
administrative bloat, 72–73
administrators, 70–71, 89–90, 144–49,
  158, 160–64; administration, 67, 76,
  80, 86–88, 91, 126–27
advancement, 41, 43, 46–47, 51
advising, 23, 29–30, 112, 115–18.
  See also mentoring
Affordable Care Act, 48, 157,
  161
alienation, 41, 52, 91–92
American Association of University
  Professors (AAUP), 121–22, 138
American Federation of Teachers (AFT),
  121–22, 138
anxiety, 90
Association for Governing Boards
  (AGB), 158, 169
atomization, 81–82
automation, 84–85, 139, 160. *See also*
  technology

Bayh-Dole Act, 14, 172. *See also*
  commercialization
benefits: of contingent faculty, 45–47,
  50–51; eligibility, 17, 27; of grad
  workers, 62–63; lack of, 1, 15, 36, 80,
  91; negotiation of, 124, 127–28,
  135–36, 140–41, 156–57, 161,

166–68; portable, 166–67; of
  postdocs, 56–57; of staff, 39–40;
  unemployment, 44

Coalition of Contingent Academic
  Labor, 130
Coalition of Graduate Employee
  Organizations, 131, 134
collective bargaining, 121–26, 133–36,
  140, 144, 151–56; more collectivist
  collective bargaining, 153–54
commercialization, 14, 172. *See also*
  Bayh-Dole Act
community, 3–9, 37, 76–98
contingency: under academic capitalism, 16–22, 25–26, 80–81, 87,
  151; combating against, 132–33,
  136–37, 146, 165–67; of contingent
  faculty, 43–44, 50–51; of graduate
  workers, 63–64; of postdocs, 54–56;
  of staff, 39
contracts: of contingent faculty, 43–45,
  49, 52, 100, 103; of grad workers, 63;
  independent, 15–22, 26–28, 32–33,
  166; negotiations, 122, 124–26,
  128–42, 158, 166; of postdocs, 57; of
  staff, 40–41; subcontract, 20–21, 31,
  33, 81, 138, 162. *See also* outsourcing
corporatization, 6, 14, 76, 85–89. *See also*
  academic capitalism
custodial staff, 90, 177

debt, 24, 66–67, 125, 162–63, 169.
  See also student debt
Department of Labor, 61, 129

depression, 65–66
deprofessionalization, 15, 24, 36, 48–50, 78, 136, 148
discrimination, 10, 20, 31–33, 57, 159–60

economic risk, 27–28
employee engagement, 92–94, 149–52
employment benefits. *See* benefits
entrepreneurialism, 19, 25, 30, 76–78, 82–84, 147. *See also* micro-entrepreneur

faculty-student interactions, 97, 115–16; and academic self-confidence, 107–8; and academic self-efficacy, 107–8; and first-generation students, 114; and low-income students, 114; and mattering, 110; and racially minoritized students, 114; and sense of belonging, 110–11; and student academic performance, 103–4; and student graduation, persistence, and retention, 103; and student support, 100–101; and student transfer, 104; and validation, 108–9; and vicarious learning, 107. *See also* social learning theory
fear, 41, 81
first-year experiences, 100–103, 114–15
flexibility (institutional), 27, 29
for-profit institutions, 74, 169
Foucault, 19, 25
freelance, 82, 147–49
funding, 48–57, 77–83, 162–64

gender, 22, 32, 33, 64, 159–60
gig economy, 16–21, 26–35, 133, 141, 146–48
gig logic, 77–96. *See also* academic capitalism
governance, 86–87. *See also* shared governance
grade point average (GPA), 113
graduate assistants, 60–67; students, 4–5, 7–8
graduate students, 1–5, 16, 36–37, 60–67, 91, 168–69; union (organizing), 88, 120, 122, 125–35, 140, 142–43, 154–56
graduation rates, 99–103, 113–17

hiring, 26–29, 39, 43–49, 69–73, 94–96, 137–39, 159–67
hyperproductivity, 38–39, 46, 51, 57, 62–63, 79

Integrated Postsecondary Education Data System (IPEDS), 50
interest-based bargaining, 154–55
intersectionality, 159–60

Janus v. AFSCME, 153, 167

Labor Center at UC Berkeley, 15

managed professionals, 36, 78
market, 14–15, 17–18, 20, 25–27, 31, 33–35; marketization, 6, 76, 78
mattering, 107–10
mental health, 65–66
mentoring, 4, 79, 115–18. *See also* advising
metropolitan strategy, 132–35
micro-entrepreneur, 24–26, 82–84. *See also* entrepreneurialism
middle-level professionals, 67–71, 89–90. *See also* new professionals
morale, 90–96, 142, 153

National Center for the Study of Collective Bargaining in Higher Education and the Professions, 122–23, 126
National Education Association (NEA), 121–43
National Labor Relations Act (NLRA), 125, 128. *See also* Wagner Act
National Labor Relations Board (NLRB), 120
National Research Council, 53
National Science Foundation, 53, 58
neoliberalism, 2, 6, 13–35. *See also* academic capitalism
New Faculty Majority, 130, 156, 165
new professionals, 67–71, 89–90. *See also* middle-level professionals

online education, 28–30, 47–48, 84–85, 138–39
organizing, 120–22, 129–35, 143; faculty, 122–23; goals of, 135–39; graduate students, 125–27; impact of, 139–43; postdoctoral, 127–29; staff, 123–25; strategies of, 152–56. *See also* power; unions
outsourcing, 20, 31, 40–41, 47–48, 81, 138, 146

Pacific Lutheran, 130–31
part-time faculty, 8, 15, 43–49, 50–53, 74, 100–104
pedagogy, 104–5
persistence, 99–103
portable benefits, 166–67
postdocs, 53–60, 91–92, 120–29
power, 1–35, 4, 6, 7–8, 15, 24, 30, 34, 120–69; concentration of power, 36–37, 80, 86–87; managerial power, 69; transition of power, 42–43; worker power, 20, 77, 88. *See also* organizing; unions
professional development, 48, 92–93, 100, 135, 137, 141–42, 148
professional staff, 12, 38–42, 67–71, 89. *See also* staff
promotion, 41, 43, 46–47, 51. *See also* advancement
public funding, 71, 162–63

race, 22, 32–33, 64–66, 73, 159–60
reprofessionalize, 137
research faculty, 50–53
responsibility-centered budgeting, 83–84
retention: employee, 94–95; student, 99–103
risk, 27–28

salary, 36, 94; administrator and professional, 70, 71, 72; contingent research faculty, 51, 52; contingent teaching faculty, 43–46; graduate teaching assistants, 61–62; postdoc, 56; staff, 39–40
satisfaction with workplace, 37, 41, 52, 90–94, 142, 153

sense of belonging, 110–11
Service Employees International Union (SEIU), 123–32, 165
shared governance, 86–87
social cognitive theory, 110–11
social justice unionism, 120–35
social learning theory, 105–19
social movement unionism, 120–35
staff, 12, 38–42, 67–71, 89; interactions with students, 117–18. *See also* professional staff
student aspirations, 113
student debt, 66, 150, 162–64
student outcomes, 99–105
student support, 28, 147–49
supervisors, 70–71, 89–90, 144–49, 158, 160–64
surveillance, 30, 42, 68, 139
surveys, 92–94

teaching, 43–49
technology, 84–85, 139, 160; integration, 160; transfer, 78, 113. *See also* automation
turnover, 94–96,

Uber, 18–19, 27–35
unbundling, 22–24, 81, 137
unions, 120–22, 129–35, 143, 152–56; faculty, 122–23; goals, 135–39; graduate student, 125–27; growth, 120–22, 129–35, 143, 152; impact, 139–43; postdoctoral, 127–29; staff, 123–25. *See also* organizing
United Auto Workers (UAW), 126–43

validation, 109
vicarious learning, 107, 117

Wagner Act, 20, 125, 128. *See also* National Labor Relations Act (NLRA)
women, 25, 31, 32, 58, 64–65, 91, 159–60
worker misclassification, 20–22
workload, 41, 42, 46, 51, 57, 62, 95
workplace democracy, 149–52
workplace safety, 42, 138, 151

Yeshiva, 131